FOR KIDS OF ALL AGES

FOR KIDS OF ALL AGES

The National Society of Film Critics
on Children's Movies

EDITED BY

Peter Keough

ROWMAN & LITTLEFIELD
Lanham • Boulder • New York • London

Published by Rowman & Littlefield
An imprint of The Rowman & Littlefield Publishing Group, Inc.
4501 Forbes Boulevard, Suite 200, Lanham, Maryland 20706
www.rowman.com

6 Tinworth Street, London, SE11 5AL, United Kingdom

British Library Cataloguing in Publication Information Available

Library of Congress Cataloging-in-Publication Data

Names: Keough, Peter, 1952– editor.
Title: For kids of all ages : the National Society of Film Critics on children's movies / edited by Peter Keough.
Description: Lanham : Rowman & Littlefield, [2020] | Includes bibliographical references and index.
Identifiers: LCCN 2019010237 (print) | LCCN 2019019557 (ebook) | ISBN 9781538128596 (electronic) | ISBN 9781538128589 (pbk. : alk. paper)
Subjects: LCSH: Children's films—United States—History and criticism.
Classification: LCC PN1995.9.C45 (ebook) | LCC PN1995.9.C45 F57 2020 (print) | DDC 791.43/6523—dc23
LC record available at https://lccn.loc.gov/2019010237

For my parents, who took me to the movies

CONTENTS

ACKNOWLEDGMENTS

I'd like to thank Elisabeth Weis, Justin Chang, David Sterritt, Peter Rainer, Michael Sragow, and all the members of the National Society of Film Critics for their support, encouragement, assistance, and wonderful submissions. Also thanks to Chaz Ebert; Kym Wilner of the *New York Times*; Anne Elizabeth Moore of the *Chicago Reader*; Erica Varela of the *Los Angeles Times*; Thomas Doherty; Langdon Kessner; and my publisher at Rowman & Littlefield, Stephen Ryan. And, of course, thank you to Alicia Potter for her editing skills and for being the light of my life.

INTRODUCTION

Why a book about children's movies by film critics, who might approach the topic in the worst possible way—taking it too seriously?

Because, for better and worse, critics are the most childish people you'll meet. As the essays and reviews in *For Kids of All Ages* indicate, the fundamental response of even the most hard-core film critic is that of a kid who has just fallen under cinema's spell.

As for myself, I don't recall the first movie I saw. Maybe my parents had taken me with the rest of the family to the Blue Hills Drive-In in Canton to see *Heaven Knows Mr. Allison* (1957) or Sam Fuller's *China Gate* (1957). One of my sisters distinctly recalls how she got grossed out during the latter film, an early foray into the Vietnam morass, when Nat King Cole stepped on a punji stick. Now that I probably would have remembered.

But I do remember a few years later going to the Rialto, the second-run theater in Roslindale Square on the outskirts of Boston, and the thrill and terror of watching war movies, like an already well-worn rerelease of Dick Powell's *The Enemy Below* (1957). It is a tense and realistic action drama about a duel between a U.S. destroyer and a Nazi U-Boat, and has its share of shocking moments—holy cow, that guy's arm is blown off! But Robert Mitchum as the destroyer's canny, unflappable skipper restored calm and resolution.

That blown-off arm looks tame compared to the movie mayhem of today. But although less graphic, older movies hold their share of terror and thrills, for some reason *The Wizard of Oz* (1939), in its own way the most frightening of movies, was for years deemed appropriate holiday fare. Dutifully, the family gathered around the TV set, and I would ritualistically undergo the beloved classic's terrors. The tornado that inspired recurrent dreams of "twisters" chasing me under my bed, where there was no escape. Flights of flying monkeys filling the skies like waves of Soviet bombers bearing death. A dismembered Scarecrow, later set afire, proving beyond doubt the vulnerability of the human body, at least when made of straw. And then the most hideous revelation of all [SPOILER!]: It's all a dream.

Other films, seen on TV and at the Rialto in a time before DVD, Netflix, or VOD, added to my vicarious experience of life's joys and tragedies. *Old Yeller* (1957) confirmed to me, as well as many others for generations to come, the inevitability of loss and grief, and the injustice of fate. And one afternoon at the fragile age of thirteen, I watched Robert Aldrich's *The Last Sunset* (1961) on some weekend TV movie show and laid eyes on the love of my life, nineteen-year-old Carol Lynley, somehow knowing my heart would forever be broken, because she was only figment, a mass of electrons on the screen of our Zenith TV.

It's no wonder I, like most critics and movie fans in general, fell in love with cinema as a kid. In retrospect, maybe "love" does not quite describe the experience. Awe, terror, wonder, grief, desire, hope, as well as love, vicariously entered my life through movies. They opened to the real world beyond the limitations of my own, and a world beyond that world.

Also, like most critics and movie fans, I never outgrew that initial adoration of and addiction to movies, the wondrous immersion into another world on a screen in the dark. The trick is to figure out a way of preserving that initial, primal response—and turn it into a profession.

Sigmund Freud made a similar observation when he applied his analysis to the role and status of the artist. In his *New Introductory Lectures on Psycho-Analysis* (1933), he explains how writers, painters, musicians, actors, and probably film critics, if he had thought of them, have discovered the secret of transforming childhood play into aesthetic expressions valued by society. In so doing, Freud concludes they achieve "honor, power, riches, fame, and the love of women."

Setting aside Freud's relevance today as a scientist (he would have made a good film critic), he makes a valid point. Not to claim any status as artists, film critics have also discovered how to turn the idle delights of childhood into a commodity. Although any hope of thereby gaining honor, power, riches, or love is usually delusional, critics can still get by on their ability to draw on the make-believe of children and apply it to the understanding of what remains the world's most important art form—the movies. At their best, they can combine the joy that first stirred their cinephilia with their compulsion to understand what it means.

Given that approach, this book isn't just a consumer guide for parents, offering recommendations of what to pop into the DVD player to keep the kids occupied for a couple of hours. To be sure, it does offer many suggestions, ranging from such familiar films as *E. T. the Extra-Terrestrial* (1982), and *Black Panther* (2018), to more obscure masterpieces that will enrich the lives of both children and parents, for example, Hayao Miyazaki's *Spirited Away* (2001), Jafar Panahi's *The White Balloon* (1995), and Charles Laughton's *The Night of the Hunter* (1955).

More importantly, this book tries to explain how to watch a movie critically. That may not sound like a lot of fun, but when criticism springs from that first initiation into the medium, the results can be illuminating—for not only parents who want to guide their child's viewing, but also anyone who loves film—especially when the passion and insights are expressed by talented writers who have seen thousands of movies, possess acute analytic skills and formidable cinematic and cultural knowledge, and are among the most respected professionals in their field.

Such is the case with the contributors to this book, all of them members of the National Society of Film Critics. Since 1966, the group has been one of the foremost such organizations in the United States, its membership once including such late luminaries as Pauline Kael, Andrew Sarris, Richard Corliss, Jay Carr, and Roger Ebert (the latter two are represented here by essays). Other prominent members are Peter Travers of *Rolling Stone*, Stephanie Zacharek of *Time* magazine, Kenneth Turan of the *Los Angeles Times*, Carrie Rickey of the *Philadelphia Inquirer*, and many others.

This book follows in a long, distinguished line of such collections published by the NSFC in a span of four decades on various themes, with titles including *Foreign Affairs: A Guide to Foreign Films* (1991), *The A List: 100 Essential Films* (2002), and *The B List: The National Society of Film Critics on the Low-Budget Beauties, Genre-Bending Mavericks, and Cult Classics We Love* (2008). They have rewarded film scholars, cinephiles, and film fans alike.

More so than in these previous volumes, however, the contributors to *For Kids of All Ages* have tapped into their own personal memories and experiences. That is particularly true in the first chapter, "From Child to Critic," which includes recollections of first film encounters, and the last chapter, "From Critic to Child," which applies those lessons learned as a kid to understanding films made for children.

The other eight chapters focus on the different conventions, genres, and themes that distinguish films for and about children. These include "Adventures in Animation," about the fundamental importance of that medium in the world of children's movies; "Beast Fables," a look at films that feature our often-anthropomorphized fellow creatures; "Dreams, Fantasies, and Nightmares," about the therapeutic and entertainment value of such movies; "Well Adapted (or Maladjusted"), about the difficult process of translating children's and other literature from page to screen; "Matters of Life and Death," a look at films in which childhood innocence confronts sometimes traumatic experiences; "Ordinary Heroes," discussing films in which common people, both kids and adults, meet uncommon challenges; "Extraordinary Heroes," in which uncommon people, usually in tights and capes, go about their superheroic business as usual; and "Home Movies," covering the fundamental social unit, the family.

The age groups these essays address range from preschoolers to teenagers. Some of the film choices might, at first glance, seem too challenging for kids. As they say, viewer discretion is advised. To help assess their appropriateness, the Motion Picture Association of America rating for each film mentioned is included in an appendix whenever available. But even if the films seem too adult for the kids, there's no reason the parents shouldn't see them. Then they can judge for themselves when and if they can share the experience with their children.

With such diversions as video games, iPhones, Instagram, YouTube, and other wonders of the digital age rivaling cinema for the attention of today's children and adolescents, perhaps this book will serve as a reminder of what movies on the big screen—or little screen, as the case may be—offer that these other amusements cannot. We hope that in some small way *For Kids of All Ages* might help keep that magic connection between childhood and film alive for generations to come.

The Cyclops and Kerwin Mathews (as Sinbad) in *The 7th Voyage of Sinbad*

1

—m—

FROM CHILD TO CRITIC

What do kids want? People in Hollywood make a lot of money trying to figure that out. In this chapter, critics ponder the question and find that the answers lie in their own memories of what moved them as children discovering the medium that would become such a big part of their lives.

Gerald Peary was already figuring out what he wanted to watch on the screen at the age of three or four when he saw *Goldilocks and the Three Bears* in a church basement (a film he swears he saw but of which no record can be found). In his essay "From Toddler to Auteurist: A Film Critic; the Early Years," he relates how the film-struck child evolved into a veteran critic.

For James Verniere, the discovery of his love for cinema and the beginning of his transformation from child to critic occurred while watching a monster movie. "I was born in 1951," he recalls in "Children of the Hydra," "but born again the night my mother's brother, almost a kid himself, took me to see my first film in a real movie theater, *The Beast from 20,000 Fathoms* (1953)."

Later he would learn that the person who had frightened him so much was Ray Harryhausen, the legendary special effects master. When Verniere experienced Harryhausen's magic again in *The 7th Voyage of Sinbad* (1958), he was hopelessly hooked on movies. He was on a voyage of his own to discover what they mean, how they are made, and the myths that they are made of.

In "How Seeing *Airport* (1970) as a Kid Grounded My Critical Sensibility," Charles Taylor describes his first time watching a "real" movie—the big-budget, star-studded adaptation of the Arthur Hailey best seller. Although he now recognizes the film's flaws, he recalls being haunted by a single performance: Van Heflin as the middle-class provider brought low and forced into a desperate act. It reminded him that at any moment, the stability he enjoyed could just as easily be swept away by circumstances.

"Every pained look on his face mirrored my worst childhood fears," Taylor writes. "Now, when kids are raised in such a protective bubble, how many of them are getting the experiences that told earlier generations of moviegoers something about the adult world we had only guessed at?"

In "Revisiting *Old Yeller* (1957) and *Yellow Submarine* (1968)," I recall my own worst childhood fears and wonder if two movies I saw at the time might have made things better—or worse. "Did films that touched on inner turmoil only bring back the pain of past experiences," I write, "or did they provide a safe forum to confront them, work out conflicts, and find some resolution?" Whichever the case, I became a film critic, and now can employ the skills and insights of my profession to better understand myself as well as the movies I watch.

For J. R. Jones, the film *Wonder* (2017), about Auggie, a young boy with a facial deformity, also had a special resonance with his own life. In "Light in Auggie," he writes, "I come to this review highly credentialed because, growing up, I paid some of the same dues as young Auggie. When I was born, my left ear was only a nubbin of flesh, and from age four to eleven, I underwent thirteen plastic surgeries to construct something that looked halfway normal." Because of this experience, he says, he can be less sentimental about the subject matter than others. "So you can take my word for it that the movie, adapted from a children's book by R. J. Palacio, treats its young protagonist and his craniofacial deformity with respect and common sense."

Jonathan Rosenbaum takes a more detached point of view as he focuses on the experience of wonder rather than an evocation or exorcism of the past as the key to what kids, and adults, want in movies. In his essay "The Many Kinds of Movie Wonder," he tries to elucidate that elusive quality. "Wonder is closer to a feeling than a thought," he writes, "and one that we associate both with children and with grown-ups recapturing some of the open-mouthed awe and innocence that they had as children."

As these essays indicate, many critics are born from their first experiences watching movies as children. But as Robert Horton suggests in his essay "Infant Cinema: *Querelle enfantine / A Childish Quarrel* (1896)," cinema itself was born from pioneering filmmakers watching their children. When two of the first movie pioneers, brothers Louis and Auguste Lumière, were looking for subjects to shoot for some of their minute-long *actualités*, they settled on what parents have indulged in ever since—their own children. Auguste's two daughters star in the brothers' "A Child's Quarrel," and the siblings' dinnertime spat, Horton argues, established most of the basics of movies as we know them.

—ɷ—

From Toddler to Auteurist: A Film Critic; the Early Years
Gerald Peary

I'm in a hot library basement on a chair low to the floor, among squealing, restless, sweaty children. On a pull-down screen in front of us is projected a moving picture, in black and white, of *Goldilocks and the Three Bears* (I am *certain* this film exists although, alas, there seems to be no record of it). It's a live-action story, which, at age three or four, I was quite familiar with. What I see is a girl with luscious curls who seems too old to be Goldilocks and three bears in human clothes who stand erect. When Mama and Papa Bear discover Goldilocks snoozing in their bed, an amazing pillow fight ensues. Everyone whacks everyone else, until the pillows burst open and feathers—in slow motion?—float enchantingly about the screen.

Cinema!

I am mesmerized. Tap, tap on my shoulder. Mommy and Daddy are there to take me home, and before the movie is over. Not that I know what "over" means.

Did I imagine seeing this? Whatever, I will never be the same, and especially not when I learn that there are actual movie houses, where wonders like *Goldilocks and the Three Bears* play routinely. Each and every day. When I was five or six, walking through town with my mother, I'd suddenly drop her hand, bolt, and disappear. A movie theater! On tiny legs, I would scoot past the ticket booth and into the magical darkness.

"When were you first obsessed by movies?" I'm asked often as an adult. My answer is, "Always." I was a toddler, then I was a cinephile.

Did your parents set in motion a devotion to cinema? Certainly not my dad, a Russian-born biologist with zero interest in the movies. He went when my mother made him go. I don't recall him ever mentioning a film he liked or the name of a Hollywood star. A good picture for him was one with animals in it. He'd had a pet raccoon as a child, and he brought into our home as potential pets two baby alligators and a monkey. While most of us at a film warm to the actors and get involved in the narrative, my dad sat passively, waiting for the chance appearance of dogs, cats, cows, or horses. He'd written his PhD dissertation on the water buffalo, and *The Good Earth* (1937) had some of those, plowing in the background. For my father: ecstasy!

My mother had been a silent movie fan growing up in Bucharest, Romania. She'd gotten frightened by the German horror film *Waxworks* (1924), and Pola

Negri had been her favorite actress. As an immigrant in New York, she took a subway from the deepest Bronx to work as a hostess at Longchamps, a glamorous midtown restaurant. Among her regular clientele were actor Franchot Tone, a "very nice man," and Mrs. Henry Fonda, later a suicide, eating lunch with her two small children, Jane and Peter.

There were no film stars where, far from New York, my parents resided after they married. First, Jackson, Mississippi. Then Mountain Lake, North Carolina. My parents were both Jewish refugees from Hitler, and my father took whatever job he could find. For five years, that was teaching at a religious Baptist college in the hills of West Virginia. We lived nearby the college on Faculty Row. In the valley below, across a covered bridge, was the tiny town of Philippi. We were the only Jews, we believed, for hundreds of miles.

We didn't have a car. The coal city of Pittsburgh, sixty miles away, was out of our cultural reach. We did find ourselves once in Charleston, West Virginia's, hilly capital. While my father was attending a science conference, my mother got an opportunity to see a movie of her liking. She revisited a favorite from years before, *Les Misérables* (1935). She brought me with her, and I, about age four, suffered dreadfully along with Fredric March's Jean Valjean. It was too much for my system, the way he, such a decent guy, was hounded by Charles Laughton. I remember lying in my mom's lap afterward, certainly in shock.

Was the classic 1930s *Les Misérables* really exhibited in a first-run theater in 1950? I don't think I'm misremembering and that time had stopped in backwater West Virginia. This I'm sure of: In one of the two movie houses in downtown Philippi, the 1939 *Jesse James* played as a single feature in 1951. The next week, *Jesse James* was replaced on the marquee by its 1940 sequel, *The Return of Frank James*.

My mother, who had intelligent taste (her favorite picture: Federico Fellini's 1954 masterpiece *La Strada*), was put off by the kind of movies that trickled into Philippi. In this blue-collar, mountaineering town, what we got was practically all genre fare, and often of the lowest caliber: Ma and Pa Kettle films, the Francis the Talking Mule cycle, the oeuvre of rube comedian Judy Canova. Also double features of every cowboy in existence, bookended by lots of trailers and a chapter each week of a cheap, melodramatic serial. For me, what was not to love?

I recall one family trip to the cinema to see Abbott and Costello starring in *Jack and the Beanstalk* (1952). It was for the entertainment of my little brother, Danny, who'd been born in Philippi. At age three, Danny went crazy for it, giggling for weeks about Abbot's character with the sublime name Mr. Dinkelpuss. When he got older, Danny, too, would become a rabid cinephile. But in Philippi, I normally went to movies alone.

Alone. This is hard even for me to believe, living now in a predatory age. But in those days, movie theaters were safe havens for children. Even my protective parents, my hysterical mother, thought nothing of seven-year-old me sitting in the dark by myself. And it wasn't just rural West Virginia. I went solo later on in Miami Beach, Philadelphia, and Columbia, South Carolina. I remember a neat double feature of *The Little Kidnappers* (1953) and *The Adventures of Robinson Crusoe* (1954), which I saw with my cousin, Luba, on West 95th Street in New York. I recall no adult escort, and we were nine.

There was only one incident where a parent might wisely have intervened. One day, some friends drove our family to the neighboring West Virginia town of Clarksburg. I was dropped off at a movie house. Emboldened by this adventure, I strode to the concession stand, plunked down a nickel, and bought a giant Tootsie Roll to gobble while I watched the movie. Corn syrup, hydrogenated soybean oil, artificial flavors, a yucky simulation of chocolate. I threw up in the car on the drive home to Philippi. "Your eyes were bigger than your stomach," my dad lectured me. My last Tootsie Roll ever.

Back in Philippi: a sublime diet at the movies of Roy Rogers, Gene Autry, William Boyd's Hopalong Cassidy, Rocky Lane, Lash LaRue. "Hoppy" was weirdly white-haired. No one remembers Rocky Lane. LaRue was the sharpest cowpoke with his dark clothes and lethal bullwhip. Rogers was small and lithe, and hit hard with his fists. Autry emerged as my favorite: pie-faced and pretty gentle, and he rode Champion, a classy, beautiful horse. I knew the word: a "sorrel." And Roy Rogers's Trigger was a "palomino."

Besides seeing Autry on-screen, I listened religiously to his radio program. Each week I struggled to comprehend the fourth line of his theme song, "Back in the Saddle Again." As an adult, I found it instantly on the Internet: "Where the longhorn cattle feed / On the lowly jimsonweed." Jimsonweed was not in a seven-year-old's vocabulary.

The cowboy movies I saw in the valley were played out by the kids on Faculty Row. I had a monopoly on Gene Autry. My next-door neighbor, Stanley, got to be Roy Rogers, great for gunfights. But that meant he got strapped with Patty, the only girl in our posse. Patty was Dale Evans, Roy's loving wife. Ugh! But when it came to a cowboy suit, a present for my eighth birthday, I opted for Hopalong Cassidy's all-black outfit, with sequins and silver buttons. I have a vivid memory of me opening my front door and, in full Cassidy regalia, strutting about the front porch, keeping the peace with my drawn six-gun.

Yet, as great as the cowboy stars were, their sidekicks were even more appealing. They were riotously funny. I'm talking of Pat Buttram, with his patented squeaky voice, who moved from hanging out with Rogers to, in later movies, turning up with Autry. (Check out Buttram's 1990 Community Bank commercial on YouTube.) Smiley Burnette, Autry's most longtime pal, got laughs from me when he'd climb in his jeep, Nellybelle, and stupidly put it in reverse, sending Smiley flying. And, of course, George "Gabby" Hayes, forever stroking his geezer's white beard, and with the chops to play second banana to almost any gunslinger coming down the pike: Cassidy, Rogers, Autry, also Randolph Scott and John Wayne. I loved "Gabby," and I'm happy he's got a star on the Hollywood Walk of Fame.

A Philippi birthday party. A dozen children are fed ice-cream cake and taken to a movie: *Desperate Search* (1952). Here is a wonderful story of a brother and sister who shuttle by airplane between their divorced parents. This time, the plane crashes, all the adults are killed, including the pilot and friendly stewardess. The siblings are the only survivors. In the frozen wastes of British Columbia.

They have a bunch of harrowing adventures; and just when they are about to be ravaged by a mountain lion, their mother appears on one side of the screen, their daddy on the other. Someone with a rifle shoots the mountain lion, and the children fall into their parents' open arms. There is an especially appealing ending. The parents renew their love and decide to give their marriage one more try. Children deserve two parents.

If only every movie was this positive. But children also need to be confronted with Snow White's evil queen and the deaths of Old Yeller and Bambi's mother. They need to discover through art that evil things happen, that the world is not always a just, trustworthy place. I know that I found these things out, and painfully, at the movies. Including movies I otherwise adored. For example, *The Greatest Show on Earth* (1952), a major Hollywood film that, to my delight, played in Philippi. It presented bad news in so many ways and climaxed in a tumultuous train crash, upending and killing many circus performers.

I couldn't fathom why Jimmy Stewart's kindly clown is taken off by the police at the end and he must give his dog away. So sad! So unfair! And there's the plight of Cornel Wilde's virile trapeze artist, the Great Sebastian, falling from above and crashing to the ground. If that wasn't awful enough, Sebastian comes out of the hospital with a jacket covering his arm. The jacket is ripped away, and on-screen in close-up is Sebastian's maimed, withered hand. The horror!

I suffered with *The Greatest Show on Earth*. But two movies so frightened me that I had screaming nightmares for months afterward. *The Boy with Green Hair* (1948) persuaded me that I too would wake up with my brown locks the color of grass. Just as lethal was *In Old Chicago* (1938), which dramatized the leveling of the Windy City by Mrs. O'Leary's cow. Traumatized, I believed that our house would flame up in the night like the 1871 Chicago fire. And there was one spooky movie I've never been able to track down. A Joan Crawford–looking dame played Typhoid Mary. In a seminal scene, Typhoid Mary takes a drink from a water fountain and walks away. A few seconds later, a lamb-like little girl skips to the bubbler and also drinks. And this was in the age of polio!

Finally, a movie experience of the most intense disappointment. Like life itself. Occasionally, Alderson Broaddus College offered 16mm screenings on campus. At one of those, I'd been blindsided by the burning buildings of *In Old Chicago*. But things now looked up because I heard that *The Count of Monte Cristo* (1954) would be showing there. That meant sword fighting! Villains with pointy beards getting stabbed! Fantastic. I pushed my parents to get us there on time for the evening screening. The lights went down, the movie started up. I'd misheard! There was no Alexandre Dumas swashbuckler. The movie title was *The Countess of Monte Cristo* (1948), and it was a drab ice-skating comedy starring Sonja Henie. Blinded by anger, I made it through fifteen minutes of this effete atrocity. I couldn't take anymore. I pushed my parents to walk out.

Pouty though I was, I was right to exit *The Countess of Monte Cristo*. It was not only a lame story, but also, I know now, helmed by a filmmaking nobody, Frederick de Cordova, who was better suited to his later career as a TV director. What I've determined in the years since is that, as a kid, I had impeccable movie taste. I was, without knowing it, a proponent of the "auteur" theory, admiring cinema made by filmmakers with a distinct personal style. Cecil B. DeMille made *The Greatest Show on Earth*. Even better, Joseph Losey directed *The Boy with Green Hair*. *Desperate Search* turned out to be by "B" cult director Joseph H. Lewis. *The Adventures of Robinson Crusoe* (1954) was a work by Spain's master, Luis Buñuel. My West Virginia days, which ended in 1952, laid the aesthetic groundwork. While in sixth grade in Pennsylvania, and in junior high in South Carolina, I fell hard for Nicholas Ray's *Johnny Guitar* (1954) and *Rebel without a Cause* (1955), Howard Hawks's *Land of the Pharaohs* (1955), and Otto Preminger's *River of No Return* (1954). Best of all were the four matinees in a row in Miami Beach, when I became totally enraptured by John Ford's western *The Searchers* (1956). It was my favorite film as an eleven-year-old and remains so.

One more West Virginia anecdote. Movies were also special to me for a reason I haven't mentioned. Not one person in Philippi owned a television set. So here's my final remembrance, a show of how my media consciousness was molded by cinema.

In that golden era, each movie played repeatedly during the day and evening, with the shortest of breaks between screenings. No one shooed customers out of the theater, no usher entered to sweep up popcorn. So, if you missed, for instance, the first fifteen minutes of a film, no worry. You'd stick around and watch as the movie started up again. In fact, people often arrived in the middle of a film and stayed on for the next screening. They'd exit when they got to the familiar part, where they came in.

I absorbed all of this.

When I was seven in 1951, our family took the long, long trip by train from nearby Grafton, West Virginia, to Boston, with a switch of trains in Washington, DC. It was my mother's first cousin's wedding, and a party was held afterward in the home of the bride's relatives. There was a paneled den away from the celebrating, and in that den was the first television I'd ever seen, tuned to a western program. As I began to watch, a cowboy rode his horse into a valley. After about ten minutes, the cowboy rode again into that valley. I asked someone to turn off the TV. That's where I'd come in.

—————ɯ————

Children of the Hydra: *The 7th Voyage of Sinbad* (1958) and Special Effects Master Ray Harryhausen

James Verniere

I was born in 1951, but born again the night my mother's brother, almost a kid himself, took me to see my first film in a real movie theater: *The Beast from 20,000 Fathoms* (1953). The creature in it, a ravaging "rhedosaurus" with a lively tail created by special effects master Ray Harryhausen, left an impression on me more indelible than any I can remember from early childhood. (I also remember being perplexed when my uncle laughed uproariously while the "Beast" devoured a New York City policeman, but that's another story.) Early childhood has faded. But the "Beast" remains, in part because I have seen the film, helmed by Jean Renoir's former production designer, Eugène Lourié, and based on a story by Harryhausen's lifelong friend, Ray Bradbury, many times since. Rewatching Harryhausen is a sacred ritual for true believers.

Who knows how films become a part of us. I think a key is that films are so much like dreams. They open a window to another world, and in that dreamworld they show us things we have glimpsed only in our imaginations. Like dreams, they also transport us from a river to a desert in the wink of an eye (or a wipe or a wash). Films can take us from our real world to a world of pure fantasy—from dreary Cold War–era United States to a magical, mythic past and the island of Colossa in the Arabian Sea in *The 7th Voyage of Sinbad* (1958).

In Bruno Bettelheim's book *The Uses of Enchantment* (1976), the pioneering child psychologist and Holocaust survivor discusses the impact of fairy tales on children and their usefulness in helping children cope with harsh realities. Escapist cinema has its uses, too, and fantasy films, featuring stop-motion animation and fanciful creatures, are a beloved and inspiring staple of movies, especially the movies children love, cherish, and remember for all their lives.

Stop-motion animation is just that: a form of animation, bringing something inanimate to life before our eyes by photographing an object or a molded figure on an armature, moving it frame by frame, and then turning the result into a continuous shot and, in the case of *The 7th Voyage of Sinbad*, Harryhausen's first color film, also combining it with live-action, using a three-layered, split-screen technique that the artist and inventor dubbed Dynamation.

You can use stop-motion to "animate" a rhedosaurus, a "Corpse Bride," or a girl named Coraline, and because of the painstaking processes involved and flipbook element of the results, stop-motion has more in common with puppetry and conventional 2D animation than live-action films—although stop-motion is filmed with live-action cameras. When such artists as Georges Méliès, who was a trained magician, Willis O'Brien, or Ray Harryhausen combined stop-motion with live-action, they made it possible to bring to life the creatures of fairy tale, myth, lore, and legend on a movie screen in a way that is vastly superior to mechanical props or anything that had come before. These processes transformed filmmakers into modern-day wizards, commanding battalions of dragons, dinosaurs reawakened by nuclear testing, and sword-wielding skeletons.

The 7th Voyage of Sinbad, arguably the most important (and inspired) fantasy film of the post–World War II period, was a stunning showcase of such film wizardry. Screenwriter Ken Kolb (writer for such '50s TV series as *Have Gun—Will Travel*), director Nathan Juran (1957's *20 Million Miles to Earth*, also with Harryhausen), and Harryhausen adapted elements from the Arabian Nights tales of Sinbad the Sailor (and quite likely from Lotte Reiniger's *The Adventures of Prince Achmed*, a 1926 silent Weimar-era fantasy film featuring animated silhouettes and creatures from Arabian myth and legend). Also adding immeasurably to the power of *The 7th Voyage of Sinbad* is an electrifying score by Bernard Herrmann, admittedly inspired by Nikolai Rimsky-Korsakov's 1888 symphonic suite *Scheherazade*.

The result suggests that the admixture of Juran, Harryhausen, and Herrmann could bring to life on the screen anything that could be imagined, however chimerical. And this was long before the advent of today's computer-generated imagery—a process that turns special effects into imagery that is arguably more realistic but often cheesy and less dream-like.

Not that Harryhausen was the first to achieve such movie magic. His creations came as the culmination of an evolutionary chain linking Georges Méliès's early silent cinema fantasies, Willis O'Brien's monster saurians in *The Lost World* (1925), George Pal's 1940s-era "Puppetoons," and the simian superstars of *King Kong* (1933) and *Mighty Joe Young* (1949), on which Harryhausen served under the original stop-motion master, "Obie" O'Brien.

The 7th Voyage of Sinbad, with its cyclops, fire-breathing dragon, its dancing blue-skinned serpent woman (a forerunner of Harryhausen's Medusa in 1981's *Clash of the Titans*), its two-headed giant roc and its offspring, all conceived, sculpted, painted, manipulated, and photographed frame by frame by the special effects maestro, jolted my childhood senses. The cyclops was especially unforgettable. It is one thing to read about the mythological Polyphemus in *The Children's Homer* (1918), as I did along with thousands of other children of the '50s, with illustrator Willy Pogany's human-like Cyclops. It is quite another to behold Harryhausen's howling, one-eyed giant. It is a thing out of a nightmare, with a sharp single horn above its large single eye, pointed ears, three-fingered claws, goat-like legs and hindquarters, cloven hooves, and a taste for human flesh.

Harryhausen, ahem, cannibalized the armature (the jointed, metal endoskeleton) he used for the Martian "ymir" in *20 Million Miles to Earth* to create the cyclops. Making its oddly sprung, wobbly entrance to the blast of Herrmann's shrieking horns (pipes?) and licking its lips as it turned a victim on a skewer, the cyclops is an unforgettable vision out of hell (model kits still available on eBay).

Anticipating the groundbreaking motion-capture performances of Andy Serkis (Gollum of *The Lord of the Rings* series, Caesar of the *Planet of the Apes* films, among others), Harryhausen's creatures had a crude personality. Undoubtedly, this was another lesson learned from *King Kong* (and even earlier from Boris Karloff's Frankenstein's monster and the pitiable Quasimodo of Lon Chaney).

Give your "monster" an aggrieved, alienated, or wounded personality, as well as a writhing-in-agony death scene, and moviegoers—especially children—will clutch it to their hearts. Even the cop-gobbling dinosaur from *The Beast from 20,000 Fathoms* (1953) looks like a lost, angry canine at times, and it's sick to boot, thanks to the atomic bomb that awakened it. The misplaced rhedosaurus, ymir, and allosaurus of *The Valley of Gwangi* (1969) just wanted to go home or back to the peaceful slumber or solitude from which they had been rudely interrupted by humans. Even Medusa was, according to Ovid, a formerly beautiful mortal maiden ravished by the lustful god Poseidon and horribly transformed by a vengeful Athena. This homesick-monster angle would achieve pop apotheosis in Steven Spielberg's *E.T. the Extra-Terrestrial* (1982).

But supernatural beasts alone don't make Sinbad an archetypal childhood experience. The human element contributes as well. That includes Sokurah the Magician, the diabolical villain marvelously played by stentorian British actor Torin Thatcher (1953's *The Robe* and 1946's *Great Expectations*), who would have made a great Darth Vader; the beguiling Princess Parisa, animated, if you will, by Kathryn Grant's alluring voice, face, and form; a genie in the guise of the freckle-faced then-boy actor Richard Eyer; and finally the intrepid and affable, if rather stiff, scimitar-wielding title hero played by Kerwin Matthews. (Could the young George Lucas have been so inspired by the scene in which Sinbad and Parisa swing over the river of lava that he re-created it for his 1977 *Star Wars*?)

Also hearkening back to *King Kong*, Harryhausen's fantasies boast a beautiful heroine, who is provocatively dressed and undressed (à la Fay Wray) to show the audience that adventure isn't all monsters, genies, and sorcerers. Adding to the film's stature are live-action scenes shot on location at the ninth-century Palace of the Alhambra, in Grenada, Spain. Mix all these ingredients together and you have high-grade kiddie crack cocaine in motion-picture form.

How did Harryhausen—who received an honorary Academy Award in 1992 and died in 2013, at ninety-two—become the only special effects master whose name sparks the same brand recognition as Hitchcock, Disney, and Spielberg?

He first recognized his vocation when he saw *King Kong* at the age of thirteen. It changed his life. He saw an ape-like monster, unlike any ape ever seen or heard before. Heard, especially. Kong roared with the recorded roars of a lion and tiger combined and played slowly backward. In addition to such powerful sound effects, the Max Steiner score intensifies the suspense and evokes a deliriously romantic sensibility.

Harryhausen likely first learned to appreciate the impact of music and sound watching (and rewatching) *King Kong*. He also probably recognized that Kong was not just some ape out of a zoo, but a denizen of the dark, Jungian, collective unconscious, a terrifying, tangible entity with weirdly bristling fur (reportedly, O'Brien wanted the beast to look more human). Kong was a figment from a dream but, because of the stop-motion animation, also overwhelmingly real.

Transformed into a CG image in Peter Jackson's otherwise worthy 2005 remake, the ape loses this aura of tangible otherness and is just another big ape—anatomically and zoologically correct but without the evocative strangeness and power of the dreamworld original. CG strives for verisimilitude, a pixel image made to look real down to the last follicle. But stop-motion brings the unreal—a rabbit fur-covered, wire-wrapped, jointed armature—to life. As much as I have enjoyed Peter Jackson's *The Lord of the Rings* (2001–2003) trilogy and *The Hobbit*

(2012), a part of me clings to the idea that stop-motion is the ideal venue for Tolkien's stories, as well as most fantasy subjects.

Perhaps what CG needs is a Harryhausen of its own. Stanley Kubrick died before the evolution of the computer technology needed for his version of *A.I. Artificial Intelligence* (made by Spielberg in 2001). To see what a master can do with CG combined with makeup and animatronics, look at Guillermo del Toro's modern classic *Pan's Labyrinth* (2006). Del Toro's vision is intensely strange and phantasmagorical, not realistic at all. His CG fairies aren't winged runway models in Victoria's Secret outfits, but odd-looking "dirty fairies" (his words) with leaves for wings.

But the gulf between the spell of stop-motion and the literalism of CG might be too much for a single genius to overcome. Harryhausen used mechanical means and did everything himself: sculpting, painting, lighting, manipulating, shooting, and matching stop-motion images to live-action. CG is a digital process, requiring dozens, if not hundreds, of artists and even multiple companies, each with a specific task to accomplish on a computer. Harryhausen's art is a singular, analogical vision. CG is a collective effort, taking place in an entirely digital realm. Stop-motion is rooted in the real world. CGI is the ghost in the machine. It is what is used to create such 3D-animated films as the landmark Pixar achievement *Toy Story* (1995). But compare the CGI-created Shrek films and the Disney smash hit *Frozen* (2013) to the stop-motion works *Coraline* (2008), *Corpse Bride* (2005), and *ParaNorman* (2012), and the difference is almost palpable.

Proponents of today's CGI might disparage the herky-jerky-ism of stop-motion and the sometimes-imperfect match between live-action and stop-motion images. But these supposed flaws make the stop-motion action appear that much more otherworldly and dream-like.

That's how it seemed to audiences in 1958, when *The 7th Voyage of Sinbad* was a huge, surprise hit (and again when rereleased in 1975), spawning numerous copycat Sinbad movies. One of these, *The Magic Voyage of Sinbad* (1962), was a dubbed and recut (with dialogue rewritten by Francis Ford Coppola) version of *Sadko*, a 1952 Soviet production directed by Harryhausen-like Soviet filmmaker Aleksandr Ptushko. Another was *Captain Sindbad* (1963), directed by Byron Haskin, with special effects by Tom Howard (*2001: A Space Odyssey*).

Fans seeking another Harryhausen in these films were disappointed. Harryhausen himself tried to recapture lightning in a bottle with the follow-ups *The Golden Voyage of Sinbad* (1973) and *Sinbad and the Eye of the Tiger* (1977). They weren't quite the same. But much of the old magic returned with *Jason and the Argonauts* (1963), an adaptation of the Greek myth with special effects by

Harryhausen and another Herrmann score. Since a duel between Sinbad and an animated skeleton in *The 7th Voyage* had caused such a sensation (British censors felt it was too frightening for children), Harryhausen figured he should up the ante in *Jason*, animating an entire platoon of skeletons in the famous "children of the Hydra" sequence in the new film.

That scene thrilled me, but not as much as when I saw *The 7th Voyage of Sinbad* for the first time. I also recall being floored by the late entrance of one of the greatest movie dragons ever, a Narwhal-horned, green-skinned, spike-tailed wonder that I bet author J. K. Rowling first beheld as a spellbound English girl long before she dreamed of Harry Potter. Harryhausen held back one of his best creations for the final act of the movie.

After being amazed by *The 7th Voyage of Sinbad* on the screen, I was inspired to seek out all things Sinbad in my Nutley, New Jersey, parochial school's small library, presided over by a tall librarian with the eerily apt name Miss Troy (also curator of the town's Annie Oakley Museum), where I learned of the variant spellings of Sinbad/Sindbad's name. There I found a *7th Voyage of Sindbad* in the print that differed a lot from the film—although it does feature birdmen and an elephant king. Later, I would voyage farther afield to the larger Belleville, New Jersey, town library, one of my first solo outings away from home as a child.

In a way, Harryhausen's films sent me on a 1950s–1960s suburban variation of Sinbad's journeys, featuring unknown streets and strange, if not wizard-like, librarians. In this quest I found Greek and Roman mythology to feed my hunger. In what I would later learn was a favorite Jorge Luis Borges metaphor, libraries became my own private Colossa. One of my discoveries, *The Tales of the Arabian Nights*, with Art Nouveau illustrations by Edmund Dulac, remains a treasured possession and a gift I often give to children in my family.

It was not much of a leap from Edith Hamilton and *Bulfinch's Mythology* to books about fantasy films. One of the best and most influential was *An Illustrated History of the Horror Film* (1967), an insightful and scholarly work by Havana-born, Sorbonne-educated Carlos Clarens. Reading it I experienced for the first time the thought that I, too, might write about film professionally one day. Later, as a young film critic in New York City, I was lucky enough to meet Clarens.

Even luckier, a few years later, I found myself assigned to interview Harryhausen himself for a story about *Clash of the Titans*. More than two decades after seeing *The 7th Voyage of Sinbad* for the first time, I was having a working lunch with the master himself in the Oak Room at the Plaza Hotel. He did not have goat legs and was very reserved and soft-spoken. He answered my questions, accepted my respect and admiration, and kindly signed a copy of *Cinefantastique* magazine featuring him on the cover that I'd brought with me.

How many times have I revisited Harryhausen's Colossa since first seeing *The 7th Voyage of Sinbad*? As a working film critic, I could say every day. I'm still addicted to Harryhausen's magic and my boyhood sense of awe and wonder. What is *Game of Thrones* if not a Ray Harryhausen movie in modern cable television series form? Long live the children of the Hydra.

—⚹—

How Seeing *Airport* (1970) as a Kid Grounded My Critical Sensibility
Charles Taylor

My dad worked as a manager for a supermarket chain for almost forty years, running stores, making displays, unloading trucks. The Boston suburb he and my mother moved to when I was two and lived in until she died of ovarian cancer after fifty-four years of marriage is a town they couldn't afford to move to if they were a young couple now. Things were always tight in the middle of the week before payday, and since my mother didn't work, I knew we were dependent on my dad's well-being. There were a couple of times when an upcoming union vote on whether to strike was a black cloud over the house. But even when an accident put my father out of work for twelve weeks—an aluminum sliding ladder he was standing on to paint the house collapsed; he fell to the ground and the ladder fell on top of him, breaking both his wrists—there was still food on the table. Looking back, I realize I must have spent a good part of my childhood practicing the trick of not admitting the worst—that we might be poor—as even a possibility.

I didn't talk about any of this, maybe because I believed that talking about it made it more likely to happen. And given my parents' desire to protect me, an impulse I colluded in, I knew they'd just brush away the possibility, which wouldn't have alleviated the fear in the first place.

This may be why I've never had any patience for sneering at middle-class aspirations, or at the pleasure middle-class and working-class people take in new possessions. Those easy swipes at American consumerism never understand that that pleasure is less about the things than about the security and pride those things instill in their owners. I remember the unspoken sense of security my folks and I shared when it came time to get a new car and we were able to do so. Just as I remember the underlying nervousness when times were leaner, and my dad was trying to find a deal on a new car before the one he'd been driving fell apart on him. Going into my parents' kitchen and seeing the same oven that was there for almost forty years, looking, due to my father's faithful cleaning of it after every meal, pretty much as it did when it was delivered, told me something about the pride people take in being able to maintain a nice home. Of course, the downside is the nagging sense that what you've got isn't good enough. But if you've ever felt not just pleasure, but also a sense of accomplishment in being able to get a new easy chair or a new oven, it's not easy to dismiss.

And it has a lot to do with the reason that, when I was eight or so, *Airport* (1970) hit me so hard.

Airport was the first movie I saw in the theater that wasn't a cartoon or a musical or what director Joe Dante called those "flying rubber professor movies." My mom, who'd read the Arthur Hailey novel, had already seen it, but my Aunt Vera, who was visiting, hadn't. So, she, my mom, my dad, and I went to our neighborhood theater, where it was near the end of its run. And I was overwhelmed. It seemed very grown-up to me, exciting in a way the movies I'd seen hadn't been.

And it was Van Heflin, the bomber who puts the central drama of the movie into motion, who both terrified me and to whom I felt closer than any other character. Heflin plays a businessman at the end of his rope who plans to blow up a plane and leave his wife (Maureen Stapleton) the insurance. This was a white-collar worker with a job higher up the food chain than my dad. What scared me was how low he could be brought. It wasn't that low—but to a sheltered only-kid in a suburban home, it looked dicey enough.

Every detail of Heflin's scenes drilled their way into my head: the doily on the bureau in his apartment, which I immediately understood was someone's attempt to give a comforting touch to this shabby place. I remember the below-street level diner where Stapleton worked as a waitress (this was someone whose wife had to work) and the way she dug into her tip jar to give Heflin money to get to the airport. And I remember the look Heflin wore as he accepted the money, a look that told you exactly what it cost him to put a good face on things. Only he couldn't any longer and looked as if he was being eaten alive from the inside out. (It's the face I fear I'm getting on bad days.) And every pained look on that face reflected my worst childhood fears—just as years later, Vittorio De Sica's *Umberto D.* (1952) put my worst adult fears right in front of me.

Airport was a big G-rated hit, critically derided as the type of movie for middle-class Americans who felt shut out by the pictures Hollywood was making in a desperate appeal to the counterculture market. Most of the attention went to Helen Hayes's god-awful performance as a cutesy old-lady stowaway. The movie's musty *Grand Hotel* (1932) scheme swamps even the likes of Burt

Lancaster and Dean Martin, a man who was as relaxed in front of a camera as any performer has ever been. There's panic beneath the surface of the movie, a desperation on the part of the filmmakers (the director was George Seaton) and the studio (Universal) to bring back a Hollywood they could comprehend.

And in the midst of this, there's the hounded look on Heflin's face, the face of a weary animal about to give itself up to the dogs on its trail. And there's Maureen Stapleton, whose final scene is simply astounding, one of those potentially over-the-top moments that, in the movies, create their own reality that is so strong it renders everything around it phony. Stapleton has figured out her husband's plan and gotten to the airport too late to stop him. At the end of the movie, after a shaky landing and as the passengers safely make their way off the crippled plane, Stapleton stands by the gate, greeting each one with an anguished, tearful apology. Thinking she's a crazy woman, they pass her by.

Nothing I'd ever seen in a movie prepared me for that. And the scene still gets to me. Now, when kids are raised in such a protective bubble that their parents are afraid to give them inorganic milk, I wonder how many of them are getting the experiences, even from bad movies, that told earlier generations of moviegoers something about the adult world we had only guessed at?

—∞—

Revisiting *Old Yeller* (1957) and *Yellow Submarine* (1968)
Peter Keough

When I was seven years old and living in the town of Stoughton, Massachusetts, my family adopted a collie, Shep, that had been owned by a group of nuns who could no longer care for him. Shep looked like Lassie, with silky hair that smelled like lanolin. One day I was walking with my friend Billy down Pine Street, and Shep ran into the street just as dump truck full of gravel rumbled by. It hit him, and he exploded.

Fur covered the bloody pulp, spread out like a carpet. I remember the sound, a loud pop and a splash. The stain on the road was still there when we moved a year or so later to Roslindale, a neighborhood in Boston, and a strange, hard-to-describe odor hovered there. It wasn't unpleasant, but whenever I catch a whiff of it now, or think I do, I'm seized with horror. It didn't help much when I suggested we pray for Shep's soul and someone, a priest, told me dogs don't have souls and that he ceased to exist.

Perhaps that experience contributed to the depression I fell into when I was seventeen. I dropped out of college for a while and spent time in mental hospitals. I was prescribed many pharmaceuticals and celebrated my twenty-first birthday, my mind a blank, staring at a cup of coffee and a glass of orange juice on a place mat that read, "You are at St. Elizabeth's Hospital and have just had an ECT treatment."

I suppose the ECT helped. I gradually got better. But I wonder what effect movies might have had on my mental health, for better or worse. Did films that touched on inner turmoil only bring back the pain of past experiences, or did they provide a safe forum to confront them, work out conflicts, and find some resolution? In particular, *Old Yeller* (1957) and *Yellow Submarine* (1968) come to mind as movies that might have triggered flashbacks to these dark moments. I remember seeing them and recall them having an impact, but the shock treatments affect my memory and the details are foggy. To find out what happened when I first saw them, I decided to watch them again, hoping that my expertise as a film critic would help me understand what they meant to me.

I remember first seeing *Old Yeller* (directed by John Stevenson, who, perhaps, feeling remorse for traumatizing a generation of children, went on to direct *Mary Poppins* in 1964) a few years after Shep died, probably at the local second-run movie theater, the Rialto, in Roslindale Square. At the risk of a spoiler, the dog of the title dies in the end. Almost sixty years later, about to watch the movie on Amazon Prime, the prospect of seeing that ending again filled me with trepidation.

It begins with a theme song celebrating the "best doggone dog in the West" and shots of post–Civil War Texas. Jim Coates (Fess Parker), an ex-Confederate soldier struggling to feed his family on their hardscrabble farm, heads off to spend four months on a cattle drive to earn some Yankee dollars. Left back at the ranch are his wife Katie (Dorothy Malone, who went on to play the Virgin Mary in the 1965 biblical epic *The Greatest Story Ever Told*) and two boys, stern Travis (Disney fixture Tommy Kirk, later a Hollywood pariah when he was found out to be gay) and his rascally younger brother Arliss (Kevin Corcoran, who would play Kirk's younger brother in four more films).

Fess Parker. Bad sign. As Davy Crockett, he inspired a generation of kids to wear fake coonskin caps and believe in immortality. He was last seen in *Davy Crockett: King of the Wild Frontier* (1955), which was regularly broadcast on the Walt Disney TV show. In the movie, Davy is the last man standing at the Alamo, swatting Mexican soldiers with his rifle butt as the screen faded to black.

Did he survive? Do dogs have souls?

Actor/writer Stephen Tobolowsky best describes the impact of this shocking scene on young fans in his 2012 memoir *The Dangerous Animals Club*. "How could Disney do this to me?" he writes. "It wasn't just the end of the story. . . . It was the end of something I looked up to. Something with real meaning. It was the end of decency, reason . . ."

It was a sadistic betrayal. Setting kids up with expectations of everlasting glory only to smack them down with the tragic reality they would inevitably face.

Just seeing Fess Parker on the screen made me angry and anxious. So, my mind wandered to the film's oedipal subtext, a case study in conflicts and neuroses that was undoubtedly unintentional. Say what you will about the scientific validity of Freud's theories, he would have made a great film critic. I think he might have suggested that Old Yeller symbolizes Travis's desire for his mother. But Travis resists this taboo, drives the dog away, and even threatens to shoot him if it comes back—foreshadowing the tragedy to come.

But Travis's brother Arliss takes an immediate liking to Old Yeller. And when Old Yeller attacks a bear threatening to kill Arliss—the bear representing, oh, I don't know, Travis's thwarted desire for his mother metamorphosing into a new, more powerful incursion of the id, which also tries to fulfill a latent sibling rivalry wish–fulfillment fantasy—Travis bonds with the dog. He "masters" it and turns it into a helpmate, a protector, an extension of his ego.

Enter Burn Sanderson (played by another familiar face, Chuck Connors of the TV show *The Rifleman*, onanistic master of the phallic lever-action Winchester rifle), and if this were a more adult western, say, directed by Anthony Mann or Budd Boetticher, Katie might have done more than serve Burn a home-cooked meal. Even so, Burn looks sinister, especially when it turns out that Old Yeller used to be his dog, who he had banished because of a persistent egg-sucking problem.

Just as Travis has his oedipal compulsion under control and integrated it usefully into his psyche, here comes this father figure to disrupt everything. But for now, Burn is a nice guy. He lets Travis keep the dog, even though this seeming kindness, in the long run, doesn't do anyone any favors.

More conflicts between ego and id follow. Old Yeller rescues Travis from wild boars. And he fights off a wolf that Travis needlessly antagonizes. That last encounter proves fatal. The wolf turns out to have "hydrophobia," or rabies, and after the long, anxious, desperately hopeful quarantine of Old Yeller in a corn-crib, the dog goes mad, snapping at the heartbroken Travis.

Come to think of it, maybe the poor mutt didn't even have hydrophobia. Maybe he just got fed up because he figured that after giving up eggs and saving Arliss from a bear, a wild boar, and a wolf, he'd get a better deal than being locked up for weeks in a corn crib. What does a dog have to do to catch a break from this family? I'd be mad, too.

Either way, it doesn't matter. The time for Old Yeller and Travis to part has come. Travis must become a man, and the dog must die. Travis sticks the barrel through the slats and fires a shot. In a typical Disney-esque gesture of decency and good taste, the audience is spared the sight of Old Yeller's death.

But that's not the way I remember it, and this was the part of the movie I was sure I had not forgotten. I remember Old Yeller jumping up and down, writhing and snarling and frothing in agony in the distance when Travis fires the fatal shot. That scene is in fact from *To Kill a Mockingbird* (1962), a film I saw later. Another dog with hydrophobia is endangering a community, and seeming greenhorn Atticus Finch grabs a gun, takes off his glasses, and plugs the writhing dog one hundred yards down the road with one shot. The kids, Scout and Jem, are stunned, not because their dad killed an animal, but because he had it in him to do so, that he was, as one of the locals comments, the best shot in the county.

Now it all came back to me. Unlike in *Old Yeller*, the dog in *To Kill a Mockingbird* died in the open, on the road, like my own dog. I had transposed the scene to the earlier film, suggesting to myself that the traumatic memory of Shep's death had been exiled for good into the corn crib with Old Yeller, where it would never bother me again.

In a way, the dead dog in the corn crib emerged again for me about ten years later, when I had my nervous breakdown.

I got drunk at a New Year's Eve party during the Christmas break as a college freshman. I looked into a mirror, and the abyss swallowed me whole—an inverse, irreversible epiphany, a palpable immersion into nothingness. Typical teenaged stuff. For a while I believed the world, myself, and everyone else did not exist. Then for a while I believed only I existed.

I was paralyzed by depression. My first therapist, Dr. Shapiro, prescribed a variety of the then-new miracle drugs: Elavil, Stelazine, Trazodone, Mellaril, Marplan, Trilafon, Tofranil—it was the golden age of tricyclic antidepressants. Plus talk therapy. "People do not become depressed for existential reasons," he said when I whined about the futility of life and inevitability of death. He suggested I stop reading depressing, metaphysically disorienting books, like *The Painted Bird*, *Nausea*, and Jorge Luis Borges's *A Personal Anthology*, and stop watching such distressing movies as *The Seventh Seal* (1957), *El Topo* (1970), and *Performance* (1970).

How about *Yellow Submarine?* I asked. I avoided it when it first came out, and it was playing in a revival at the Brattle Theatre. Dr. Shapiro had no objection.

Why would he? An animated bonbon based on the Beatles' silliest, perkiest tune? So I watched it. What happened?

Probably nothing bad, judging from my second viewing. But there are a few treacherous moments. It is much dippier and more un-Beatley than I expected (this was director George Dunning's first and only feature film). For example, the song "Strawberry Fields" ("Let me take you down, 'cos I'm going to Strawberry Fields / Nothing is real," etc.). Now that's the kind of trippy stuff that will get an unstable mind working overtime. You can still buy a *Yellow Submarine* coffee cup on Amazon and eBay with the logo "nothing is real" printed on it.

But neither the song nor that line are in the movie. I was sure they were—like the death scene in *Old Yeller*, I was positive I remembered this correctly.

I was also disappointed that, except for a two-minute live appearance at the end, and the songs on the soundtrack, the Beatles aren't in the movie at all. For example, the animated Paul is voiced by Geoffrey Hughes, an actor who went on to roles in several British TV comedy series, had a part in Spike Milligan's 1973 farce *Adolf Hitler: My Part in His Downfall*, was awarded the post of Deputy Lord Lieutenant for the Isle of Wight, and died in 2012, at the age of sixty-eight. And John Clive, the faux John, went on to bit parts in *The Italian Job* (1969) and *A Clockwork Orange* (1971), and, in 1972, played the first gay character in the British *Carry On* comedy series. He died in 2012, at age seventy-eight, thirty-two years after Lennon was murdered by John Hinckley Jr. In short, despite the adorable Liverpudlian accents, this faux four did not match up well with the Fab Four.

On the other hand, the animation enhances the songs with sometimes haunting effect. A montage of grim "lonely people" in the "Eleanor Rigby" sequence engaging in repetitive actions (a '60s version of today's "gif") revitalizes a tune that by now has degenerated into kitsch after decades of overuse. The "Sea of Holes" sequence played entertaining head games with visual and spatial paradoxes, which, had not the rest of the film maintained a tone of fizzy inconsequentiality, could even now plunge me into an old habit of angst-filled, compulsive circular thinking. It also features one of the best lines in the film, when Ringo (voiced by Paul Angelis, who would do a lot of TV and appeared in the 1981 Bond film *For Your Eyes Only* as "Karageorge") says, "I've got a hole in me pocket." Very droll given the context.

For the most part, however, and this may not be a criticism, the animation comes off as defanged Terry Gilliam, with none of the Monty Python genius' gleefully oneiric and surreal monstrosities (credit the film's Czech avant-garde designer, Heinz Edelmann, whose other claim to fame is creating the 1992 Seville World's Fair mascot, "Curro").

The wild card in the movie, appropriately enough, the one most likely to rattle the cage of a disturbed young mind, is George, the mystical Beatle. He's played by Paul Batten, who turns out to be a figure even more elusive than George himself. As the *Guardian* newspaper reported in "The Fake Four," an August 23, 1999, article on the film, at the end of the production, "Batten was in bed with one of the young women on the production team when the military police burst in and arrested him for desertion. He has not been seen or heard of since."

Maybe that's why George has only one tune in the picture, "Only a Northern Song." As one verse puts it,

> If you think the harmony
> Is a little dark and out of key
> You're correct
> There's nobody there.

How true. And George/Batten repeatedly mutters the most unsettling line, over and over again: "It's all in the mind, you know."

It still gives me a passing chill. But after the innocuous Blue Meanies; the soothing Sea of Green; a nonthreatening Sea of Nothing; the annoying, rhyming polymath Jeremy Hillary Boob, PhD, aka the Nowhere Man; and the endless bad puns I no doubt parroted later with my fellow would-be hip friends I probably thought to myself back then the same thing I do know—no big deal. Movies were all in your mind as well. They were ephemeral and illusory and fun. Maybe life was that way, too.

—⁂—

Light in Auggie: In *Wonder* (2017), a Deformed Child Isn't the Only Flawed Character
J. R. Jones[1]

August Pullman, the ten-year-old boy at the center of Stephen Chbosky's *Wonder*, is severely deformed: The bridge of his nose reaches to his forehead in a straight line, the corners of his eyes are pulled down in a perpetual sob, his cheeks are traced by scars, and withered ears peek out from under his long hair. One dreads to think what he might have looked like before the twenty-seven plastic surgeries he mentions near the beginning of the film. Auggie's devoted mother, Isabel (Julia Roberts), has been homeschooling him since he was small, but the time has come for Auggie to join the world. As the story opens, he, Isabel, and Auggie's gentle, laid-back father, Nate (Owen Wilson), are anxiously preparing for the first day of class at the local public school, where Auggie will be dropped into the shark-infested waters of fifth grade.

I come to this review highly credentialed because, growing up, I paid some of the same dues as young Auggie. When I was born, my left ear was only a nubbin of flesh, and from age four to eleven, I underwent thirteen plastic surgeries to construct something that looked halfway normal. These involved skin grafts from my legs and, later, in a more invasive procedure, cartilage extracted from my ribcage. Seeing one's body carved up and reassembled can be horrifying for a child; I still remember the grinning doctor who, having painfully cut through and plucked out the stitches in my chest and drawn out a length of black surgical thread, handed me the tweezers and asked if I wanted to finish the job myself. At some point there was talk of drilling a hole through my skull to create an auditory canal, but when I was in sixth grade, my parents decided enough was enough and the surgeries ended, leaving my ear like an unfinished swimming pool.

Because of that history, I may approach *Wonder* less sentimentally than other viewers (at least that's my excuse this time). So you can take my word for it that the movie, adapted from a children's book by R. J. Palacio, treats its young protagonist and his craniofacial deformity with respect and common sense. The film delves inside not only Auggie and his overlooked older sister, Via (Izabela Vidovic), but also several of their classmates, who are much easier on the eyes but have as much trouble looking in the mirror as Auggie. So while Auggie's experience in school doesn't exactly square with mine—the kids at school bully him for his disability, which was considered uncool even when I was growing up—I have to admire a storyteller who recognizes that emotional flaws can be every bit as debilitating as physical ones.

One thing Chbosky gets right is the discomfort of being stared at by strangers. "You're gonna feel like you're all alone, but you're not," Nate tells Auggie when the family drops him off at school—loving words but a paltry defense against the sea of eyes widening with sick fascination as Auggie ventures through the playground and the crowd parts to let him pass. This shot from Auggie's perspective wouldn't be nearly as haunting if the director hadn't already played on our voyeurism in the opening scenes, where Auggie (a science whiz and *Star Wars* fanatic) romps around the family's house in a spherical white astronaut's helmet whose black visor hides his face. Chbosky gives us an uncertain glimpse of Auggie in his bedroom at night when the boy pulls off his helmet and his face is reflected in the darkened glass of a window, but only the next morning, when his parents take him to meet the principal, are his features fully exposed.

Wonder takes place in a school full of wise, with-it teachers and cruel, clueless children, which doesn't really square with the more complicated social terrain I remember. The principal, Mr. Tushman (Mandy Patinkin), appoints a trio of kids, including Jack and Julian, to welcome Auggie to the student body, although they mainly pull away from him once classes have begun. Jack (Noah Jupe) connects with the new kid immediately but takes his social cues from rich, handsome Julian (Bryce Gheisar), whose personal antagonism toward Auggie progresses from smart remarks ("Do you eat special food?") to physical bullying to vicious notes and cartoons stuffed into Auggie's locker. All of that can and may well happen, but in my own school experience from kindergarten onward, hassling someone because of a physical deformity was considered obnoxious (and unnecessary, because in fifth grade you can get hassled for nothing at all). I had more trouble from well-meaning but incompetent teachers who'd single me out in class and invite the other students to pity me.

My relationships with my siblings were all shaped (perhaps misshaped) by the inordinate amount of attention I got from my parents, a dynamic to which *Wonder* is well attuned. After sticking with Auggie for a while, Chbosky turns to Via, a high schooler whose identity has been defined by her younger brother. Via loves and looks out for Auggie, but she craves the attention of her mother, who's even more preoccupied with the boy now that he's caught up in the social crises of middle school. Via's best friend, Miranda (Danielle Rose Russell), returns from summer camp and inexplicably freezes her out, although Via keeps this heartache to herself ("I just knew my family couldn't take one more thing," she explains). Her life brightens when a classmate named Justin (Nadji Jeter) urges her to audition for the school play with him and they edge toward romance. Via is so delighted to be the object of his gaze that she deletes Auggie from her life, telling Justin she's an only child.

This being a family film, Auggie triumphs at the end, winning not only a place for himself in the school, but also a medal, awarded at the last assembly of the year, for the positive influence he's exerted on the student body. Apparently, nothing can stop educators from singling out a kid for his disability and using him as part of their lesson plan. Prior to that scene, however, *Wonder* levels the social playing field by widening its narrative frame to focus on Jack, Julian, and Miranda, each of whom hurts as much as Auggie and his family. In one scene, Miranda—who lives alone with her divorced, bitter, and lonely mother—stands outside the Pullman's house, spying on them through a window as the happy foursome decorates the Christmas tree. Like Auggie, Miranda has serious problems, but hers are invisible to others, and those are usually the kind that get you in the end.

—∽m⌁—

The Many Kinds of Movie Wonder

Jonathan Rosenbaum[2]

Wonder is closer to a feeling than a thought, and one that we associate with both children and grown-ups recapturing some of the open-mouthed awe and innocence they had as children. Many of us experienced some of this as kids watching the classic Disney cartoon features or certain live-action fantasy adventures, like *King Kong* (1933) or *The Thief of Bagdad* (1940).

Other generations, for that matter, might recall feeling a comparable emotion before the vast spaces of the 1916 *Intolerance* (whose gigantic Babylon set would eventually be redressed for *Kong's* Skull Island) or the 1924 *Thief of Bagdad* or the 2005 *King Kong*—or even in that hokey opening line, "A long time ago, in a galaxy far, far away . . ." Or what about the hushed sense of reverence that we bring to the virgin wilderness of *The Big Sky* (1952), whose very title expresses our feeling of astonishment? It's a primal emotion, particularly as it relates to cinema in the old-fashioned sense: 35-millimeter projection in palatial theaters, the screen invariably much larger than us (*Bigger Than Life*, as the title of Nicholas Ray's 1956 melodrama in CinemaScope has it). Of course, with the advent of digital video, smaller screens, home viewing, and a more detailed interest on the part of the public in understanding how various visual effects are achieved, some of this innocence and involvement has been altered. But our primal sense of wonder tied to the cinematic experience remains, despite everything, and without it I'm not even sure if we'd still be watching nearly as much.

If we consider the role played by our imaginations in "completing" a film's image and sound filling in the dark spaces that appear between the film frames without ever consciously seeing them, and doing pretty much the same thing with off-screen spaces, for example, responding creatively to suggestive soundtracks by filling in additional images of our own, this shouldn't be at all surprising. "I want to give the audience a hint of a scene," Orson Welles said early in his career. "No more than that. Give them too much and they won't contribute anything themselves. Give them just a suggestion and you get them working with you." In fact, he was referring explicitly to theater and implicitly to radio when he said this in 1938, not to cinema at all. But the sense of wonder he brought to movies soon thereafter in *Citizen Kane* (1941) and *The Magnificent Ambersons* (1942) had a lot to do with adapting some of the discoveries he'd already made about other dramatic forms to express a certain wonderment about America in the late nineteenth century. One might even add to this that the medium for expressing this wonderment is secondary; it's the feeling itself that remains primary—the experience of remaining an infant basking in the warmth and expanse of a maternal screen and wondering where all this bounty comes from.

The military term "shock and awe" could be viewed as a kind of perversion of cinematic wonder, sought after and applied with the aggressive assault of a blunt instrument. There's always been this brutal side to movies as well, although I think it would be lamentable to associate this kind of coercion too closely with wonder. The best kinds of wonder in movies are the ones that invite and encourage idle speculation rather than those that are designed to settle disputes, stop conversations cold, or simply intimidate. Wonder is a kind of question mark from which fear is not so much abolished as held in an exquisitely sustained abeyance, allowing the mind, in a relaxed state, to fill in the gaps with all sorts of possibilities. Terrifying and brutalizing the spectator, by contrast, has zip to do with soliciting the gentler responses of wonder.

Charles Laughton's sublime *The Night of the Hunter* (1955), charting the nightmarish pursuit of two children by an insane and deadly preacher (Robert Mitchum) across an Expressionist version of rural Depression America, certainly has its chilling moments. Yet, these are mainly experienced as secondary to the sense of poetic wonder felt by these children about the world they're inhabiting and sometimes rushing through. There's a sinister edge to the preacher's nocturnal silhouette on horseback as seen by the boy protagonist from a distant hayloft while he hears the villain faintly singing "Leaning on the Everlasting Arms." Yet, it's the boy's relatively calm sense of wonder about this threat—"Don't he never sleep?"—that leaves the most profound impression. If fear were all he was experiencing, we wouldn't end up with any sense of wonder at all.

Another emotion that needs to be sharply distinguished from wonder is curiosity—especially the kind that killed the cat and leads us remorselessly through whodunits. Let's call curiosity, in this case, a very limited kind of wonder, restricted mainly to details of plot and character that fill out an incomplete jigsaw puzzle. Wonder is more spiritual and all-encompassing than that, and therefore less geared as a rule to straight-ahead storytelling. As gifted a storyteller as Steven Spielberg is, the moment in *Close Encounters of the Third Kind* (1977) when we arrive at the massive landing of the huge alien spaceship is basically a stretched-out moment when the story stops and the spectacle takes over. I'm reminded of the term used by American film theorist Tom Gunning, the "cinema of attractions," which links early movies to carnival sideshows rather than serial cliffhangers. Both are, of course, essential aspects of our experiences of movies, but the elements that provoke our wonder are more apt to exist as spectacle than plot or action: the landscapes in an Anthony Mann western like *The Naked Spur* (1953) or *Man of the West* (1958), or the fairy-tale waterfall in Nicholas Ray's *Johnny Guitar* (1954).

And when we turn to independent cinema and art cinema, a sense that people and life are ultimately unknowable—or at least unfathomable—lies behind the sense of wonder about the world and the human condition conveyed in very different ways by Michelangelo Antonioni, Robert Bresson, John Cassavetes, Carl Dreyer, and Atom Egoyan (to restrict my list to just the first five letters of the alphabet).

Late science fiction writer Damon Knight titled his excellent 1956 collection of science fiction criticism *In Search of Wonder*, and it's certainly true that it's a sense of quiet amazement and bemusement that draws us to both SF and fantasy, either on the page or on the screen. It's the main thing we bring away from outer-space yarns as disparate as *Forbidden Planet* (1956) and *2001: A Space Odyssey* (1968), and stories about androids and future cityscapes as different from one another as Fritz Lang's *Metropolis* (1927), Ridley Scott's *Blade Runner* (1982), and Spielberg's *A.I. Artificial Intelligence* (2001). On the other hand, wonder isn't at all what we bring away from such SF satires as Stanley Kubrick's *Dr. Strangelove or: How I Learned to Stop Worrying and Love the Bomb* (1964) and *A Clockwork Orange* (1971), or Paul Verhoeven's *RoboCop* (1987) and *Starship Troopers* (1997), because sarcasm and wonder rarely make compatible bedfellows.

The sense of immensity and monumentality conveyed in SF films like *Things to Come* (1936) isn't necessarily just a function of the way we feel about the future. There's another string of films conveying a similar sense of bottomless mystery about the historical past, ranging from Howard Hawks's 1955 bombastic and campy but awestruck spectacular *Land of the Pharaohs* to Kubrick's more muted and melancholy 1975 *Barry Lyndon* (a kind of variant of Welles's aforementioned *Ambersons*)—or from Stanley Kwan's exquisite Hong Kong biopic *Actress* (1991), with Maggie Cheung as Ruan Ling-yu, the Chinese Garbo, working in the Shanghai film industry of the '30s, to Richard Linklater's underrated saga about a Texas family of 1920s bank robbers, *The Newton Boys* (1998).

Some filmmakers, for instance, Alain Resnais and Andrei Tarkovsky, take us on guided tours of metaphysical worlds, mysterious and uncharted labyrinths of the mind. I'd call them quintessential directors of wonder, above all because their appeal remains sensual and emotional rather than intellectual, while plumbing the depths of our inner lives, the kinds of secrets and hidden desires we sometimes keep even from ourselves. If you misread Alain Resnais and Alain Robbe-Grillet's *Last Year at Marienbad* (1961) or Resnais and David Mercer's *Providence* (1977) as intellectual or cerebral puzzles, you aren't likely to catch their poetic handling of nocturnal moods and the imaginative, dream-like drifts that course through both like uncanny, subterranean tunnels.

There's another sense of the uncanny found in Tarkovsky's *Solaris* (1971) and *Stalker* (1979), both deceptively derived from SF novels of ideas. I would argue that both films have relatively little to do with these ideas—and quite a lot to do with the gut feelings and intuitions of someone experiencing both spiritual desolation and a feeling of awe about the universe he inhabits.

Apart from the church hymn sung by Mitchum, I haven't yet said anything about music. Yet, this clearly plays a substantial role in establishing our gaping sense of wonder in many of the aforementioned examples—the "Blue Danube Waltz" of Strauss in *2001: A Space Odyssey* and the eerie organ music resembling a spooky silent film accompaniment in *Last Year at Marienbad*; the romantically lush, Hollywoodish Miklós Rósza score in *Providence* and the ecstatic burst of the choral climax of Beethoven's Ninth Symphony in the final sequence of *Stalker*.

Which makes it only logical that some of the ultimate expressions of amazement in movies come to us courtesy of actual musicals. Consider the awe-inspiring geometric shapes of chorus girls in Busby Berkeley production numbers, the astonishingly gaudy spectacle of Marilyn Monroe and Jane Russell in *Gentlemen Prefer Blondes* (1953), or even something as relatively modest as Donald O'Connor dancing wildly around a park pavilion in roller skates in *I Love Melvin* the same year. For the truth is, we can only gape at such soulful visions of glitz, grace, and synchronicity, making us gullible kids all over again.

—◊—

Infant Cinema in *Querelle enfantine / A Childish Quarrel* (1896)
Robert Horton

When movies were inventing themselves, the subject matter for an *actualité* could be almost anything; Louis and Auguste Lumière famously transfixed their early audiences with short films of a train arriving at a station and workers exiting a factory. Given the possibilities of the new medium, there is nothing remotely surprising about the fact that the Lumières immediately turned their camera in the direction of children. Their first public program in Paris in December 1895, featured *Repas de bébé* (*Baby's Dinner*), a minute-long glimpse of Auguste and Marguerite Lumière dining with their infant daughter. Showing children in their natural habitat, with predictably unpredictable consequences, was one of the easiest bets a filmmaker could make.

One of the Lumière's most delightful *actualités* is *Querelle enfantine* (*A Childish Quarrel*; 1896), which features the typical attributes of a Lumière film in its brevity, unmoving cameras and neutral viewpoint, and interest in documentary-style naturalism. The film, lasting fifty seconds or so, consists of two young children (evidently Auguste's daughters, Andrée and Suzanne) sitting side by side in their high chairs. The film may be set up as a documentary, but it quickly becomes melodrama: Andrée, the older girl, bosses Suzanne, eventually winning a tug-of-war over a spoon.

Even with its brevity, *A Childish Quarrel* provides some basic principles of what the cinema of childhood would become. These revelations include (1) that watching movies about childhood conjures up twin responses for most grown-up viewers: memories of one's own youth (with the attendant nostalgia for or identification with the action) and adult amusement in observing children; (2) that childhood behaviors mirror adult behaviors; and (3) that child actors can be uniquely charming and complex on-screen, with a spontaneous quality that has resulted in some of the most astonishing performances in cinema history, from performers both experienced and completely untrained.

Contained in the running time of *A Childish Quarrel* is a huge range of human deportment: aggression, passivity, the will to dominate and acquire, regret, contrition, and the urge to reconcile. There's also slapstick comedy. As though planned for a Buster Keaton routine, that wrestled-over spoon ends up inadvertently bopping Suzanne in the face, an outcome that seems inevitable once the sisters begin tussling. Think of that spoon as carrying the significance of the tapir bone in *2001: A Space Odyssey* (1968). Both objects embody a breakthrough: In *2001*, it's that the bone is a tool, and a key to warfare; in *A Childish Quarrel*, the spoon triggers the discovery of property, injustice (Whose spoon is it? Why does the older, stronger sibling get to keep it?), and the existence of the cosmic joke—a utensil hitting you in the forehead just when you were in the middle of a serious disagreement. At the end, elder sister Andrée taps Suzanne's hand with the spoon, as though trying to establish contact with her bawling sister. Or maybe it's an apology. Or basic primate triumph.

The action is located in the real world, on some sort of outdoor patio, not a stage or studio. The mise-en-scène is pleasing, the sunlight spreading evenly over the scene, a jumble of plants in the background; at the right top corner, effortlessly balancing out the composition, some coats are piled casually over a chair, a little marker of domestic simplicity. It's a peaceful setting in every way, just waiting for the disruption of youth. The children are surrounded by ordinary objects from a kid's life—a stuffed sheep and a metal cup—all perfectly natural-istic, but we might sense the hint of directorial interference in how those things are precariously balanced on the sisters' trays, as though inviting chaos, like a banana peel placed in the road as a silent-film comedian approaches.

As will be true for so much of film history to come, no matter how much cinematic craft is on display, the performers draw focus. The sisters' expressive in-teraction points the way to one of the great mysteries of film acting, which is how so many on-screen children can convey such deep, truthful behavior. How great kid performances happen—from Jackie Coogan in *The Kid* (1921) to Margaret O'Brien in *Meet Me in St. Louis* (1944) to Jean-Pierre Léaud in *The 400 Blows* (1959) to four-year-old Victoire Thivisol in *Ponette* (1996)—must surely vary from film to film, but the fact is they keep happening. Does this say something about the camera's ability to capture truth, or about its ability to let the viewer project his or her own feelings and ideas on actors who are, by definition, unso-phisticated and unworldly?

Whatever the answer is, it gets to the heart of acting for the camera, an art that relies at least as much on personality and unfiltered presence as it does on training. A child can be both a personality actor and a pro, of course; Shirley Temple was innately exuberant *and* a shrewd little technician. And there are exceptions—kids who are listless by nature, or those made self-conscious or arti-ficial by acting classes or stage parents. The girls in *Querelle enfantine* have sheer, unfettered presence, a demonstration of how children, these great screen actors, cut right through to the essentials of personality. More than a hundred years of film history, and countless YouTube videos uploaded by proud parents, have only underlined the point.

Rango (voiced by Johnny Depp) in *Rango*

2

ADVENTURES IN ANIMATION

As fans of *Family Guy* and *Rick and Morty* know, animation is not just kids' stuff anymore. Nonetheless, animated films still initiate many children into the world of movies, and with their unlimited means of expressing the imagination, they turn that first impression into a lasting love. The essays and reviews in this chapter discuss the ways animation works its magic, in films from well-known Disney classics to present-day Pixar favorites, from the best of conventional Hollywood fare to the eye-popping offerings of Japan's Studio Ghibli.

Disney's *Bambi* (1942) has probably made the biggest impression of any film on the most kids for several generations, but it would still be a spoiler seven decades later to explain why. In his review, Michael Wilmington sums up the film's accomplishments succinctly: "Walt Disney's *Bambi* is one of those classic family movies that children never forget, that adults still love, and that tends to make children of us all as we watch it."

Lauded for revolutionizing animation with its CGI process clumsily called "PhotoRealistic RenderMan" when it released its first feature, *Toy Story*, in 1995, Pixar also revitalized such old-fashioned values as character, plot, and narrative craft. Curmudgeon that I am, I was less impressed in my review of the Pixar hit *Up* (2009) by the newfangled 3D than by its "limpid storytelling, thrilling visuals, endearing characters, and respect for its audience." In "Of Eternity and Beyond," John Anderson finds that *Toy Story 3* (2010) might take respect for the audience to the point of intimidation. "[It] contains a vision of eternal damnation that will be positively hair-raising, particularly for smaller children," he warns. "What will unnerve their parents even more, though, is the existential dread that underscores the entire movie."

The dread that unnerves Andy Klein as he reviews *The Lego Movie* (2014) is of the dubious source material. "If there's one starting point for a film project even worse than a video game, it's a line of toys," he writes. "Legos? A world of interlocking plastic bricks?" Indeed. These humble cubes serve as talismans to stir the imagination to life, creating a world "in which conflicts are revealed as an imaginative little boy's fantasy." And an adult's as well. Notes Klein, "[The movie] is shot through with references that play off decades of cultural touchstones, particularly goofing on *The Matrix* (1999) and *The Terminator* (1984)."

As *The Lego Movie* indicates, not all animated features are conventional Hollywood products. Some are meta-Hollywood, like Gore Verbinski's reflexive shaggy critter story *Rango* (2011). "A Wild West show that sends up movie westerns as they've rarely been sent up," Michael Wilmington writes in his review, "and does it with style, wit, and lots of playful, if occasionally perverse, imagination." Wilmington thinks the kids will like it even though some of the grotesquerie, intertextuality, and in-jokes might be over their heads. "I'm sure I would have liked it as a kid," he surmises, "although I might have been startled by the violence and scatological humor."

Other animated films have roots neither in Hollywood nor meta-Hollywood, but in different countries and cultures. These films delight with their strangeness and enlighten with their familiarity. The weird world of French director Sylvain Chomet's *The Triplets of Belleville* (2003) is epitomized in the city of the title, which Gerald Peary describes as a "magical animation creation: a baroque metropolis that is seemingly a composite of Paris, New York, Montreal, and Quebec City."

The triplets, once a hip, young jazz-singing trio, are now, as Peary puts it, "three white-haired shopping-bag ladies" living in an apartment that "sports an unflushed toilet deep in dung and swarming with flies. Their nightly cuisine is frogs and more frogs: frog soup, frogs on a stick, frogs squirming, frogs dead, frogs half-alive. Gross!" Peary thinks that such ickiness is the "stuff of nightmares for impressionable children." Frankly, I don't think there is a kid in the world who wouldn't have fun with a movie that featured frogs and maybe even a little poop.

In the Franco–Belgian–Luxembourgian coproduction *Ernest & Celestine* (2012), Benjamin Renner, Stéphane Aubier, and Vincent Patar posit an alternative universe that, like *Belleville*, is both fantastic and oddly recognizable. Ernest is a street musician and Celestine an artist, and both have rebelled against their bourgeois families. She's a mouse and he's a bear, but it's not a problem—at least for them. Not for us, either. Writes Michael Sragow, "It's about the power of friendship *and* imagination to conquer everything."

Some animated films use whimsy, wit, and comedy to help younger—and older—audiences face harsh realities. John Anderson found that to be the case in *The Boxtrolls* (2014), a surreal and satiric tale of an oppressed race of homunculi in a fantasy world with shades of Dickens. "It's fantastical, fast-paced, and droll," Anderson writes. "But it's also an allegory about xenophobia, class war, and political fear-mongering."

One of the world's greatest animation artists, Hayao Miyazaki, doesn't bother with allegories in *The Wind Rises* (2013) but cuts directly to the historical facts. He tells the true story about a Japanese kid "whose dream," writes Michael Sragow in his review, "was to create beautiful airplanes. [The film] sees him through the 1923 earthquake, the Great Depression, his days as a student engineer, and his entry into the professional ranks of Japan's aeronautical engineers at Mitsubishi." That's where he designs the Zero, the warplane that bombed Pearl Harbor on December 7, 1941. The inventor is horrified to see his dream turned into a tool of destruction. Miyazaki combines breathtakingly realistic imagery, mercurial fantasy, and complex and sympathetic characters to make this grim historical tragedy comprehensible, and even uplifting.

Dutch animator Michaël Dudok de Wit is an admirer of Miyazaki, and his *The Red Turtle* (2016) was coproduced by Miyazaki's Studio Ghibli. In it de Wit has taken the master's sensibility and transformed it into his own unique vision. The story of a shipwrecked sailor and the giant sea creature of the title, it takes on the quality of a folk tale or elusive allegory. In his review Peter Rainer describes how the "film moves ever more decisively into transcendent realms of fantasy" and evokes a "hushed evocation of nature's mystic mysteries." It is that "rare 'children's film' that works equally well for adults. . . . It doesn't have the easily definable meanings that often attach to classic fairy tales. . . . Dudok de Wit respects our imaginings. He allows them to take shape right alongside his own."

The Ageless Wonder of *Bambi* (1942)
Michael Wilmington[1]

Walt Disney's *Bambi* (1942) is one of those classic family movies that children never forget, that adults still love, and that tends to make children of us all as we watch it. Now, I don't want to come across as too much of a softie or an easy mark for Disneyfied sentiment. Perhaps to reestablish my cynic's credentials I should include a joke reference to that brutal little 1969 toon *Bambi Meets Godzilla*, in which Godzilla, or his immense foot, stomps little Bambi. But aw shucks, how can you help it? This lush 1942 film adaptation of the classic Felix Salten book—available on Blu-ray, with every color shimmering, every brush stroke gleaming, every animal character (from Bambi, his regal dad, and his loving and lovable mother, to that fussbudget old owl and Bambi's charming, stalwart chums Thumper the bunny and Flower the skunk) absolutely aglow with life—plays just as well and just as beautifully as it did more than seventy-five years ago, on its first release.

Spoiler Alert

It's one of the great movie nature stories and one of the great rite-of-passage children's tales—and like *Lassie Come Home* (1943), *The Yearling* (1946) and *The Red Pony* (1949), it's one of a great cycle of animal movies from the '40s. Thanks to Disney and his matchless animation team of the 1930s and 1940s—headed here by director David Hand—the movie unforgettably gives us the times and seasons in the life of the princely little deer Bambi: his widely celebrated birth (as the future Great Prince of the Forest), his first faltering bent-legged steps, the tenderly wise tutelage by his mother (while his dad is busy with his princely duties elsewhere), his meetings with his forest friends and future wife, the russet-colored falling leaves of autumn, the cold snows of winter, crisis and tragedy, and, finally, poetically, the new spring. There we find the problems of "twitterpation" (a Disney term for emerging sexuality), and, at long last, the renewal and birth of the next Prince.

End of Alert

Of course, Disney's classic feature cartoon tale of animals in the forest, the cycles of life, of mothers and fathers and their young, has a proecology theme that's gotten even more powerful and topical throughout the years, especially when we watch the movie's lovely, painterly forest being ravaged and burned, and Bambi's parents and friends threatened or harmed, or even killed, by the carelessness and brutality of the movie's chief villain: that shadowy, menacing, rifle-toting, mostly unseen but always dangerous figure who the animals shudderingly call "MAN!"

The movie offers an animal's-eye view of the beauties of nature and the threats to it, and of the hunt, and it's probably done as much throughout the years to make movie audiences conscious of that beauty and that which threatens it as any nature-loving film endeavor right on up to those other great popular masterpieces of the ecology cinema canon: the wondrous David Attenborough / Alastair Fothergill BBC documentaries *The Planet Earth* (2006), *The Planet Earth II* (2016), *The Life of Birds* (1998), *The Life of Mammals* (2002–2003), and *The Blue Planet* (2001). (If you haven't seen these movies on TV or DVD, you've missed a cinematic revelation.)

But those British movies—splendid, educational, and knowingly and enthusiastically narrated (by Attenborough) as they are—don't have, as *Bambi* does, a guaranteed pipeline to our heart: characters we feel we know, life experiences that become our own, a great sacred natural cartoon domain that becomes our spiritual homeland, as well as Bambi's. They don't have the little spotted fawn Bambi hiding behind his mother from his first (and last) crush Faline; or the bashful, little, self-conscious skunk Flower (Pepé Le Pew's unlikely American nephew?); or Bambi's great, self-sacrificing mom nestling and protecting him, and calling for him frantically as the hunters go on their rampage in the Meadow. They don't have the little deer's groovy, chubby, smart-aleck little sidekick Thumper to keep thump-thump-thumping and wisecracking away, offering such pearls of forest wisdom as his defiantly noncorrect version of his dad's doggerel homily, "Eatin' greens is a special treat. It makes long ears and great big feet. . . . *But it sure is awful stuff to eat!* (I made that last part up myself.)"

Bambi was the last of the five great animated features with which Disney impressively kicked off his and his studio's feature cartoon filmography, and which, in many ways, Disney and the studio have never surpassed (or equaled) since. And, like the others—1937's *Snow White and the Seven Dwarfs* (also directed by Hand), 1940's *Pinocchio* and *Fantasia*, and 1941's *Dumbo*—it's a still-luminous showcase for the genius and craft of his artists, their talents meshing back then in a grand synergy that still seems amazingly personal (Walt's personality, of course), staggeringly ambitious, and amazingly accomplished. It took barely a decade, after all, for the Disney studio to go from the "primitive" black-and-white line drawing style of *Steamboat Willie* (1928) and *Plane Crazy* (1928) to the incredible color, detail, and lushness of *Snow White* and the others. A decade!

Bambi is a movie that has never lost its own youth, even as the ages and seasons pass inevitably in the movie itself. For many years, *Bambi* and most of the rest of the great first five were regularly rereleased to succeeding generations of children and their parents, until we all seemed to know them, and until the relative financial failures of some of those movies on first release (notably *Pinocchio* and *Fantasia*) were finally wiped out. Like the cycle of nature, the theme reworked in the Bambi-like 1994 hit *The Lion King*, these movies were always renewed and renewing, always returning, forever young.

I first saw *Bambi* as a child (with my mother, of course) in the 1950s. I saw it again as an older (old?) man in a brand new, restored 35mm print at Chicago's Museum of Contemporary Art, accompanied by a Q&A session with a current Disney Studio animator and by the actor who, as a boy, voiced young Bambi, the still vigorous and sharp retired U.S. Marine Donnie Dunagan. It was probably the last time for me to see *Bambi* in a 35mm print in a theater, and maybe the last time for me to see it ever. (I always hoped I'd see it one day, however, with kids of my own.)

But the movie, unlike the Prince of the Forest, hasn't aged. Most of it never will. And what has aged in it has become sometimes even more precious. *Bambi*, whether in 35mm or on DVD or Blu-ray, or not, whatever the format, whatever your age, whatever the season, is a picture that should be seen and reseen—especially by us, humanity, MAN.

—————

Raising the Art of Animation to a Higher Level in *Up* (2009)
Peter Keough[2]

No one these days tells stories as cinematically as do the people at Pixar—at least for the first half-hour of their films. The opening of *WALL·E* (2008) might have been a lost masterpiece of silent cinema; it is visually rapturous and witty, relating its touching fable with precise and evocative images and brilliantly elliptical cuts, and with no dialogue other than sound effects and some clips from *Hello, Dolly!* (1969). It is that rare film that allows the intelligence and imagination of the audience, young and old, to fill in the gaps.

Up similarly boasts a tour de force opening. Written and directed by Pete Docter (who cowrote *WALL·E*) and Bob Peterson, it evokes *Citizen Kane* (1941), *King Kong* (1933), and *The Wizard of Oz* (1939) in its first five minutes alone. A mock newsreel tells the story of the great explorer Charles Muntz (Christopher Plummer), who has returned from Paradise Falls, a lost world somewhere in Venezuela, to present his discovery, a prehistoric monster, on stage à la Kong. But Muntz turns out to be more like the man behind the curtain in Oz, or so say the experts, who denounce him as a phony. He disappears, vowing to be vindicated.

Young Carl Fredricksen watches this newsreel in a movie theater, and he can't believe it. He and fellow Muntz fan Ellie (Elie Docter, Pete's daughter)

bond over their belief in the Paradise Falls myth. The montage of wordless images that follows traces their lives together: a wedding, a house, a dream deferred,
a hospital bed. It ends with Carl (Edward Asner) somehow transformed into a
curmudgeonly widower beleaguered by developers who are after his property, the
precious house that's the last vestige of his beloved Ellie.

Here is the point at which some Pixar pictures go astray. Not this time. Just
when *Up* seems about to descend into treacherously trite narrative and thematic
terrain, Docter and Peterson trim the sails and turn the film in an unexpected
direction.

That starts with Russell (Jordan Nagai), the "wilderness scout" who shows
up on Carl's doorstep hoping to earn a merit badge by aiding the elderly. At first,
he's merely annoying, but by the time the two set sail in Carl's balloon-powered
house, Russell has become irresistible and irrepressible. In the same way, the
talking dogs (Muntz rigged them up with high-tech translating collars) who
appear later in the film would come off as contrived if the details of their canine
behavior were not so precise.

That's also the case with the film's signature image, Carl's house. At times,
the banal structure, sprouting a huge, radiant bouquet of balloons, resembles a
canvas by Magritte. At other times, it seems like an image from Samuel Beckett
as it hangs suspended inches above the ground and Carl drags it, Sisyphus-like,
to its final resting place. Near the end of the movie, Russell touches on the key
to the film's power of metamorphosis. He reminisces about his life and concludes
that the boring stuff was the best. *Up* masters that boring stuff and so has the
right to transform it into something magical. Such magic owes nothing to the
film's hyped 3-D format. It's a distraction. 3-D may or may not be the future of
movies. But *Up*'s limpid storytelling, thrilling visuals, endearing characters, and
respect for its audience are.

Of Eternity and Beyond: *Toy Story 3* (2010)
John Anderson[3]

At a time when every soulless movie multiplex might well have "Abandon all
hope . . ." emblazoned on its portals, Pixar has represented a source of consis-
tent joy. There may have been a minor misstep or two throughout the course
of its history (2006's *Cars*—maybe), but this Disney-owned CGI animation

wonderland has largely been busy producing one mini-masterpiece after another—*The Incredibles* (2004), *Monsters, Inc.* (2001), *Finding Nemo* (2003), and the sublime *WALL·E* (2008). As of 2019, the studio has won fifteen Oscars and released twenty-one features.

Among the best is *Toy Story 3* (2010). It does not mark the end of the trail for Woody the Cowboy (Tom Hanks) and the posse at Andy's playroom, whose story continues in *Toy Story 4* (2019). But it feels valedictory. It seems like the culmination of all that preceded it in the franchise/series that started the Pixar coffers chiming with glee in 1995. *Toy Story*, the first entirely computerized animated feature, signified a victory for cutting-edge entertainment technology and made it, in a sense, antihuman. But, of course, humanity is what it was all about. The photo-realist visuals may have been both new and dumbfounding (how are they doing that?), but the film was also an immersion in the familiar: We knew the toys, we knew the conflicts (personal dynamics, ego, loss, purpose), and we certainly knew the characters. They could have been a 4-H Club, a ladies' sodality, a group of mah-jongg players in San Francisco, or a B'nai B'rith chapter in New York City. They also may have been springy and plastic, but hey—no one's perfect.

And imperfection was, and is, what makes the *TS* characters who they are, and the movies what they are. Woody's precarious dominance over the playroom is a constant source of tension and something he blusters his way through. Buzz Lightyear's egomania (batteries not included) is a reliable source of fun; the Potato Heads are constantly bickering; Rex the Dinosaur is paralyzed by neuroses; Slinky Dog is leashed to an inferior intellect. Hamm? A salty character at best.

Like the characters, we know the basic structure of the *Toy Story* movies: They begin with a fantasy conjured in Andy's head as he plays with his beloved toys; they end with a chase-and-rescue executed by the toys themselves. These sequences have gotten wilder and more virtuosic throughout the course of the series, and the *TS3* sequences are among the best, at least in terms of choreography and wit. What's curious this time around is the edginess of the story. The ending of this latest film contains a vision of eternal damnation that is positively hair-raising, particularly for smaller children. What will unnerve their parents even more, however, is the existential dread that underscores the entire movie.

The crisis? Andy (John Morris) is going off to college, and his toys are going—well, that's the thing. His mother (Laurie Metcalf) wants Andy's room cleaned out; his covetous sister (Beatrice Miller) would like Andy gone, too, and quickly, so she can annex his bedroom. Andy is torn about his toys. For a pregnant moment, he stands with Buzz (Tim Allen) and Woody poised over his college-bound suitcase before he finally drops Woody in and consigns Buzz to the plastic bag with the rest of the gang. You feel bad for Buzz. It's like Dorothy telling the Scarecrow she's going to miss him most of all. Pass the oil can. And hand that lion a hankie.

Anyway, the rest of the toys are intended for the local day-care center, except the bags get mixed up. Mom puts the toys on the curb for garbage collection, and Woody (as always, putting others before himself) has to undertake the kind of plaything-salvaging mission that's been the core drama of all the films in the series.

This is the first *TS* in 3-D, but apart from the cumbersome glasses, you might not notice. The Pixar style has always implied three dimensionality, and the "3-D" boast is more about marketing than effect. Still, the action is superb, the humor is abundant, the slapstick is inventive—Woody's little balancing act on an unrolling tube of toilet paper is worthy of Buster Keaton. Barbie (Jodi Benson)—who finally gets her fifteen minutes and a date with Ken (Michael Keaton)—is hilarious. But underlying the comedy and the tenderness are some disturbing suggestions about mortality, meaning, and, despite the fiery images of the film's finale, what hell might really be.

These toys have no life expectancy and no heavenly expectations. For them, ultimate happiness means having a child to love and amuse. Being put in a bag in the attic for an indefinite period of inactivity/disconnection apparently holds no terror for the toys. But it does for us. What would eternity be like for a conscious being with no hope of a hereafter, no purpose, no contact? Is there anything more terrifying? What the toys represent is not something human or subhuman, but superhuman: beings for whom the only salvation is an existence rooted in charity itself, without other reward, without freedom through death. Children won't get it. But it's hard to imagine adults who won't.

The entire *TS* series has been marked by a certain darkness. The absence of a father has gone unexplained, and silence implies misfortune. In the first film, the family is moving for undisclosed reasons, but one gets the sense they're downsizing. The toys have had to contend with several incarnations of evil: Sid, the malicious toy-abuser of *Toy Story*; Al (of Al's Toy Barn); and Stinky Pete in *Toy Story 2* (1999). In *Toy Story 3*, the bad guy is Lotso (Ned Beatty), aka Lots-O'-Huggin' Bear, the neo-Stalinist leader of the Sunnyside day-care center, where an entrenched hierarchy maintains a kind of enslavement of newer toys in the playroom of the youngest kids (where pain and chaos reign).

Joe Morgenstern, the film critic for the *Wall Street Journal*, has compared Beatty's performance to Andy Griffith's in Elia Kazan's 1957 film *A Face in the*

Crowd, and the comparison is apt: a folksy facade masking instinctive ruthlessness. Unlike other *TS* villains, however, Lotso is imbued with a psychology: He was abandoned by his first owner and suffers from a kind of posttraumatic stress disorder. But he is also beyond redemption, which makes him a rare thing in what is ostensibly a children's movie, a character without hope.

That may sound oxymoronic, but much about *Toy Story 3* is. The ostensibly inanimate objects are far more animated than most movie stars. They certainly have more soul. Plastic may not biodegrade for several millenniums, but the characters still struggle with questions of obsolescence and a kind of mortality. They may be the possessions of a kid just going off to college, but they are aging Boomer toys. At the beginning of the series, few real-life children had ever related to the gang in Andy's playrooms, except as the fictional characters in the film: the talking action figure with the pull string (Woody), his female counterpart (Jessie, voiced by the great Joan Cusack), the Slinky Dog, the Potato Heads, the little army guys who provide the toy room's Swiss Guard. These are, in fact, now recognizable to children thanks to the movies and the unholy Disney–Mattel alliance, but they were, originally, aimed at their parents' nostalgia for innocence. There's not an Xbox in sight; the Mario Brothers make no appearances (that would have been a rights infringement of the type Disney would never tolerate against itself). It is Barbie, and Barbie alone, who spans the generations with any ease, and she has her own poignant story in *TS3*. She finally meets Ken, and Ken turns out to be a rat. You wonder how many mothers of little *Toy Story 3* devotees will be nodding sympathetically as Barbie tries to make Ken into the anatomically correct man he ought to be.

But such are the story points that make *Toy Story 3* something other than the child mollifier of its marketed image. The characters, specifically Woody, are confronted—even in a milieu that should be free of such crises—with unavoidable choices that test their moral mettle. Once again, Woody is offered a kind of paradise (college with Andy) and turns it down because the greater good depends on his selflessness and leadership. He is not quite Jesus in the desert, but neither can he turn from his mission or his sense of duty, nor can he deny the love/responsibility with which his existence has been blessed.

The heavy subtexts of *Toy Story 3* are perhaps like the undercoat on a Rembrandt, something that makes the surface brightness pop. There is nothing chiaroscuro about *TS3*. It's sunny and warm and well-lit by the selflessness and small-caliber courage of its characters. Were the toys themselves casually heroic, the storyline would not mean that much. That they have to work so hard to do the right thing makes them very recognizable and worthy of affection.

—៣—

Spinning Gold from Plastic in *The Lego Movie* (2014)
Andy Klein

If there's one starting point for a film project even worse than a video game, it's a line of toys. Corporately designed merchandising concepts are about as far from art as you can get. Michael Bay's Transformers films—mediocre and slapdash as they are—at least had the advantage of a universe already populated with characters. But Legos? A world of interlocking plastic bricks? Yes, there are characters in the Lego world, but the majority are licensed from other movie franchises—including such obvious choices as *Star Wars* (1977), *Batman* (1989), and *The Lord of the Rings*.

Given such a dubious source, the filmmakers' accomplishment is nothing short of remarkable. Phil Lord and Christopher Miller seem to be the go-to team these days for fashioning silk purses from the tattiest of sows' ears. In and around the production of *The Lego Movie* (2014), they found time to turn the less-than-stellar '80s TV show *21 Jump Street* into two features that were far more entertaining than the concept deserved.

The general outline of *The Lego Movie*'s plot is identical to every by-the-numbers heroic epic of the last thirty-five years. Emmet Brickowski (voiced by Chris Pratt) is a typical construction worker in a universe composed completely of off-the-shelf Lego pieces. Like most of his coworkers, Emmet has no idea that their supposedly benevolent leader, President Business (Will Ferrell), has plans to lock everyone and everything permanently in place, using a secret weapon called the Kragle. The Kragle is [SPOILER!] actually a tube of Krazy Glue with some of the letters worn off. (Almost as frightening is the solvent President Business calls the "puh-lish remover of Nah-eel"—that is, a bottle of nail polish remover.)

Emmet is our Everyman, a normal guy who is forced into the role of hero one evening when he pulls from a junk pile the film's equivalent of Excalibur—the Piece of Resistance, prophesied to be the only weapon that can conquer the Kragle. (In reality, it's [SPOILER!] a Krazy Glue cap.) In the movie's most daring move, this throws Emmet into a trance-like vision—a vision that includes brief flashes of real actors in live-action footage.

This sets us up for the climactic sequence in which Emmet has a spiritual awakening, suddenly perceiving a higher, photographic level of reality—one in which his conflicts are revealed [SPOILER!] as an imaginative little boy's fantasy of getting his rigid father (Ferrell again) to loosen up.

It's a nice bit of thematic sleight of hand, but it's merely one creative element in an hour and a half of first-rate entertainment. The filmmakers have clearly studied the Pixar playbook as a model. (And who wouldn't?) That is, they've neatly combined humor designed to appeal to kids with a large amount of adult-targeted material likely to go right over younger heads. At any given moment, there's something for all manner of viewers. The jokes fly fast enough that there's no way to catch all of them in a single viewing.

The result is shot through with references that play off decades of cultural touchstones, particularly goofing on *The Matrix* (1999) and *The Terminator* (1984). And let's give props to another group of behind-the-scenes geniuses—the lawyers who managed to clear permission to use characters from all the films listed here and dozens of others. (Even Milhouse, from *The Simpsons*, shows up.) In several cases, Lord and Miller were able to get the original actors to provide the voices.

It's no surprise that Will Arnett comes up with a hilarious parody of Christian Bale's brooding, self-absorbed Batman; however, it is a surprise to discover how funny Liam Neeson (who voices Bad Cop, Good Cop, and Pa Cop) can be, given the chance.

——꿈——

The Spirit of the West Is Alive and Well in *Rango* (2011)
Michael Wilmington

Rango (2011) is a fast, funny, sometimes gorgeous-looking cartoon feature by director Gore Verbinski—a Wild West show that sends up movie westerns as they've rarely been sent up, and with style, wit, and lots of playful, if occasionally perverse, imagination. In this puppet-ish spoof—in which Johnny Depp plays (or voices) a gabby chameleon masquerading as a deadly gunslinger named Rango—Verbinski and his screenwriter, John Logan (2000's *Gladiator* and 2004's *The Aviator*), and their all-animated, all-animal cast, have fun with movie westerns of everyone from John Ford to Sergio Leone, from *Shane* (1953) to *The Wild Bunch* (1969), and from *High Noon* (1952) to *The Good, the Bad, and the Ugly* (1966).

The setting is the desert, a Monument Valley–ish sort of sunbaked wasteland off the highway somewhere: a sandy land where water is precious and desert critters of all kinds make up the dramatis personae. The actual boss gunslinger is the fearsome Rattlesnake Jake (voice courtesy of Bill Nighy), who has a Gatling gun where his rattles should be. The love interest, a looker prone to what seems epileptic freeze-ups, is a lizard lass named Beans (Isla Fisher). And there's Bad Bill (Ray Winstone), Balthazar (Harry Dean Stanton, by God), and the Carlos Castaneda–spouting run-over armadillo Roadkill (Alfred Molina).

And there's the mayor of the desert town of Dirt, of course, a wheel-chair-bound tortoise voiced by Ned Beatty with the throaty purrs and left-handed eloquence of John Huston in *Chinatown* (1974), who hires Rango to be the town sheriff because he knows he's a phony. The plot? Someone is cheating these beasts out of their water. That someone will pay.

Rango may have prehensile tongue in scaly cheek from start to finish, but it's obviously a movie made by people who know and love westerns, and that's what makes it fun. It's as entertaining a movie western as I've seen lately—not as good as the Coen brothers' grimly poetic, classically structured *True Grit* (2010) but definitely funnier. *Rango* is yet another cartoon feature done with the style and smarts that our adult movies often miss.

I'm sure I would have liked it as a kid as well, though I might have been startled at the violence and scatological humor. It should perhaps be emphasized that this is a movie as much for adults as children, in fact, probably *more* for adults than children. That was already the case, of course, with some of the recent Pixar movies (2008's *WALL·E*, 2009's *Up*), and I suspect it's a trend that will continue, as long as these moviemakers are sharp enough to keep broadening their appeal, while the makers of "adult" movies keep dumbing down their movies.

There have been plenty of great cartoon features and lots of great movie westerns. But, until *Rango*, I can't think of many great cartoon westerns—other than the peerless Czech stop-motion puppet animator Jirí Trnka's little masterpiece *Song of the Prairie* (1949). That intoxicating gem was a western-lover's delight: Trnka took almost all the plot, imagery, and jokes for *Song of the Prairie* from John Ford's 1939 *Stagecoach*, although he added a romantic singing Gene Autry–style cowboy hero of a kind Ford never used. (The songs in Ford's westerns—and there were some Mexican ballads in *Stagecoach*—were usually confined to the Sons of the Pioneers and their occasional warbling appearances.)

It's *Rango*'s contrasts between delicate fantasy and gruesome horror, gentle humor and bloody havoc, that make it so memorable—as well as its multi-pop-cultural fluency. (At one point there's an aerial assault modeled on the 1979 Francis Coppola film *Apocalypse Now*, complete with Wagner's "Ride of the Valkyries.")

The violence in *Rango* is more extreme than we're used to in cartoons, and the characters, modeled on real reptiles, look more vulnerable. I suspect that's why the movie has gotten a few "tsk-tsk" reviews from critics worried that *Rango* is too harsh, violent, or grotesque for susceptible children. Maybe. But what about the Brothers Grimm, Disney's early feature cartoons, and many other children's tales we consider classics or classics-to-be—for instance, the Harry Potter books and movies?

Listed as Rango's visual consultant is the Coen brothers' cinematographer, Roger Deakins, who shot their *True Grit* and *No Country for Old Men* (2007). This is the kind of dangerous beauty and frontier grandeur many of us like to see in westerns, and we should be glad to see it here—the visual virtuosity, playful creativity, weird beauty, and intense love of movies—saturating the computerized but old-fashioned-looking, wonderful 2D flat images Verbinski creates with production designer Mark "Crash" McCreary and Deakins. These images of desert vistas, sun-scorched cliffs, and the ramshackle little town Dirt are largely modeled on the look of Leone's westerns (just as Hans Zimmer's score takes many of its cues from Ennio Morricone's Leone scores), and they turn out to much more beautiful—stunning in some cases—than the fuzzier, darker 3D stuff that's become the feature cartoon movie norm.

This movie also has a superb cast—including Abigail Breslin, Stephen Root, cowriter and storyboard artist James Ward Byrkit (in seven roles), and Timothy Olyphant in a dead-on Eastwood impersonation as the Spirit of the West. Using a method he calls "emotion capture" (suggesting the "motion capture" in Robert Zemeckis's 2004 film *The Polar Express*, among others), Verbinski shot a live action movie of his actors on actual sets, which he then used to help design the character animation for the movie. Whatever the method, it produced one of the liveliest, most memorable cartoon ensembles in years.

And it takes its lead from Johnny Depp. He long ago learned how to simultaneously maintain a child's and an adult's sensibilities; it's the method of those Tim Burton films *Alice in Wonderland* (2010), *Charlie and the Chocolate Factory* (2005), and *Edward Scissorhands* (1990). A childlike quality even lingers in a Burton–Depp movie that's certainly not for children: 2007's *Sweeney Todd: The Demon Barber of Fleet Street* (also written by Logan).

In *Rango*, we can see the real Depp in both the voice and the movements of the little chameleon: the accident-prone clown, lovable humbug, ad hoc hero, and cock-eyed legend. Like Danny Kaye in *The Court Jester* (1955), he's a play-acting hero who becomes a real one because he doesn't want to let his audience down. And he doesn't. Neither does the movie.[4]

—ɯɯ—

Weirdness for Both Kids and Adults: *The Triplets of Belleville* (2003)

Gerald Peary

The first images of France's *The Triplets of Belleville*, Sylvain Chomet's sublime 2003 feature, are immediately magical: a shimmering, knowing homage, drawn by Chomet's cartoonist staff, to the beginnings of sound animation. A scratched piece of black-and-white celluloid unwinds on-screen. It's a wobbly, primitive, early 1930s-style cartoon in which a crudely caricatured audience at a vaudeville house bobs and wobbles in rhythm to the live show. Onstage, a Fred Astaire figure lithely tap dances, a Django Reinhardt look-alike strums some hot-licks gypsy guitar, and, in the spotlight, a trio of odd-looking female siblings partake of Andrews Sisters–style harmony. The song they are crooning concerns a mythical city of Belleville. The language? It's what everyone speaks in the movie: a sort of muffled, pidgin French.

The picture fuzzes and turns to static, and the camera pulls back. What we have been watching is a cartoon-within-a-cartoon, playing on a black-and-white TV screen on a mammoth television console. *Triplets*, ever animated, turns to color, and we are in a house somewhere in France in what appears to be the mid-1950s (the only historical clue: a TV appearance later in the movie of a speech-ifying General Charles de Gaulle, all proboscis but not yet French president, an election that occurred in 1958).

Whereas the opening animation was frenetic, herky-jerky, *Triplets* now slows to a pensive, storybook-reading pace, and the images resemble ink and watercolors discovered in finely illustrated children's books. (I think of that 1931 Gallic classic children's book, Jean de Brunhoff's *The Story of Babar: The Little Elephant*.) The two characters who live in this house are three-dimensional, carefully individualized. Our protagonists: an aging Madame Souza, with failing vision and thick spectacles perched high on her wrinkled forehead, and Champion, her pudgy, serious little grandson in shorts, with melancholic saucer eyes and a squiggle of a chin.

Triplets is, by careful design, extremely low on dialogue, 99 percent visual. So there's no conversation about how Madame Souza and Champion came to be living together, or what happened to Champion's parents. But the lad is obviously lonely, a problem alleviated by Grandma. She purchases Bruno, a hound dog puppy, who coaxes a tiny smile from Champion. Better, she buys Champion a tricycle, which he quickly becomes obsessed with, peddling it everywhere.

A grandmother, a dog, a petite boy? *Triplets* has in place the ingredients for a crowd-pleasing family cartoon. But playing to a G-rated audience was not Sylvain Chomet's ultimate plan. *Triplets* is neither cutesy nor sentimental. None of the characters are there to win your mainstream heart. The film is "alternative adult," as if there was such a category, but unusual kids will adore its weirdness.

Bruno grows into a daft, clumsy, overweight canine whose hours pass in a doggy way, with him trotting a hundred times to a window and barking at a passing train. Meanwhile, Champion, almost nonverbal, grows tall and thin but with muscular balloons for legs. He's gone from kid tricyclist to adult competitive bicyclist, and Madame Souza has become his trainer.

There's a second-act plot. Champion competes in the Tour de France. When he's climbing through the hills, he and two other racers run afoul of kidnappers. They're placed in a truck, then an ocean liner bound across the water for . . . ? Madame Souza and Bruno go in pursuit, following Champion's scent, crossing the sea in a paddle boat.

My favorite animated sequences are scattered throughout *Triplets*. The topsy-turvy vaudeville opening, described earlier. A long, very funny scene (everyone who has ever had a pet will recognize it) in which Bruno anxiously walks around the dining room, trying, by odd mutt noises and body language, to nudge his distracted owners to fill his food bowl. And the spiritual moments on a painted ocean, when Grandmother and Bruno toss and turn through a Melvillean storm, riding atop a biblical whale to the soaring sounds of Mozart's Mass in C Minor.

The sudden insertion of this Mozart passage—as if providence is talking—is something borrowed by the *Triplets* filmmakers from the theistic French filmmaker Robert Bresson and his 1956 masterwork, *A Man Escaped*. Also, *Triplets* offers allegiance to the French comic genius Jacques Tati, with a poster from his 1953 *Monsieur Hulot's Holiday*, and also a scene on a television of Tati, appropriately on a bicycle, in his 1949 film *Jour de fête*. But *Triplets* is surprisingly free of direct references to famous cartoon movies. When there are visual homages, they're invariably to French live-action pictures, that is, the deep-blue dreamscape of 1995's *The City of Lost Children*.

For the third act of *Triplets*, everyone—kidnappers, the kidnapped, Madame Souza, and Bruno—abandon ship for the titular city of Belleville. Here's another magical animation creation: a baroque metropolis that is seemingly a composite of Paris, New York, Montreal, and Quebec City. How can Grandmother and

Bruno rescue poor Champion from there? With the help of the eponymous Triplets of Belleville. Decades have passed, and the popular 1930s singing trio (the beginning of the movie) are, in the 1950s, three white-haired shopping-bag ladies who share a slum apartment. And here's where the grotesque comes in, the stuff of nightmares for impressionable children in the *Triplets* audience: Their chaotic flat sports an unflushed toilet deep in dung and swarming with flies. Their nightly cuisine is frogs and more frogs: frog soup, frogs on a stick, frogs squirming, frogs dead, frogs half alive. Gross!

Still, Madame Souza, Bruno, and the icky Triplets to the rescue of Champion! They plunge into a den of thieves!

The movie ends happily, with one and all driving into the countryside past a road sign, "Belleville—Thank You for Your Visit! Come Again!" I'd like to. I don't require another *The Lion King* or *Pocahontas*. But here's wishing for a *Triplets of Belleville 2*.[5]

Bear Meets Mouse in *Ernest & Celestine* (2012)
Michael Sragow[6]

A delicate portrait of an artist as a mouse meets a scruffy portrait of a bear as an all-out entertainer in *Ernest & Celestine* (2012), a witty and original cartoon feature. It's about the power of friendship *and* imagination to conquer everything, including violent interspecies prejudice.

The story has bite, in more ways than one. Young mice, who live in a sophisticated underground city, scurry through the bears' village at night to gather ursine teeth for rodent dentists. Mouse society, they're told, is based on the strength of their incisors.

Bears, meanwhile, are vulnerable to a sweet tooth. In one house, the Papa Bear runs a sweet shop downstairs, and the Mama Bear runs a tooth shop across the street. (He decays teeth; she replaces them.) She tells her son that the "little mouse fairy" plucks baby teeth from bears' nightstands when, actually, she scoops them up herself, to sell.

Our mouse heroine, Celestine, the budding sketch artist, falls behind in her tooth-gathering because she spends too much time drawing fantasies about a bear befriending someone just like her. One night she lands in a trash can outside the sweet shop—and Ernest, a jovial bear who performs as a one-man band, thinks he's found a dainty morsel. She convinces him to raid the sweet shop instead of swallowing her whole. When he's nabbed for theft, she springs him from the police wagon and persuades him to bring her a bulging bag of bear teeth from Mama Bear's store. They become pals on the run, ultimately hiding out in Ernest's rural hibernation house. They complement one another. Ernest is all wild-eyed appetite and big heart. Celestine boasts a surprising, fetching sensibility.

Misfits in their own communities, they match up perfectly as a twosome. Ernest has rebelled against the family business—he's become a bohemian street performer rather than a distinguished judge. Celestine prizes the kind of creativity that has no value in the more Spartan, puritanical, and scientific mouse world.

With ingenuity and ease, the trio of directors (Benjamin Renner, Stéphane Aubier, and Vincent Patar) pulls off the kind of jokes about ingenuity and scale that Jerry Seinfeld sweated over hard in *Bee Movie* (2007). The mouse police and the bear police at times perfectly and hilariously mirror one another, especially when squads of them back off from one another in fear and amazement.

Visually, the film is full of mini-marvels. Some have a bent logic: In one workout area, mice have turned mousetraps into exercise machines. Others are more surreal. At one point, hordes of helmeted mice scamper out of their headquarters from exits that are not immediately apparent, as if the precinct is somehow both solid and porous. The bears, of course, are natural slapstick comedians, and the chase scenes rejuvenate gags as old as the Keystone Kops.

The movie's style is full of personality. It reflects Celestine's character and accentuates Ernest's. The cartooning has a liquid grace and light, fluid coloring, but Ernest's bounding figure gives it bounce. In the film's artistic high point, Ernest pushes a hollow pipe through a blizzard-blotted window so Celestine can paint the winter. As Ernest plays his fiddle, Celestine daubs out whorls of color that turn from snow-blue to spring-green. It's as if his music and her eye make beautiful images together.

—⟨⟨⟨—

Underground Comedy in *The Boxtrolls* (2014)
John Anderson

A magnificent bit of steam-punky stop-action from 2014, *The Boxtrolls* was criminally underappreciated upon its release (despite an Oscar nomination for

Best Animated Picture). But the film also arrived before its own prime time. The work of two directors, cartoonist-animators Graham Annable and Anthony Stacchi, it's fantastical, fast-paced, and droll, with dialogue delivered via English accents so thick you half expect a crouton to come floating by. But it's also an allegory about xenophobia, class war, and political fear-mongering. Subtitles might not have been the worst choice, or headphones, because only on repeated viewing does the film's wit fully reveal itself. As does its Trump–Brexit–Putin-era relevance.

If parents want to prep a child adequately for his/her first *Boxtrolls* screening, they might start with (1) David Lean's 1948 *Oliver Twist* (for the orphans and the accents), (2) the 2011 PBS special *Shalom Sesame! Be Happy, It's Purim* (for the theme of biblical genocide), and (3) any anti-immigration tweet by the president of the United States. If that sounds like too much trauma for a kid to handle all at once, cut straight to the movie. But sit together. And be prepared for questions.

Stop-action animation can be a mixed bag, an acquired taste, and is a genre often pigeonholed as kids' stuff. But for every old episode of *Gumby* rolling around the Internet there's a *Coraline* (2009) or a *Fantastic Mr. Fox* (2009) or whatever Nick Park confection you want to pick out of the "Wallace & Gromit" box, all of which can be appreciated by children without their having a full appreciation of the nuances involved. The *Boxtrolls* visuals are stunning; the putative monsters are adorable; the characterizations are spot on (forgive the British-ism, it's that kind of movie). But it's the film's unabashed trashing of hate, bigotry, opportunism, snobbery, and self-delusion that elevate it above standard-op pop extravaganza.

It begins with a kidnapping. Or what seems like one. The "Trubshaw baby" disappears one night in the arms of a boxtroll, a member of a race of gargoyle-ish scavengers who live beneath the streets of Cheesebridge, in what appears to be early nineteenth-century England. (The atmosphere feels intentionally Dickensian, although the Alan Snow's 2005 sourcebook *Here Be Monsters!* never really spells it out.) The "abduction" provides an excuse for the story's villainous social climber, Archibald Snatcher (a virtuoso voice-over by Ben Kingsley), to make an offer to the unctuous Lord Charles Portley-Rind (Jared Harris), city elder and head of the Cheese Guild: I will, Snatcher vows, rid Cheesebridge of every last boxtroll, in exchange for a white hat—the symbol of the guild and the passkey to its "tasting room," where bits of yellowed curd are adored like the Baby Jesus and eaten like the eucharist.

What it really means for the Cockney-accented, lactose-intolerant evildoer to exterminate the boxtrolls is the social elevation for which Snatcher so deeply hungers—despite being violently allergic to cheese in any form. "A white hat? You? Never!" exclaims Portley-Rind. Yet, the campaign of fear by the déclassé Snatcher convinces him to make the deal.

For the next ten years, Snatcher perpetrates a regular series of pogroms against the boxtrolls, abetted by a cretinous, homicidal maniac named Gristle (Tracey Morgan), and the two humorously conflicted henchmen, Mr. Trout and Mr. Pickles (Nick Frost and Richard Ayoade, respectively). The latter pair ponders what they suspect might be a morally dubious campaign. "You think these boxtrolls understand the duality of good and evil?" asks Mr. Trout, to which Mr. Pickles answers, "Why else would they hide from us? We're the good guys." A lot of Germans and ICE agents have thought the same way.

During this time, the lamented "Trubshaw baby"—whom Snatcherian propaganda has declared was eaten by the boxtrolls—has been reared, lovingly, in an underground lair that resembles a pastel carousel, and something out of Rube Goldberg. There, the boy in question, Eggs—rechristened after the old box he wears—is parented principally by Fish, one of the many trolls who specialize in the nocturnal gleaning of anything useful, attractive, or curious left on the Cheesebridge streets, which is then brought below and put to use. The montage in which Eggs grows up, being tutored and even chastised—running about without one's box is a no-no, the naughtily naked boy is warned—is a small masterpiece of silent filmmaking (with opera buffa soundtrack), to say nothing of a stop-motion tour de force.

But *The Boxtrolls* is many things, including a Holocaust allegory, a Dickens homage, and *Tarzan of the Apes*—Eggs is, understandably, under the impression that he, too, is a troll, having spent his entire life among them and with no exposure to humans (or light, for that matter). His Jane arrives in the person of Winnie (Elle Fanning), neglected daughter of Lord Portley-Rind and a girl morbidly obsessed with the supposedly murderous creatures living beneath her streets. "Did they eat your family and let you watch?" she asks Eggs when they meet. "I mean *make* you watch?" Eggs (Isaac Hempstead Wright) is completely nonplussed.

Winnie orchestrates Eggs' entrée into Cheesebridge society, which is a sequence of low comedy, as is the Cheese Guild's enchantment with Madame Frou-Frou—Snatcher in drag—who works the old gents for all they're worth. "A woman like her," sighs Portley-Rind, "is like a fine brie. Raw. Dangerous.

Maybe a little stinky." They're not just *fromagers*, they're idiots—one percenters, brain-damaged by milk fat: Rather than a children's hospital, they instead fund the purchase of a "Brie-hemoth," an eight-foot wheel that helps nourish the semi-slapstick climax of the movie, but that also, of course, represents the let-them-eat-cheese politics of Cheesebridge's ruling class.

The subtexts of *The Boxtrolls* remain, like its grotesque little heroes, subterranean: It's hard to call the film pure fun, but it's definitely an adventurous film and has caused several children I know to become completely entranced. Literary awareness, provocation, politics, none of this gets in the way of the entertainment, but it gives adults something to chew on while the kids, like Winnie, are made rapt by the action and grossness (overripe exploding cheeses and all that). If there's a bone to pick with *Boxtrolls*—much like Winnie, imagining the trolls picking over the bones of the Trubshaw baby—it is the way it buys into certain Holocaust stereotypes. "They drag us away, and we do nothing," Eggs complains about his passive brethren, to which Snatcher replies, "They ain't gonna run. You can't change nature."

Unlike its historical antecedents, however, *The Boxtrolls* ends happily, with even a few lessons learned.

"Are you pest exterminators or evil henchmen?" Winnie asks, confronting Trout and Pickles, who responds with a remorseful, "I knew that's how people saw us . . ." It's nice to think that, if there should ever be a sequel (*Boxtrolls II: Nuremberg*), Trout and Pickles will have turned state's evidence.

—〰—

Ideals Crash to Earth in *The Wind Rises* (2013)
Michael Sragow[7]

The Wind Rises (2013), Hayao Miyazaki's turbulent story of a beautiful dreamer who gets caught up in war—the engineer who turned Japan's airmen into a fearsome military force—is more animated than most other biopics, and not just because it's a feature-length cartoon. Combining fiction and history, Miyazaki creates a romantic adventure that's even more remarkable and unexpected than Martin Scorsese's *The Aviator* (2004). Its hero is a natural gentleman, not an eccentric firebrand like Howard Hughes. The poetry in his soul goes straight to our hearts.

The title comes from a ringing line in a Paul Valéry poem: "The wind is rising! . . . We must try to live!" In the film, these words become a declaration of struggle—against privation, mortality, and political storms—and they italicize each incident in the hero's story. Jirô Horikoshi (Joseph Gordon-Levitt) is a scholarly idealist who fights for every inch of his creative independence. His childhood goal of becoming a pioneering aviator seems far-fetched because of his myopia. Then he shares a dream with ebullient Italian engineer Caproni (Stanley Tucci), who catalyzes his belief that designing planes is more magical than piloting them.

Few movies use dreams as daringly as Miyazaki does here. He exploits their playful ambiguity: Is Caproni entering Jirô's dream, or is Jirô invading Caproni's? Miyazaki evokes their menace, too. In his sleep, Jirô terrifies himself with visions of a zeppelin releasing bombs and missiles manned by bogeymen, or billowing biplanes burning and crashing in World War I.

Caproni insists that planes are "beautiful dreams"—and that engineers turn dreams into reality. (He later admits, "Aircraft are destined to become tools for slaughter and destruction.") Jirô hangs on to his desire to "create beautiful airplanes." It sees him through the 1923 earthquake, the Great Depression, his days as a student engineer, and his entry into the professional ranks of Japan's aeronautical engineers at Mitsubishi. He swiftly shows his mettle by transcending the hazing process of his harried supervisor (Martin Short)—and winning the man over with his super competence. He soon applies revolutionary principles to designing planes, based on his study of gull wings and mackerel bones.

The movie's story and visuals are all of a piece. The incidents are layered; the wind reveals their secrets. Jirô's romance with his true love (Emily Blunt), a painter with tuberculosis, starts with a chance meeting and a sudden gust that causes her to say, "The wind is rising," and him to finish with, "We must try to live!" The interchange charmingly suggests their love of culture and ideas; Valéry's poem appeared the year before their meeting.

Miyazaki punctuates their delayed, on-and-off courtship with other zephyrs and breezes—one upends her umbrella while she paints outdoors, another whirls his paper plane to her terrace at a summer chalet. Their romance carries all the poignancy of Zhivago and Lara's stop-and-go amour in David Lean's *Doctor Zhivago* (1965). Equally affecting—and perhaps even more unusual—is Jirô's friendship with a fellow designer (John Krasinski). They share a rare collegiality and comradeship. They persuasively demonstrate that two skilled mates can channel their competitive urges into mutual support.

The film doesn't flinch from the contradiction of Jirô staying true to his aeronautical aesthetics while foreseeing catastrophes to come. (His experiences include a terror-streaked prewar trip to Germany.) After World War II, his crowning accomplishments are buried in piles of smoking wreckage. Yet, his artistic integrity is inspiring, like his faithfulness to his wife. Even as a phantom, she never stops insisting, "*You* must live!" Both Jirô as a character and this gorgeous, piercing movie will live on as vital, unpredictable creations. They testify to the gifts of a creator even more talented than Jirô—Hayao Miyazaki, an artist who has never ceased to be the lyric *and* the epic poet of animation.

The Red Turtle (2016) Is a Myth in the Making
Peter Rainer[8]

The delicacy of the animated movie *The Red Turtle* (2016), directed by Oscar-winning Dutch-British illustrator and animator Michaël Dudok de Wit, is so quietly breathtaking that to call it a tone poem doesn't quite do the film justice. This is the first international coproduction of Japan's famed Studio Ghibli, and in its hushed evocation of nature's mystic mysteries, it summons at its best the work of the studio's founders, Hayao Miyazaki and Isao Takahata. But Dudok de Wit's sense of form and color is even more minimalist than the work of those masters. Ten years in the making, *The Red Turtle* is both homage and sui generis.

The film begins with a shipwreck in which a passenger—a sailor perhaps—is violently swept ashore a deserted tropical island in the watery middle of nowhere. His frantic attempts to build a raft from bamboo logs continually comes to naught because every time he casts off, a large sea creature—as we soon learn, a gigantic turtle with a bright red shell—splinters the makeshift vessel to smithereens.

The red turtle does not seem malevolent, just persistent. There is a reason it wants the man to remain on the island, and, after the castaway exacts his revenge on the turtle, the film moves ever more decisively into transcendent realms of fantasy. The transformation of the turtle into a beautiful young woman who will become the man's mate is as satisfying as anything in a Hans Christian Andersen fable.

This transformation is doubly welcoming because, up until this point, Dudok de Wit has achingly evoked the man's deep, spooky aloneness. We've seen this situation before, from *Robinson Crusoe* to *Cast Away* (2000), but more than almost any other film I've ever seen, *The Red Turtle*, which is entirely word-less, although with a soundtrack vibrant with the rush of wind, water, and birds, expresses the isolation of being forbiddingly alone with nature.

With its lush greens and barren beaches, the island is teeming with tiny sand crabs that scurry sideways, like little windup sentries. The ocean is flush with creatures that are like underwater emissaries from some aqueous kingdom. When the man looks up at a starry night sky and hallucinates, seeing a string quartet playing on the moonlit beach, he is swooned by both the beauty and terrors of his predicament.

Dudok de Wit and his cowriter, Pascale Ferran, don't sentimentalize the man's predicament, even after he and his wife have a playful baby boy. The dangers of the island—the rocky crevices from which one can slip from great heights into near-inescapable pits—are ever-present. And because we have witnessed the transformation of the red turtle into the red-haired woman, we are always aware that the story carries a fantastical dimension.

The film may run only eighty minutes, but it seems longer—and I mean that in a good way. Shots of the island are often held for their own sweet sake, to let the stillness of the mood sink in. The people are often filmed from high angles to emphasize their insignificance in nature's grand scheme. When something explosively dramatic occurs, such as a tsunami that wipes out much of the island, it's as if paradise itself has been despoiled.

But this paradise was never halcyon—this is not *The Blue Lagoon* (1980). Behind even the movie's most transcendent tableaux is the lurking fear that this communion will vanish as abruptly as it arose. Perhaps this is why Dudok de Wit has chosen for so much of his film a grayish palette inspired by Japanese ink and watercolor prints. He wants the look of the film to have a ghostly evanescence, and what is remarkable is how, using such a minimal color scheme, he is yet able to convey such beauty.

The Red Turtle, a rare "children's film" that works equally well for adults, doesn't have the easily definable meanings that often attach to classic fairy tales.

At times, it can seem overly elusive, starting with its main character—a man with unplaceable origins who, from first to last, is a blank slate. But as I eased into the film's hypnotic swing, this ambiguousness became more and not less attractive. *The Red Turtle* benefits from being open to all sorts of possibilities and interpretations because we sense that Dudok de Wit respects our imaginings. He allows them to take shape right alongside his own.

Still image from *Babe*

3

BEAST FABLES

We've all had teddy bears. We all recall with a glow of nostalgia having stories read to us about animals. And ever since then, we have never stopped anthropomorphizing them and regarding them as comforters, agents of our wishes, or manifestations of our fears. And it's just a quick step from the page to the screen when it comes to the ongoing love affair between animals and children and adults who miss the child they once were.

Michael Sragow, in his essay "Into the Wild," recalls the thrill of *The Jungle Book*, the British Korda brothers' 1942 live-action version of the Rudyard Kipling books. What better friends could a kid have than panthers, snakes, and monkeys? But it's not all idyllic, especially when human civilization encroaches. Like many films about animals, *The Jungle Book* shows the contrast between the rapaciousness of humans and the innocence and freedom of the creatures that dwell in nature.

Sragow also discusses three subsequent adaptations and finds them, with one possible exception, not up to the original. The 1967 version is a "soft-as-mittens Disney cartoon." Jon Favreau's 2016 remake tries unsuccessfully to combine Disney treacle with the tough love of Kipling's "blood-and-fang jungle law." Only Andy Serkis's *Mowgli: Legend of the Jungle* (2018) comes close to the 1942 version, which Sragow describes as a children's classic that "captures the reckless moment in a boy or girl's life when the adult world seems unbearably corrupt and nothing could be more exhilarating than escaping to the wild."

What happens if instead of children becoming animals, animals somehow become adults? Would that usher in a new order that combines both innocence and rationality? Michael Sragow ponders this in his review of *Dawn of the Planet of the Apes* (2014), the sequel to *Rise of the Planet of the Apes* (2011), the first in a remake of the old franchise that began in 1968, with the adaptation of the original Pierre Boulle novel (such is Hollywood). In this installment, apes who have rapidly evolved and now have human intelligence confront a band of human survivors for control of the planet, or at least San Francisco.

The apes' leader—the noble, super-smart chimpanzee Caesar (the "most stirring political leader you can see anywhere in contemporary movies," according to Sragow)—wants to arrange peace—but, oh, those wicked bonobos. Sadly, the waking of reason produces monsters. "Caesar finds that promoting long-term strategies and ethical behavior is harder than spearheading a great leap forward for the apes," Sragow writes. "As humans and apes revert to atavistic reflexes, the film becomes a timeless fable about the perils of tribalism for both species."

A key to the success of both new *Planet of the Apes* movies, notes Sragow, is the performance of actor Andy Serkis, through the miracle of "performance-capture" CGI. As Jay Carr points out in his essay on the classic horror movie *King Kong*, in 1933, filmmakers had no such resources. They had to rely on old-fashioned miniature models and stop-motion animation.

Somehow, that was enough to create a beast that the world will never forget, terrifying and delighting future generations of children—even those jaded by the latest gizmos. As Carr explains, these primitive effects "work better than the CGI special effects and rapid-fire editing, which have taken over the world of film fantasy . . . because in a sense the old effects are 'real' [and] seem more concrete and threatening than today's computer figments."

Whatever the technical means of bringing him to life, however, the thing about Kong that hooks kids and adults is that he's out of control. He embodies every taboo urge we repress and has the means to do something about it. The result is chaos and terror, as well as gratified desire. Because of this fantasy fulfillment factor and his tragic fall, Kong gets our sympathy, not the paltry humans. "The big guy wasn't really a monster," Carr concludes. "He was a fool for love. One walked out of the theater feeling sorry for him."

Unlike *King Kong*, French filmmaker Albert Lamorisse's haunting 1953 film *White Mane* tells a love story between human and animal that is requited—but no less tragic. Set in an untamed region in France where wild horses roam free, it tells the tale of the title steed and the boy who befriends him. In his essay, David Sterritt praises the truth and beauty that the filmmaker manages to achieve in forty minutes and asserts that he examines "conflict and jealousy in candid yet compassionate ways." Like real life, this story doesn't resolve neatly but transports its hero away from the ordinary world to a place of pure imagination. Sterritt concludes that such "fantasies and fables have unique value for teaching youngsters how to make sense out of stories, test unfamiliar ideas, and think about the world in critical, creative ways."

The human/animal bond in Chris Noonan's *Babe* (1995), on the other hand, works out well for both sides. It helps that the title pig can talk, just like most of the animals on Hoggett Farm. And he can herd sheep—a good thing, too, because unless he can prove his worth to old Farmer Hoggett, he might end up on a platter with an apple in his mouth for Christmas dinner (talking animals aside, *Babe* is realistic).

In her review of the film, Carrie Rickey explains its hard-earned moral. "In its artful way, *Babe* illustrates the suspicion and hate bred by segregation," she writes.

> On Hoggett Farm, the cat hates the dogs, the dogs hate the sheep, and everybody hates the duck. Babe changes all that. The film gently suggests that when one approaches the unfamiliar with fear, hate is a natural outcome; but when one approaches the unfamiliar with respectful curiosity, friendship is a probable result.

In the sequel, George Miller's *Babe: Pig in the City* (1998), the unfamiliar thing is the title metropolis, where our porcine hero and his farm friends have found lodgings at an animal hotel. Gone, as Stephanie Zacharek notes, is much of the bucolic innocence of the first film. "If you watch *Babe: Pig in the City* expecting the gentle, pastoral charm of its 1995 predecessor . . . you're bound to be disappointed," she warns.

> Sometimes [it] doesn't seem like much fun. But its spell of craziness can sneak up on you. It's a children's movie that pushes far beyond the boundaries of what's considered safe and acceptable—beautiful and confused and adamant in its mission to sow true chaos, as so many kids' movies are not.

Into the Wild: Four Variations on *The Jungle Book*
Michael Sragow[1]

The Korda brothers' *The Jungle Book* (1942) captures the reckless moment in a boy or girl's life when the adult world seems unbearably corrupt and nothing could be more exhilarating than escaping to the wild. This voluptuous fantasy—directed by Zoltán, produced by Alexander, and art-directed by Vincent—brings to turbulent cinematic life one of Rudyard Kipling's archetypal characters. Mowgli, the infant raised by wolves in the Indian jungle, was a prime influence on other classic figures, including Tarzan and Peter Pan. On film, no youthful hero has had a more exuberant coming-of-age or a more distinctive, impertinent freshness. The Kordas entrusted Mowgli to their studio's biggest star: one-of-a-kind child actor Sabu, who had debuted five years earlier in *Elephant Boy* (based on one of Kipling's non-Mowgli *The Jungle Book* stories, "Toomai of the Elephants") and had been an elephant boy himself in real life. In *The Jungle Book*, his signature emotion is delight, and throughout he exudes the gusto of a teenager eager to rack up daredevil escapades.

The Criterion Collection's Eclipse line includes this film in a box set called *Sabu!* complete with exclamation point. Zoltán Korda deserves his own exclamation point for translating Kipling's rhythmic, sinewy prose and poetry into earthy visual beauties. This film does for the Indian rain forests what Clarence Brown would do for the Everglades in *The Yearling* (1946): turn them into a place filled with magic and wonder. *The Jungle Book* rivals the Kordas' celebrated *The Thief of Bagdad* (1940) for storybook lushness—but this movie carries even more visceral force. The scenes of jungle wolves accepting Mowgli into their pack cast a spell precisely because they're so matter of fact. They strike the film's alternating awestruck and down-to-earth tone. When Mowgli exchanges the oath, "We be of one blood, ye and I" with wolves, big cats, elephants, and, yes, serpents, this primal vow sets off atavistic stirrings in a viewer's soul.

In Kipling's droll preface to his first *The Jungle Book* (1894), he thanks such sources as the "scholarly and accomplished Bahadur Shah, baggage elephant 174 on the Indian Register." (If you haven't read Kipling's stories since childhood, you might not remember how amusing they are.) The film's equivalent is equally playful. An Indian bard tells a pretty memsahib that if she could perceive what's in his eyes, she would understand the core crisis of his country: the struggle between the village and the jungle. Then he swiftly spins the yarn of Mowgli, who wanders into the wild as a baby after a mangy, limping tiger named Shere Khan slays his father.

In the film's main story (drawn from both volumes of Kipling's *The Jungle Book*, the second published in 1895), Mowgli, at age twelve, fascinated by humans' control of fire, ventures too close to a village. The elders seize him and place him with a widow, not realizing, in a twist unique to this film, that she is his biological mother, Messua (Rosemary DeCamp). She doesn't recognize this hardened lad as her soft little babe. The hamlet's chief hunter, Buldeo (Joseph Calleia), takes an aggressive dislike for him, especially after Mowgli befriends his nubile daughter (Patricia O'Rourke). We are astonished to observe that Buldeo is the storyteller in his prime. The result is a reverse *Wizard of Oz*–like effect.

Kids wonder how that Buldeo—the good-humored yarn-spinner in the introduction—emerged from this Buldeo, the tough upholder of rustic law. Buldeo's
malice toward Mowgli is outstripped by his avarice. His daughter lets slip that
Mowgli has led her to a deserted jungle kingdom full of gems and precious
metals. Buldeo brings two stooges with him to raid the ruins.

Critics who contend that the Kordas play fast and loose with Kipling's content may not recall the author's second *The Jungle Book*: This movie draws heavily
from later Mowgli stories, notably "Letting in the Jungle" and "The King's
Ankus." (The titles alone excite the imagination.) Laurence Stallings's script contrasts the rough justice of nature's laws and the ethics of killing for food with the
greed of men, and the amorality of killing for sport. The movie has twin villains,
one for each world—the cowardly, desperate tiger Shere Khan and the greedy,
power-mad Buldeo. Yet the film is refreshingly good-humored, with a robust
streak of comedy.

In an Old Testament stroke, the only creatures in the jungle that speak
human language are two snakes—a codger of a cobra who guards the lost city's
treasure and a self-adoring python who enjoys drawling, "I am bee-a-uuuteeful."
Like Kipling, the film catalyzes more sympathy for sleek predators than for chat-
tering monkeys. Bagheera, the black panther, emerges as a regal swashbuckler.
At one point, he leaps into Buldeo's face so nimbly that the hunter believes the
big cat is Mowgli—and that Mowgli is a shape-shifting "witch." The monkeys,
however, are infected with a funny, horrifying group narcissism. They're terribly
silly and unstable because they're in love with their own frolicking nature.

The cobra and python, and an ominous crocodile, are the sole cast members
who are actually mechanical animals. It took backbreaking care and ingenuity for
Zoltán Korda to use real beasts for the other jungle creatures and intercut them
with these witty machines.

Michael Korda, Vincent's son, writes in his memoir, *Charmed Lives* (1979),
"Despite his feeling that I ought to be kept away from movie sets, Vincent placed
The Jungle Book in a different category, more like a visit to the zoo." He recalls
how the elder Kordas built an Indian jungle on a Hollywood back lot, down to
a river rushing between fake rocks. Zoltán Korda's biggest challenge was "Kaa,"
the enormous, talkative water python, who was made of rubber stretched over
an articulated frame. Prop men moved it via wires hidden underwater. "Kaa was
supposed to swim," writes Michael, "open and close his mouth, and stick out his
long, forked tongue. He seemed unable to do things in the proper sequence, and
each take involved lowering him downstream on his wires." Visible wires ruined
multiple takes; production halted so the crew could "untangle the wires and put
a shine on Kaa's glass eyes with neutral shoe polish." Because everyone stood on

the far edge of the camera barge for each of Kaa's descents, the barge eventually capsized—and "Zoli," who couldn't swim, "was fished out of the river with one of the long poles that was used for mooring Kaa between takes."

Zoltán's daily sacrifice of dignity helped to create the movie's alchemy. Contemporary audiences respond to its affectionate, imaginative mesh of fantasy and realism. The human and animal comedy and drama are all of a piece. The most foolish villagers are, literally, baggy-pants comedians. John Qualen is dream casting as the bumbling barber, one of Buldeo's stooges. The bags under his woeful eyes are as saggy as his pants. Best of all is the movie's fabulous pictorial zoology: the frenetic outcast monkeys; the noble, wary wolves; the mighty elephants trampling the underbrush.

The Kordas' *The Jungle Book* contains far more Kipling spirit than Walt Disney Studios' soft-as-mittens animated feature (1967). A narrator on the supplements for the cartoon's fortieth anniversary DVD informs us that Disney had a "truly profound ability to take literary classics and make them his own." That's correct except for "profound." Kipling turns savage frontier banalities upside-down so that man is the most fearsome creature in the jungle. Disney simplifies and sentimentalizes everything to underline affable parallels between the boy and his beast friends. The beloved humor of Disney's *The Jungle Book* and its songs, for instance, "The Bare Necessities," comes from envisioning animals as human wannabes (the monkeys) or people in furry disguise (everyone else). Baloo, this film's singing-and-dancing bear, for example, becomes a comic synonym for a lazy, lovable uncle. His signature tune puns on ursine and *Homo sapiens'* identities and qualities: "Forget about your worry and your strife / I mean the bare necessities / That's why a bear can rest at ease / With just the bare necessities of life."

In the Disney Studios' later, hybrid *The Jungle Book* (2016), the director, Jon Favreau, attempts to fashion a bone-rattling adventure, rippling with the conflict between intuitive animal nurture and Mowgli's more self-aware and ingenious human nature. But Favreau makes the self-destructive choice to showcase three of the cartoon's eight songs (most jarringly, the monkey-see, monkey-do number "I Wanna Be Like You") while trying to hew closer to Kipling's blood-and-fang jungle law.

In this homogenized live-action/CGI reboot, with Bill Murray taking over for Phil Harris as the voice of the crowd-pleasing Baloo, Favreau leans too heavily on the old 2-D whimsy. He also eliminates any contact or clashes between Mowgli and the human community. (Even Disney's cartoon Mowgli locks eyes with a village girl.) Favreau reduces the boy's psychic friction to one strategic question: Can he conquer Shere Khan by fighting like a human, with mortal weaponry (a torch), rather than like a wolf, which must rely on the power of the pack?

Favreau chose the semiplausible thirteen-year-old Indian American actor Neel Sethi as Mowgli and fills out the cast with a digital menagerie. His CGI comes off as hemmed-in and cautious. Favreau limits the "motion capture" technology that weds the actors' facial expressions and physical movements to animated fur and skin. His big-star voices—Idris Elba as Shere Khan, Scarlett Johansson as Kaa, and Ben Kingsley as Bagheera—don't mesh with the handsome yet generic cast of mammals and reptiles.

Happily, actor-turned-director Andy Serkis, the "master of motion capture," who played Gollum in *The Lord of the Rings* trilogy and Caesar in the *Planet of the Apes* trilogy, fully exploits this technique in his rousing *Mowgli: Lord of the Jungle* (2018), produced simultaneously with Favreau's *The Jungle Book* and released two years later. Serkis's determination to bring expressive details to each animal soars beyond photo-realism. In this director's majestic vision, jungle flora grows on Hathi, the lead elephant, who resembles a woolly mammoth. The main characters remain predominantly wolf, big cat, or bear while taking on a stylized intensity reminiscent of illustrations by Arthur Rackham or John Tenniel.

Thanks to Serkis's use of "MoCap," Benedict Cumberbatch's urgency ratchets up the tension of this film's gnarly Shere Khan, while Naomie Harris's intuition and intelligence suffuse Mowgli's wolf mother with raging warmth. Serkis himself interprets Baloo as a hearty drill sergeant. Best of all is Christian Bale's haunting, mysterious Bagheera. In this film, as in Kipling's prose, Bagheera registers as a "black shadow . . . inky black all over, but with the panther markings showing up in certain lights like the pattern of watered silk." Bale and Serkis seize on all the character's tonalities: cunning, boldness, and tenderness. Bale pulls off the most delicate acting of his career when Bagheera sneaks into the village to share his history of captivity with the imprisoned Mowgli. Bale tinges Bagheera's every syllable with sorrow and regret.

Serkis films the wolves' Darwinian battles with close-ups that particularize the combat and wide shots that encompass the jungle's at-risk ecology. His moviemaking fervor and Callie Kloves's moving, trenchant script restore Kipling's ferocious grandeur. The exuberance of Rohan Chand's Mowgli rivals Sabu's, while Freida Pinto's lovely, affecting surrogate mom Messua contrasts beautifully with Matthew Rhys's great white hunter Lockwood (a Kloves addition). Pinto can radiate empathy without saying a word, while Rhys crisply embodies the practical understanding that draws Mowgli to his side—then, just as effortlessly, the cruel detachment that drives the boy back into the wild. Kloves translates the story's drama and themes into memorable images and sounds: It's both ineffable and eerie to see Mowgli wake up in a cage and hear Elgar's "Imperial March" wafting off the hunter's record player. Kloves's script prepares us for Mowgli's emergence as the leader who will save his brethren by bringing imagination to their warfare and fresh eyes to their rules and regs. This movie earns its Tarzan finish.

Still, the sight of the boy standing watch on the Council Rock in Serkis's film, no matter how satisfying, can't match the undiluted poignancy of the Kordas' climax, in which the jungle citizens flee the catastrophe set off by humankind's "Red Flower" fire. They travel by river deeper into the forest, retreating from the encroachments of the village. Mowgli and his cohort yearn for a state of raw, untrammeled purity. The jungle, in the Kordas' *The Jungle Book*, is partly a bare-knuckled Eden. The movie's theme is *Paradise Lost*.

—⟋⟍—

An Ape Shall Show the Way: *Dawn of the Planet of the Apes* (2014)
Michael Sragow[2]

In *Dawn of the Planet of the Apes* (2014), Caesar, the super-chimp who started a rebellion and founded an ape state in Muir Woods, becomes the most stirring political leader you can see anywhere in contemporary movies. He strives to organize apes of every kind into a just society. He turns a one-time circus orangutan into a teacher who tells his class that apes do not kill apes. He employs gorillas as his state's perimeter guard. He tries to civilize a scarred bonobo ape that lives only to fight. And when humans establish a foothold in an eerie, shattered, overgrown San Francisco, Caesar doesn't move to wipe them out. He works for a two-state solution.

The very existence of this subtle, dynamic, endlessly fascinating character pays tribute to the sophistication of "performance-capture" technology, which digitally records actors' movements and expressions, then turns them into fantasies of talking apes. Since the turn of the millennium, actor Andy Serkis has brought dazzling artistry to this process, whether as Gollum in Peter Jackson's Tolkien movies or the title role in Jackson's *King Kong* (2005).

Serkis outdoes himself as Caesar in *Dawn of the Planet of the Apes*. This gigantic spellbinder of a movie rests on his ability to convey power and command with his posture, and an array of emotions via his incredibly malleable face, from kingly and fatherly concern to menace, friendship, love, despair, and stinging sadness. This "performance-capture" milestone should be recognized with the awards and acclaim that too often go to actors who put on fake noses or phony accents.

In *Rise of the Planet of the Apes*, Caesar never lost his vision of bringing simians together and creating a real home for them, not even when they were fighting for their lives. At the end of *Rise*, the apes appeared safe in the redwoods while humans started to come down with "simian flu"—the retrovirus that was genetically engineered to cure Alzheimer's but instead accelerated apes' intelligence and killed people.

In *Dawn*, which takes place at least ten years later, filmmakers visualize a state fit for a Caesar. This lush, layered haven appears to have developed so organically that it's hard to separate where nature's plateaus and caves end and the apes' own handiwork begins, notably a marvelous whirling, trellised ramp leading to Caesar's lair.

More important, the movie tests Caesar's ability to improvise while maintaining his moral balance. Soon after we see evidence of the apes thriving as a unit in a thrilling deer hunt, humans stumble onto their turf. They're part of a remnant that has survived the simian flu and hopes to restart a hydroelectric dam that falls in the apes' domain. The humans want to power up the city of San Francisco, where hundreds of men and women not quite the equivalent of Caesar's roughly 2,000 apes have huddled together for strength and warmth. They aim to connect with other human enclaves and reestablish a demolished civilization.

Caesar grudgingly grants the humans access to the dam and provides limited help. But it's more difficult for him to teach his apes about peaceful coexistence than it was to unite them against mankind. The previous film peaked when Caesar used jungle instinct to establish his dominance at a primate center with apes and monkeys who acted the way they were treated—as dumb animals. Then he made them almost as smart as he was, by spraying them with that brain-enhancing retrovirus. (The circus orangutan Maurice was his one near-peer.)

Tragically, in *Dawn of the Planet of the Apes*, Caesar finds that promoting long-term strategies and ethical behavior is harder than spearheading a great leap forward for the apes. As humans and apes revert to atavistic reflexes, the film becomes a timeless fable about the perils of tribalism for both species.

Director Matt Reeves matches up ape and human forces with heartbreaking, nail-biting evenness. Each side has a violent wild card: the trigger-happy dam expert Carver (Kirk Acevedo) and the bellicose bonobo ape Koba (Toby Kebbell). The cofounder of New San Francisco, Dreyfus (Gary Oldman), helps set calamity in motion, but he's not an evil man, just a pragmatist at wit's end.

Caesar's heroic counterpart is Malcolm (Jason Clarke), the open-minded, bighearted leader of the mission to the dam. Malcolm, a widower, has a lover—a medic and former CDC employee, Ellie (Keri Russell)—and a teenage boy,

Alexander (Kodi Smit-McPhee), who retreats into his sketchbook and graphic novels because he can't accept Ellie as his stepmother. Caesar has a proud, confused adolescent son, Blue Eyes (Nick Thurston), and a loving wife, Cornelia (Judy Greer), who gives birth to an adorable baby boy.

Director Reeves makes the bonding of these characters credible by tying it to their individual needs and skills. You never catch the human characters overacting fear or wonder—they're simply, enthrallingly, in the grip of it. Serkis and his troupe use the apes' sign language, yelps, and yowls, and rough-voiced verbal speech, to hit operatic high notes, and sometimes grace notes, too. In a wonderful surprise, Kebbell's scarifying Koba gets to play moments of stunning black comedy (the film could have used more). And it's extraordinarily moving to see Alexander dive into a graphic novel with Karin Konoval's wise, literate Maurice.

The movie does suffer from an overemphatic musical score. So it's a balm to the ears when the Band's "The Weight" ("Take a load off, Fanny") wafts through the redwoods via the sound system of a revived 76 gas station. Happily, Reeves doesn't stint on ravishing visual harmonies, not even in the middle of pitched battles.

The apes' attack on San Francisco is as potent as the siege sequence in *Ivanhoe* (1952), and the prolonged continuous shot of Koba gaining control of a runaway tank tracks a fiery parabola of destruction. Reeves and Serkis pour so much feeling into Caesar's final close-ups that his melancholy gaze seems to follow us out of the theater.

Long Live the King: *King Kong* (1933)
Jay Carr

King Kong (1933) started out costarring with a lizard—a Komodo dragon, to be precise, the world's largest, measuring ten feet, weighing 150 pounds, and a meat-eater all the way, prowling Indonesia's jungles with a venomous bite.

But then things started happening. Like the Depression. RKO decreed that globe-trotting filmmakers Merian C. Cooper and Ernest B. Schoedsack could no longer be allotted money for an expensive expedition to Indonesia, dashing Cooper's dream of filming the clash-of-the-titans showdown between the supersized lizard and the mega-gorilla. It shut down its overbudget dinosaur film *Creation*. Studio boss David O. Selznick asked Cooper to recycle the jungle set of the just-completed *The Most Dangerous Game* (1932) with the *Creation* dinosaurs. He did just that. Some shots were filmed in New York City, but *King Kong* never got farther west than San Pedro Island, off Los Angeles.

In the film, he's twenty-five feet tall—able to take on the dinosaurs. By now anyone who cares knows that he was a model—eighteen inches of dyed rabbit fur on sponge rubber over an aluminum frame, filmed in stop-motion. Contemporary critics often condescendingly write off the film's primitive special effects. They miss the point, which is not whether they're primitive, but whether they work. Yes, they're often primitive, but yes, they work. They work better than the CGI special effects and rapid-fire editing that have taken over the world of film fantasy, as a comparison between the original Kong and the remake by Peter Jackson proves, because in a sense the old effects are "real," actual models, which through stop-motion animation, back projection, and long takes seem more concrete and threatening than today's computer figments. Inventing the techniques as they went along, the filmmakers proved resourceful and ingenious, their effects designed and executed in innovative and sophisticated ways. That is why *King Kong* looks more alive than most high-tech monster-making. Films are faces and faces are eyes, and it's the King's eyes that lure us over to his side.

Two separate, larger heads were built for their shared close-ups. Other body parts were built as needed. A giant foot, for instance, was created for scenes in which Kong stomps his victims. An eight-foot crane, covered in material to make it seem the palm of the King's hand, was built for Fay Wray to perch on while he looked her over up close. Who held whom in the palm of whose hand soon becomes all too tragically clear, although not to Kong. A giant bust of Kong's head, neck, and shoulders, covered in bearskin, was large enough to contain three men, who used levers, hinges, and an air compressor to control the mouth and facial expressions, including eyeballs twelve inches in diameter. When the big guy picks Wray's Ann up, obviously besotted, his face is a mix of bewilderment and dopey bliss.

Back on Skull Island, when he places Ann safely on a rock ledge outside a cave while he turns his attention to decking a T-Rex bent on eating her, he doesn't just drop her there. He places her tenderly. Still, she only has eyes for Bruce Cabot's Great White Lover, and the career break promised by Robert Armstrong's Great White Filmmaker. And things soon go downhill for Kong, when he's captured, chained in the hold of a freighter, and carried back to Manhattan. After a boffo opening night, in which he's exhibited in a theater in chains, he breaks out and embarks on a damage-strewn search for Ann, whom he finally plucks from a hotel.

Although listed as codirectors, Cooper and Schoedsack's styles didn't mesh, so Cooper directed the scenes with the miniatures and Schoedsack directed the action scenes. Both had a workout. So, yes, the King did go on the odd rampage, but that was mostly in New York City, where lots of people were determined to get between him and Wray. The big guy wasn't really a monster. He was a fool for love. One walked out of the theater feeling sorry for him, wishing he had swatted down the biplanes firing at him (one of which was piloted by Cooper himself) as he clung to the top of the Empire State Building.

The publicity department downplayed the fact that this was a love story, a Beauty and the Beast tale. The posters depicted Kong as vicious and crazed with destructive impulses. But he didn't want to demolish a subway car full of screaming passengers or squash hapless bystanders with his big, hairy feet. He just wanted Fay Wray—even though she screamed a lot.

He never wanted to be at the center of one of the iconic monster movies. But he was, bless his little aluminum heart. There have been spin-offs (including one by Schoedsack and Cooper) and remakes, and the King's title was usurped for a while by an upstart named Presley. But there's only one King of the twentieth century, and his name is Kong. Accept no substitutes.

—⁓—

No Reining in *White Mane* (1953)
David Sterritt

Everyone who cares about family movies should get familiar with French film-maker Albert Lamorisse, the only writer-director since the age of silent cinema to earn international fame with pictures less than an hour long. His favorite theme is friendship between a boy and an unlikely companion, and his best-known picture is *The Red Balloon*, a free-floating fantasy from 1956 about a six-year-old's relationship with an intelligent inflatable flying high over the Paris streets. But the movie that launched Lamorisse was the 1953 adventure *White Mane*, a different kind of fable solidly grounded in France's undomesticated Camargue region.

In its native France, *White Mane* is known as *Crin blanc: Le cheval sauvage*, which literally means "White Horsehair, the Wild Horse." The title character enters at the beginning, running with his herd in the Little Camargue, a patch of boggy land in southeastern France. Wild horses have dwelled there longer than anyone can remember, and the region's cowboys—who raise bulls destined for Spanish bullrings—love the way they compensate for their modest size with a strength and agility bred into them by the slippery everglade in which they've always lived. White Mane is a prime specimen of the breed, but as the off-screen narration tells us (in the English language version provided by the great critic James Agee), he isn't very fond of humans. His dim view of our species doesn't brighten when cowboys catch him and try to break his spirit.

The boy in the story, Folco, lives with his grandfather, a fisherman. He's dazzled when he sees White Mane in the corral where the cowboys have penned him, and when the beautiful stallion manages to escape, Folco follows him. The men do their best to catch him again, but White Mane outwits them, and they give up the chase, telling Folco that if he manages to get hold of the wayward horse, he can declare himself the proud owner. Folco gets a rope around White Mane, but the stallion drags him through a swampy area where he almost drowns before the lasso slips out of his grasp and White Mane gallops away, returning to his herd.

White Mane has good reason to dislike humans, but it turns out his independent spirit makes it hard to get along with other horses, too. Deciding to leave the herd and live on his own, he now changes his mind about Folco, evidently thinking the boy would be a good companion in his new life. The cowboys return to the chase, however, forcing the stallion in their direction by setting fire to the undergrowth. Folco jumps on White Mane and they race to the sea, while the cowboys shout panicky warnings, aware that anyone entering the rapid currents will surely perish. But their alarm goes unheeded. "They swam straight ahead, straight ahead," the narrator says. And the wonderful horse, the voice continues, "carried his friend, who trusted him, to a wonderful place where men and horses live as friends, always."

White Mane and *The Red Balloon* have a lot in common. Both deal with conflict and jealousy in candid yet compassionate ways, confronting their young heroes with outside forces that threaten to break up their treasured new relationships. Both films also have open-ended conclusions, not solving the story's problems but transporting the human heroes away from the ordinary world to a place of pure imagination. That place seems utterly real thanks to the clarity of Lamorisse's camera, which benefits from the experience he gained as a photographer and documentary filmmaker before turning to fiction movies. Along with Edmond Séchan, who did the camerawork, he portrays the marshy environment in astonishing detail, capturing the vigorous moods of its rougher areas, as well as the delicate beauty of land covered by just enough water to cast a twinkling reflection of the boy and horse moving along it.

Even more impressively, Lamorisse conveys the personality and behavior of White Mane—who's played by several horses—with a minimum of editing tricks, knowing that the camera eye and the skills of thirteen-year-old Alain Emery, who plays Folco, will bring the story alive no matter how fanciful it becomes. Emery had never sat in a saddle or even acted in a movie before he signed on for the film, but his bareback riding is so nimble that you'd think he was doing it before he could walk—although Lamorisse did bring in a double for the scene where Folco gets dragged through the swamp, doing that stunt himself.

Not everyone thinks *White Mane* is excellent. The great French filmmaker François Truffaut, who sensitively probed the world of childhood in such classic films as *The 400 Blows* (1959), *The Wild Child* (1970), and *Small Change* (1976), didn't care for it, saying it lacked "emotional truth" and accusing the title character of being a "counterfeit horse" like animals in Walt Disney's poorest movies. Cultural critic Philip Kennicott, who won a Pulitzer Prize in 2013, complained in a 2007 article that both *White Mane* and *The Red Balloon* take place in a "world of lies," using the allure of fine camerawork to prop up a wrongheaded moral system almost as unsophisticated as that of "Santa and the Easter Bunny," based on a "blunt promise of rewards for good behavior" and geared toward "indoctrinating kids in a worldview that will lead only to bitter disappointment." On the flip side of the debate, renowned French critic André Bazin applauded Lamorisse for making White Mane two creatures in one—a "real horse that grazes on the salty grass of the Camargue" and also a "dream horse swimming eternally."

Skeptical reviews won't bother viewers who believe that fantasies and fables have unique value for teaching youngsters how to make sense out of stories; test unfamiliar ideas; and think about the world in critical, creative ways. With their unpredictable plots, appealing characters, and colorful settings, *White Mane* and *The Red Balloon* are movies in the best sense of the word, telling their stories through vividly photographed pictures and keeping words to a bare minimum. *White Mane* packs enormous visual and emotional power into its forty-minute running time, and it deserves the honors it won—including the Jean Vigo Prize and the Grand Prize for best short film at the Cannes Film Festival—when it premiered in 1953. Just three years later, *The Red Balloon* earned the Academy Award for Best Original Screenplay (quite an achievement for a movie where hardly a word is spoken) and garnered the Golden Palm, the highest award at Cannes, for best short film.

These triumphs apart, Lamorisse's overall career was uneven and ultimately sad. His feature-length movies—*Stowaway in the Sky* (1960), about a boy who hitches a ride on his grandpa's huge balloon, and *Circus Angel* (1965), about a burglar who acquires a pair of wings—also failed to meet his high expectations.

He scored a major accomplishment outside the movie world, however, when he designed the popular board game Risk in 1957.

Flying captivated Lamorisse throughout his life, as you can guess from the stories he chose to tell, and one of his accomplishments was inventing Helivision, a device to make helicopter filming more practical. Yet, he died at only forty-eight in a helicopter mishap in Iran, where he was working on a documentary. Using his notes as a guide, his widow and son later finished that film, *The Lovers' Wind*, and it won an Oscar nomination for Best Documentary Feature in 1978. Since then, the drama, whimsy, and beauty of Lamorisse's best short movies have kept his name alive, and many consider *White Mane* to be the finest film he ever made.

In *Babe* (1995), a Pig Shows the Way
Carrie Rickey[3]

In the inspirational vein of *Rocky* (1976), *The Karate Kid* (1984), and every Muppet movie in which Miss Piggy not only dreams, but also achieves the impossible dream, comes *Babe* (1995), a deliciously funny tale of an adventurous and highly motivated piglet. Babe doesn't know his place—which means he goes places.

You've heard of the man who would be king? Babe is the swine who would be sheepdog. And he talks. Not like Mr. Ed, who had lips that moved about as realistically as Clutch Cargo's. But like your curious ten-year-old child.

So realistic are the film's digitizing techniques, so natural the voices, that Babe and the rest of the creatures in the barnyard seem quite genuine. This is the work of coproducer/cowriter George Miller (1979's *Mad Max* and 2015's *Mad Max: Fury Road*), whose signature action shots are in evidence, and director/cowriter Chris Noonan.

By asking questions, Babe gets wisdom. And in learning how to herd from a border collie named Fly, who adopts him, Babe defies the social order of an animal farm where all critters decidedly are not created equal. Some, particularly the sheep, are more unequal than others.

At Hoggett Farm, the cat is allowed in the house and the dogs in the outbuildings, but all other animals are relegated to their respective paddocks and pens. Despite the strict segregation, Babe bravely trots where ducks and sheep fear to tread.

Because he is one of nature's optimists, possessed of a trusting temperament that earns the confidence of sworn enemies, Babe does not at first suspect that the lower you are in the animal hierarchy, the higher the probability of your becoming dinner.

Based on the popular children's book by Dick King-Smith, *Babe* is not, strictly speaking, a kid's movie. It is a preposterously funny fable that strikes a chord with adults, too.

In its artful way, *Babe* illustrates the suspicion and hate bred by segregation. On Hoggett Farm, the cat hates the dogs, the dogs hate the sheep, and everyone hates the duck. Babe changes all that. The film gently suggests that when one approaches the unfamiliar with fear, hate is a natural outcome; but when one approaches the unfamiliar with respectful curiosity, friendship is a probable result. This, you may recall, is also the message of that so-called kid's movie *E.T. the Extra-Terrestrial* (1982). And not only because of this similarity does *Babe* have the breakout potential of *E.T.*

The human/creature friendship that develops here is with Farmer Hoggett (James Cromwell), a lanky gent who's as laconic as his hoglet is chatty. One is towering, the other ground-level. One is ruddy, the other pale pink. One rarely speaks, the other rarely holds his tongue. But each grows to respect the other's difference.

This, despite Babe's grievous trespass into the Hoggett home. In a scene so gripping it exceeds the thrills of the car chase in *The French Connection* (1971) or the high-speed high jinks in *Mad Max*, Babe and Ferdinand, the devious duck, steal into the house to abscond with the "mechanical rooster" (an alarm clock) that is putting certain barnyard personages out of business. It is a scene—and a film—that redefines what we mean by, "What a Babe!"

Accidental Tourist: *Babe: Pig in the City* (1998)
Stephanie Zacharek[4]

If you watch *Babe: Pig in the City* (1998) expecting the gentle, pastoral charm of its 1995 predecessor, Chris Noonan's *Babe*, you're bound to be disappointed. Sometimes, when it looks as if director George Miller is about to break faith with the audience, this *Babe* doesn't seem like much fun. But its spell of craziness can sneak up on you. *Babe: Pig in the City* is occasionally distressing, sometimes distractingly manic, but also insanely inventive and magical, and much, much stranger than its predecessor. It's a children's movie that pushes far beyond the boundaries of what's considered safe and acceptable—beautiful and confused, and adamant in its mission to sow true chaos, as so many kids' movies are not.

Pig in the City is true to the spirit of the first *Babe*: Its message is that no one must accept his or her assigned place in the world, and that little pigs (or little people, for that matter) can achieve great things. The Hoggetts are in danger of losing their farm when Farmer Hoggett is laid up after an accident. Esme Hoggett (Magda Szubanski, here filling the main human role as James Cromwell's Farmer Hoggett did in the first picture) decides to take sheep-herding hero Babe to a big fair, hoping that the money he earns for his appearance will be enough to save the farm. A few wrong turns later, she ends up in jail, with Babe (whose winsome voice is supplied by E. G. Daily) wandering a big, strange city. In his new and unfamiliar surroundings, Babe—he of the noble gray tuft, lighthearted, brave, and true—falls in with an assortment of winged, feathered, four-legged, and two-legged friends, many of them strays.

Babe and Esme have landed at a special hotel where animals are secretly welcome, against all city regulations, and a good deal of the movie's action takes place there. (We see the creatures scampering and trotting along the staircases and landings that wind around the perimeter of the hotel's open lobby—sometimes it's as if the action is circling our heads.) The animals move and talk with the help of animatronics, but as with the original *Babe*, their animal nature is still miraculously preserved. Even the trio of singing mice maintain an air of dignity during their squeaky rendition of Edith Piaf's "Non je ne regrette rien."

Babe's other friends include a couple of showbiz chimps (their voices provided by the hilariously dry Stephen Wright and the effervescent Glenne Headly) whose facial expressions are more human than those of some human actors—a stately orangutan who wears the sadness of the universe around his baggy brown eyes, an overwound Jack Russell terrier who's lost the use of his back legs but scoots along just fine by way of a little wheeled harness, a pink poodle with fluttery eyes and Blanche DuBois mannerisms, and a mafioso bull terrier who starts out mean but ends up transformed after Babe saves him from drowning. ("A murderous shadow lies hard across my soul," he says as a way of explaining how his tough-guy nature has been bred into him.)

The plot unfolds in angles and twists that, despite seeming a little slapdash, keep the picture moving along. Babe saves the day, over and over again, and ultimately reunites with Mrs. Hoggett. (His rescue occurs at a fancy ball; Mrs. H., wearing an inflatable clown suit—don't ask—spends much of the scene bouncing along the ceiling like a Macy's parade balloon, a bobbing symbol of the movie's go-for-broke lunacy.)

But while the action is engaging enough, the small moments in *Pig in the City* are what resonate. Babe's friends have been imprisoned in a hospital lab, and he rescues them, leading them to safety. We see them in silhouette against a twilight sky, crossing a narrow upper-story walkway connecting two buildings, as a woman in a billowy white dress flutters through the alley below. In the same sequence, the animals traipse through a children's hospital ward like a ragtag parade. Their shadows pass silently along the wall as they trot past a row of iron beds; one of the children wakes up and sees them, his face lighting up with delight and wonder, and it's no less than what Miller makes *us* feel.

As with any movie, to feel something is a kind of risk: The only way I could get through some portions of *Pig in the City* was to think of it as a kind of European art film—one that I knew would have a happy ending. A sequence in which a troupe of scary animal-control officers storms the hotel wearing lab coats, padded suits, and jackboots goes on far too long, and the sight of frightened animals running in every direction, and of sweet dogs being lured to their entrapment with treats, just isn't fun. (The children in the audience I saw the movie with seemed to have less trouble with the animals-in-distress business than I did; even so, I'd hesitate to recommend it for very young or very sensitive children.)

But as anxious as the scene made me, I can't say that Miller made it cheap; he doesn't stoop to those god-awful traumatizing Disney moments. (No animals die in *this Babe*.) Miller always redeems himself just when it seems that he's going to milk us dry. At one point, we're led to believe that Flealick, the Jack Russell in the wheeled harness, has finally gone to meet his maker: He lies in the street, his body twitching, one upended wheel turning creakily, and it's too much. But, suddenly, Miller cuts soundlessly to a vision of dog paradise. We see Flealick bouncing up and down in a green field loaded with butterflies, a perfect picture of dog joy, his harness cast aside, Clara-like.

The scene—short, surreal, and hysterically funny, as well as breathtakingly gorgeous—represents exactly the kind of heaven that's hoped for by everyone who's ever lost a beloved pet. Of course, Flealick's time isn't up yet—he hears Babe calling and comes back to the land of the living, quickly righting himself, and righting the movie, too—but his brief interlude in paradise is a reassurance from Miller that he cares for his characters as much as we do.

Babe: Pig in the City is even more visually beautiful than its predecessor. Production designer Roger Ford and cinematographer Andrew Lesnie have outdone themselves: When we see the Hoggett farm in the early sequences, with its honey-toned fields and verdant stretches of grass, it's like being reunited with an old friend. Babe's foray into the city is rendered in the same paint-box colors, but they're even more fanciful—as well as being mysteriously softer and brighter—than in the earlier movie.

When Babe, lonely in the city, gazes out the circular window of his hotel, he sees a gently colored cityscape that's a magical array of every great urban landmark you've ever seen on a postcard or souvenir charm bracelet: There's the Statue of Liberty, the Golden Gate Bridge, the Eiffel Tower, the Sydney Opera House, the Hollywood Sign. The hotel is a bright, candy-like building that sits on the edge of a shimmery canal, as if the intersection of Venice and Hong Kong were a single street corner. Even the human characters are rendered in incredible colors: Mary Stein is delightful as the eccentric innkeeper who allows pets in her establishment. With her swan neck, china-doll skin, and flapper's bob, she's like a Mary Engelbreit illustration come to life.

But, of course, it is the animals that make *Babe: Pig in the City* click. As Babe rounds up his friends at the lab so he can lead them to safety, the orangutan—a clown's assistant who's used to wearing a coat and pants—quietly asks the other animals to wait for him to dress. And, patient and naked, they do. The idea of an orangutan needing his clothes to maintain his dignity is either touching or absurd, depending on how you look at it. But in *Babe: Pig in the City*, you're about as likely to scoff at it as you are to expect a pig to fly. That he can talk, of course, is already a given.

Cheryl Callaway, Gloria Castillo, Mary Ellen Clemons, Sally Jane Bruce,
Lillian Gish, and Billy Chapin in *The Night of the Hunter*

4

DREAMS, FANTASIES, AND NIGHTMARES

Like dreams, movies offer kids (and adults) a safe place to confront fears and desires that are otherwise hard to acknowledge or understand. They allow access to alien or impossible worlds that turn out to be strangely familiar or not so impossible after all. Fantasy and horror films thus are often the first genres that turn children on to cinema.

Some of those exposed to *The Wizard of Oz* (1939) at an early age (such as myself) claim it to be one of scariest films they've ever seen. (According to a study done by the University of Turin in 2018, it is also the most influential movie of all time, with the most spin-offs and the most cultural references.) In his essay "There's No Film Like *Oz*," Michael Wilmington admits to a frightening moment or two (the Wicked Witch's nasty cackle gets him every time) when watching it as a child with his family on TV, but mostly he recalls the exultant joy and poignant longing of Judy Garland singing "Over the Rainbow." "What pure, shattering emotion wrapped in rapturous show-biz kitsch and MGM bliss!" he exclaims. He concludes, "[It is] a show that never loses its power to grip us and tickle us and make us laugh and cry and [is] the greatest kids (plus adults) movie this side of the rainbow." But he also notes a sense of unease, "At least on our second time through we know that this is Dorothy's dream, brought on by the cyclone and a head-bonk, and that Oz is her creation—her fairy-tale Kansas—which is why it's both her paradise and her nightmare."

Following in the footsteps of Dorothy in *The Wizard of Oz*, the two children in Tomm Moore's animated fantasy *Song of the Sea* (2014) also seek some magical paradise beyond the stark seascape of their village on the Irish coast. As Justin Chang writes in "The Animated Enchantment of *Song of the Sea*," it is a "realm where the boundaries separating reality and myth turn out to be surprisingly porous—where rocks, boulders, and even small islands can house long-dormant spirits, and an ethereal, white-robed being called a 'selkie' can transform into a seal under water." While *The Wizard of Oz* recreates its fabulous alternative reality through Technicolor, fantastic sets, unforgettable songs, and Munchkins, Moore employs the "sheer beauty of his visual design [to pull] the viewer into a dream state where this sort of magic is at once a given and a source of continual wonderment."

The two children in Charles Laughton's *The Night of the Hunter* (1955) also engage in a desperate journey; they are in flight from the demonic preacher Harry Powell, played by Robert Mitchum in one of his greatest performances. In his essay on the film, Robert Horton extols its one-of-a-kind combination of "German Expressionism, the Brothers Grimm, the films of D. W. Griffith and James Whale, [and] Mark Twain" in evoking a childhood nightmare of evil and salvation. He also puts the preacher in a long tradition of American con men, a "character in the bullshitting tradition that extends from P. T. Barnum to Donald Trump, [someone who is] almost astonished himself at the gullibility of his prey . . . [who] convinces complacent suckers but doesn't fool [his] adversary, a child."

The film not only epitomizes a traditional villain, but also evokes the trauma of growing up in an abusive family. "People who see *The Night of the Hunter* in childhood never forget the terror of Harry Powell," Horton writes. "I think Mitchum instills fear not merely because of his cruelty, but because of his sarcasm. He's like a bad parent (literally, he's the evil stepfather) who knows that sneering mockery is at least as unsettling to children as open anger."

Like Michael Wilmington in his appreciation of *The Wizard of Oz*, Sheila Benson is struck by a thrilling performance when she watches Michael Powell and Emeric Pressburger's glorious and uncanny *The Red Shoes* (1948). But she also recognizes the dangerously seductive appeal of a menacing male figure like the Preacher in *The Night of the Hunter*. In her essay "Careful What You Wish For," she explains how she was drawn to and troubled by themes of the film: reality imitating art—an art one is willing to die for.

In it a ballerina takes the lead role in the title ballet, which is based on the Hans Christian Andersen fairy tale about a dancer who dances herself to death. Will art imitate life? Will the dream become a nightmare? When the dancer puts on the title shoes, Benson writes, "The surreal, genuinely scary ballet has . . . begun." Although the film should thrill all young novice dancers, and children, in general, Benson includes a caveat: "Ballet-mad or not, you might want to hold off on *The Red Shoes* until your very young, interested party can take it. Eleven? Fourteen? Thirty-five?"

Some of the scariest movies, like *The Night of the Hunter*, succeed because they evoke the point of view of endangered children. David Sterritt, in his essay "Between the Fantastic and the Mundane," finds this to be the case in two seemingly dissimilar horror movies, *The Curse of the Cat People* (1944) and *Poltergeist* (1982).

Both feature young girls with active imaginations and the kind of acute sensitivity that picks up on the mysteries that underlie the surface of things. In *The Curse of the Cat People* (1944), young Amy, a fey child like the girl in *Song of the Sea* in *The Curse of the Cat People*, summons up an imaginary companion upon seeing the photo of a tragic, spectral figure from the past. Her near-supernatural empathy makes possible a long-delayed reconciliation. In *Poltergeist*, the psychically attuned five-year-old Carol Anne contacts malevolent entities via TV. Sterritt points out that the film reflects producer Steven Spielberg's "fascination with the impact of unearthly experiences on ordinary people in everyday environments." And on extraordinary children.

The girl in Guillermo del Toro's *Pan's Labyrinth* (2006) is older than those in *The Curse of the Cat People* and *Poltergeist*, and, as I write in my review "Fauny Girl: Innocence Finds a Way through *Pan's Labyrinth*," the ordinary world she inhabits is more perilous and fraught with evil. Twelve-year-old Ofelia lives in post–Civil War Fascist Spain, and her brutal stepfather is an officer in the regime. Ofelia seeks refuge from this oppressive existence in a fantasy world as frightening as the real one but one potentially within her control. The two realms inevitably collide, and, as I conclude in my review, "Neither the nightmare of history nor the nightmare of childhood offers refuge from the other, but in one, at least, innocence proves triumphant."

"Beauty and the Beast Within," my essay on the various film adaptations of the perennial fairy tale, also emphasizes historical context. Analyzing the story as adapted in *King Kong* (1933), Jean Cocteau's *La Belle et la Bête* (1946), Disney's animated *Beauty and the Beast* (1991), and the 2017 live version of that film, I discuss how the title characters symbolize the politics and cultural issues of the period in which they were made. The Beast, in particular, reflects this in his scary, shaggy aspect rather than as an insipid, hunky guy. "That's the problem with the Beast," I write. "He's more appealing when beastly than when in his vapidly handsome human form. The beautified Prince is a bore."

—◊◊◊—

There's No Film Like *Oz: The Wizard of Oz* (1939)
Michael Wilmington[1]

Some movies appeal to just about everyone—like the heart-stoppingly entertaining and wonderful 1939 musical that MGM made out of L. Frank Baum's

American fairy tale, *The Wizard of Oz*. It's a movie most of us saw for the first time in childhood and then grew up with throughout the years. I was ten when CBS televised it nationally for the first time (in 1956), and I still remember the shock of joy that came over me as I watched it in the living room on Parkhurst Place, in Williams Bay, Wisconsin, with my Grampa Axel, Gramma Marie, and Mother Edna—all of whom were already very familiar with it—especially when Judy Garland, as Dorothy Gale, stared at the sky above her Hollywood–Kansas barnyard backdrop, let loose those incredible sixteen-year-old pipes, and brought down the house once again with Harold Arlen's and E. Y. Harburg's hair-raising ballad "Over the Rainbow."

What a song! What a singer! What pure, shattering emotion wrapped in rapturous show-biz kitsch and MGM bliss! For years, *Esquire* magazine made fun of that ballad in their annual Dubious Achievement issues by recounting exactly how many times Garland had sung it. (Who was keeping track?) But, in fact, I'll bet those smart alecks were sort of knocked out by it, too: the crystalline notes; Judy's yearning, faraway gaze toward a somber sky with a storm brewing; and lyrics like, "If happy little bluebirds fly beyond the rainbow, why, oh why, can't I?" Such lines should have made you snort but instead broke your heart.

Then there was her fantastic supporting trio: Ray Bolger as the flopsy-mopsy, always-resourceful Scarecrow ("I would not be just a nuffin,' my head all full of stuffin' / My heart all full of pain); Jack Haley Jr. as the metal-bod, senti-mental Tin Man ("I hear a beat! How sweet!"); and Bert Lahr as the boisterous scaredy-cat Cowardly Lion ("Yeah, it's sad, believe me missy, when you're born to be a sissy"). Meeting Dorothy one by one, singing the three parts of another Arlen–Harburg masterpiece—"If I Only Had a Brain / a Heart / the Nerve"—followed by the lusty chorus of "We're Off to See the Wizard!" the four grand companions instantly became the most appealing quartet of adventurous buddies since the Three Musketeers and d'Artagnan. (Hovering sadly over them all, how-ever, is the ghostly image of their absent comrade, poor Buddy Ebsen, cast as the Scarecrow, who cheerfully switched parts with the original Tin Man, Bolger, and then lost out completely when he got poisoned and sickened by the spray powder used to make his flesh tin.)

You'd also be stumped to find a better nasty, evil witch with a more mem-orably creepy cackle than Margaret Hamilton's supremely malicious Wicked Witch of the West, aka Miss Gulch, or a shinier good witch than Billie Burke's winningly sweetie-pie Glinda. Or a more spectacular purveyor of Midwestern humbuggery and medicine show eloquence than Frank Morgan as Professor Miracle and the Wizard himself (and three other parts, too). And what can you say about the Munchkins? (Better not say too much. This is a family movie.)

Judy Garland, just great as Dorothy, beat out the most popular child star in the United States—the most popular Hollywood child movie star ever—when she took the role away from Shirley Temple. And she makes the movie, of course; it's really one of the all-time best movie musical performances (and part of Garland's own career top three, with *Meet Me in St. Louis* in 1944 and the 1954's *A Star Is Born*). Judy's Dorothy is a perfect centerpiece and beating heart for Oz. She plays it with a stunning conviction and sparkling sincerity that sets off perfectly the glorious "Smith's Premium Ham!" (the exhortation from the film crew cheering them on) clowning and vaudeville of her three fellow travelers, and also because, at least on our second time through, we know that this is Dorothy's dream, brought on by the cyclone and a head-bonk, and that Oz is her creation—her fairy-tale Kansas—which is why it's both her paradise and her nightmare.

The Wizard of Oz was directed by two big-studio movie masters: Victor Fleming (the Oz scenes) and the uncredited King Vidor (the Kansas prelude and coda). Their styles are not really similar—Vidor was more of a populist poet, Fleming a robust yarn-spinner—yet here they fuse perfectly. Every single scene gels and works like a charm in both the movie's Kansas and Oz, and the only times I've ever gotten restive during the dozens of times I've seen this film is, occasionally, during the Cowardly Lion's florid aria, "If I Were King of the Forest" (and I can always forgive that for every other moment of Lahr's blow-away performance—Fleming and Vidor guided him, and the others, and the movie, flawlessly).

If you've read Mike Sragow's 2008 book *Victor Fleming: An American Movie Master*—and you should—you've probably bought Sragow's main thesis that the attractively macho, underrated Fleming, one of the directorial kings of MGM in the 1930s and 1940s, is a critically neglected movie genius, and that the director who made both most of *The Wizard of Oz* and *Gone with the Wind*, which were released the same year—not to mention *The Virginian* (1929), *Red Dust* (1932), *Bombshell* (1933), *Treasure Island* (1934), *Captains Courageous* (1937), *Test Pilot* (1938), and *A Guy Named Joe* (1943)—deserves more than passing mention in any Hollywood pantheon.

Fleming and Vidor together presided over one of the most charmed and charming movie ensembles ever—transforming Noel Langley, Florence Ryerson, and Edgar Allan Woolf's (among others) marvelously playful and witty script, and Arlen and Harburg's fantastic songs—along with that peerless cast—into the stuff of movie magic: a show that never loses its power to grip us and tickle us and make us laugh and cry, and the greatest kids (plus adults) movie this side of the rainbow.

I loved it when I was ten, watching it with my childhood family. I loved it last night, watching it with my incredibly brave ninety-four-year-old Mother

Edna in her hospital room with her, on a computer on her food table, as she lay dying. I love *The Wizard of Oz* still, and I'm not alone.

—⚬—

The Animated Enchantment of *Song of the Sea* (2014)
Justin Chang

Every so often in Tomm Moore's exquisitely handcrafted animated fantasy *Song of the Sea* (2014), a young boy named Ben puts on a pair of old-school red–blue 3D glasses and peers at the scenery. Why he does this is never made clear, exactly—one of the charms of the film is that it respects the natural curiosity and eccentricity of children, rather than treating mystery as something that has to be explained or apologized for. But you have to wonder if it isn't Moore's way of acknowledging, with a wink, just how thoroughly his methods oppose the prevailing trends in big-studio animation. With its sharply drawn edges, soft watercolor hues, and boldly flattened perspectives, *Song of the Sea* feels like not only a throwback, but also a mild rebuke—a triumph of idiosyncratic vision over the eye-popping, computer-generated photorealism that has become the industry standard.

An Irish animator who came to prominence with his Oscar-nominated 2009 debut, *The Secret of Kells*, Moore works in a highly personal, artisanal style that seems to have more in common with medieval woodcuts or tapestries than with anything produced by his Western contemporaries. *Kells*, which he codirected with Nora Twomey, was a gloriously out-of-time artifact; set in a ninth-century Irish monastery, it employed the ancient art of manuscript illumination as both its visual inspiration and subject. *Song of the Sea*, Moore's second feature, is no less intricately drawn or striking to behold, but its design scheme is rounder, less angular, and more subtly rendered. An inspired fusion of sensibilities old and new, it wrings something at once timeless and contemporary from the storytelling traditions of Celtic folklore.

Ben may skulk, scowl, and drown out the world with headphones like any other modern preteen, but he also inhabits a realm where the boundaries separating reality and myth turn out to be surprisingly porous—where rocks, boulders, and even small islands can house long-dormant spirits, and an ethereal, white-robed being called a "selkie" can transform into a seal under water. Through the sheer beauty of his visual design, Moore pulls the viewer into a dream state where this sort of magic is at once a given and a source of continual wonderment. Early on we see Ben, his parents, and their loyal sheepdog sharing a brief moment of happiness, their bodies framed by concentric circles; the outermost of these rings is decorated with images that, we realize later, are telling the story of the film in miniature. (It's the sort of intricate, all-encompassing tableau you might expect to find painted on a church ceiling, or etched in stone, like the Pictish carvings that inspired Moore and his collaborators.)

As in many a fairy tale, the family's peaceful idyll is short-lived. Ben's mother dies in childbirth, leaving the boy with a broken, grieving father and a younger sister, Saoirse, who is unable to speak, seemingly scarred by the tragic circumstances that marked her entry into the world. Six years later, the family continues to dwell in an old lighthouse overlooking the rugged Irish coast, a haunted backdrop that Ben and Saoirse's stern grandmother calls "no place for a family" before whisking them off to live with her in Dublin. The kids impulsively escape, and what follows is a classic homeward-bound adventure, replete with hidden enchantments, modest perils, and whimsical detours that will lead Ben on a deeper journey into his own heart.

In due time, the boy learns to love the sister he has long blamed and resented, who turns out to be more of a living embodiment of their mother's spirit than either of them initially realizes. Saoirse, in turn, brings out her brother's courage, helping him to conquer his fear of the sea and the mysteries that lurk in its depths. Emotionally relatable as these lessons are, they also have a touch of the prosaic—the sole element of the film that feels obligatory or conventional. Visually and musically, *Song of the Sea* is so eloquent that actual words can feel like an encumbrance, especially since it falls in a grand and immediately recognizable cinematic tradition of great children's fantasies.

At times there are echoes of the fairy-tale lyricism of *The Night of the Hunter* (1955), an infinitely darker tale of a brother and sister on the run. Elsewhere, the film recalls *The Wizard of Oz*, and not just because Ben and Saoirse here have their own Toto-like companion; here, as in that 1939 classic, a few key characters introduced at the outset are mirrored by their fantastical counterparts later on. In the most memorable parallel, the children's grandmother serves as an early stand-in for the witch Macha (both roles are voiced by Fionnula Flanagan), whose owl minions swoop down on their prey in perfectly symmetrical formations before turning them to stone. You may be reminded of the Wicked Witch of the West and her winged monkeys, but the truer comparison may be to Yubaba, the sorceress in Hayao Miyazaki's *Spirited Away* (2001), who turned out to be less evil than misguided—like Macha, a mother warped by her own selfless devotion to her young.

A similar generosity of spirit pervades *Song of the Sea*, and Moore, no less than Miyazaki, sees his characters and their environments as one and the same. His use of circles throughout is at once a design element and a thematic one: You see it in the roundness of the characters' faces; the tiny, glowing orbs of light that guide the children home; and the curve of a seashell that the mute Saoirse plays like a flute, giving rise to the song of the title. (The score, by French composer Bruno Coulais and the Irish folk band Kila, takes the film to another level of sustained enchantment.) Most of all, perhaps, it's there in the very arc of a journey that ends where it began, this time with a piercing sense of renewal. It's no place for a family, perhaps, but there's still no place like home.

—ɱ—

A Dream of Evil in *The Night of the Hunter* (1955)
Robert Horton

"I'll be back," the man calls out, "when it's dark." Those words are the warning, and the credo, of every monster that ever slouched through fairy tale or film. Toward the end of *The Night of the Hunter* (1955), they are uttered by Harry Powell, the evil preacher who burns through the movie like something out of an American folklore nightmare. Few monsters have embodied the shadow side of existence more absolutely than the murderous Reverend Powell. Where Harry Powell goes, it *is* dark.

For many years an unappreciated gem or a cult classic, *The Night of the Hunter* has secured its status as one of the greatest films in the American cinema. Although its web of influences can be identified (German Expressionism, the Brothers Grimm, the films of D. W. Griffith and James Whale, Mark Twain), it resembles nothing else. In the cinema of childhood, it is one of the most piercing and terrifying of titles. It stands alone as the only film directed by celebrated actor Charles Laughton, who suffered from one of the most tortured actor's psyches ever—and that's a crowded field—beset as he was by his sharp intellect, intense sensitivity, and closeted (publicly, at least) homosexuality. Laughton's achievement is magnificent: There isn't a single shot without visual interest, the pacing is certain despite the episodic structure, and the narrative tone is an amazing balancing act.

Laughton had distinguished collaborators. The film is based on a novel by Davis Grubb, whose gothic story is closely followed. To write the script,

Laughton and producer Paul Gregory chose James Agee, the film critic and author of the 1941 Depression-era classic *Let Us Now Praise Famous Men* (*Night of the Hunter* is also set during this period). Agee's detailed, overlong adaptation was edited and reshaped by Laughton—Agee himself felt that Laughton deserved a co-screenwriting credit.

Aside from an excellent cast, the other major collaborator was cinematographer Stanley Cortez, an unusual figure who also shot *The Magnificent Ambersons* (1942) for Orson Welles. Cortez was a master of shadowed filigree and black-and-white contrast, and *The Night of the Hunter* afforded rich opportunities for the play of light and shadow; but Cortez also had his hands full with the film's complex blend of naturalism (no Hollywood version of Mark Twain ever had a small-town look as authentic) and stark stylization. Cortez later counted Welles and Laughton as the two most formidable directors he worked with.

You know something is odd from the first moments of the film, when the disembodied heads of Lillian Gish and a group of children fill the screen, hanging among the stars of night. Gish's opening remarks are shaped as a parable to the children, invoking the Bible and explicitly making what follows a "tale" intended as a moral fable. "Beware of false prophets," she warns, and the film jumps to a fantastically strange sequence introducing preacher Harry Powell (Robert Mitchum). First the camera swoops down, from a great height, to see children playing in a field (hide-and-seek, apparently, which also describes the movie's plot). A boy looks in the cellar, only to stop short: A pair of legs sticks out awkwardly, almost obscenely, from the door. The cinematic memory can't help but flick to another great fable, *The Wizard of Oz* (1939), and the legs of a dead witch curling out from beneath a similar Midwestern home.

Another helicopter shot finds Harry Powell, trundling along the country roads in a Model T. The dead woman is clearly Harry's handiwork; as he admits in his conversations with the Almighty, his habit—and pleasure—is killing rich widows. In his wide-brimmed hat and black suit, he looks like an avenging angel—and we haven't even noticed his knuckles yet, which bear the tattooed letters LOVE and HATE on each hand (the film's most famous contribution to popular culture, including a reference in Spike Lee's 1989 film *Do the Right Thing*). His homicidal fingers come into play when the Reverend Powell delivers his lecture on the "little story of right hand, left hand," a dubious discourse that convinces complacent suckers but doesn't fool Powell's adversary, a child. (Pauline Kael keenly noted that Powell is a "Pied Piper in reverse: Adults trust him, children try to escape.")

A full description of this villain leads us to the actor playing him, whose finest hour this is. A notorious Hollywood bad boy, a barrel-chested stud of little respect (that is, he gave little and received little), Robert Mitchum had the kind of effortless, self-contained movie presence that better actors would die for. While always capable and credible, Mitchum pushed his persona in *The Night of the Hunter*; Powell may be a classic personification of evil, but the performance is highly original, not least because Mitchum uses humor to explore Harry's dark places. This is an absolutely modern approach, predating the sidelong wit of Norman Bates in *Psycho* (1960), the culinary bon mots of Hannibal Lecter, and the stand-up comedy of Freddy Krueger.

Mitchum's devious huckster is breathtakingly contemptuous of the rubes around him; he all but laughs in their faces as he spreads his ludicrously flimsy falsehoods. This is the all-American flim-flam man, a character in the bullshitting tradition that extends from P. T. Barnum to Donald Trump, almost astonished himself at the gullibility of his prey. Powell is often wildly funny, but the actor doesn't let the performance become a joke. Every now and then the animal in Harry comes out, in his strangled, frightening vocal howls, or the canine way Mitchum cocks his head. People who see *The Night of the Hunter* in childhood never forget the terror of Harry Powell, and I think Mitchum instills fear not merely because of his cruelty, but also because of his sarcasm. He's like a bad parent (literally, he's the evil stepfather) who knows that sneering mockery is at least as unsettling to children as open anger.

Harry Powell insinuates himself into the lives of the widow Willa Harper (Shelley Winters) and her children, John (Billy Chapin) and Pearl (Sally Jane Bruce). In prison, Harry has questioned Willa's husband Ben (Peter Graves), a robber, about where $10,000 from a bank job might be hidden. After Ben is executed, Harry sweeps into town to marry the widow and find the money. The perversions of this marriage come fast and thick: Harry condemns Willa's sexual interest during their wedding night, and she becomes a religious zealot, blaming her wicked self for her dead husband's misdeeds. (Shelley Winters is fascinating, and very fine, in the role.) Poor Willa ends up as one of Harry's victims, killed in a bedroom lighted to resemble a chapel. The viewer discovers her body in one of the film's visual coups: The camera descends through water, past the gently waving fronds of eel grass, finally finding Willa sunk like a mermaid, her hair waving in the current. Harry Powell himself is evidently impotent, but his knife serves as a violent substitute; sitting in a burlesque house, watching the grinding of a stripper onstage, his official disapproval is complicated when his knife flicks open and pricks through his coat pocket.

The second half of the film brings a remarkable shift, away from Powell's blustering and toward the pathos of the children. The Harper siblings elude Harry's grasp during an electrifying sequence in which every child's nightmare of a howling, relentless monster comes true; as critic Richard T. Jameson has suggested, in this sequence Laughton makes the preacher into a close visual and aural rhyme with Boris Karloff's Frankenstein monster, his arms stretching out of his black jacket as he reaches for the little ones (Laughton's wife, Elsa Lanchester, was the Bride of Frankenstein herself).

The children escape in a small boat and glide down the river at night. Perhaps they pass over the gently swaying corpse of their mother. Eventually they are taken in by a peculiar woman, Rachel Cooper (Lillian Gish, reappearing), who adopts "stray chicks" or "little lambs" into her brood of orphans. Laughton's approach turns to lyric poetry, as the boat floats through the nightscape, its progress watched over by animals, little creatures from a grade-school encyclopedia. A haunting song accompanies John and Pearl on this delicate journey, and music is another constant motif in the film, from folk and gospel songs sung onscreen to Harry's ominous habit of crooning, "Leaning . . . leaning . . . leaning on the everlasting arm."

Much of this is seen on obviously studio-built sets, as though an illustrated children's book had come to life (François Truffaut said the film was "like a horrifying news item retold by small children"). At this point you realize that *The Night of the Hunter* is young John's story, a tale in which a boy grows into a protector and, in a Freudian exercise, kills or causes the death of his dark substitute father. The film might be John's imaginative dream, a slumberous attempt to make sense of the loss of his executed, disgraced dad. A series of weighted signs pass through this dream: the owl that swoops down on a rabbit, the eggs dropped and broken by a girl startled by Harry's arrival, the apples exchanged by John and his surrogate mother ("ye shall know them by their fruits," as Miz Cooper has reminded us), and John's Christmas gift from Rachel, a watch—curiously echoing an unexplained throwaway scene from the beginning of the film, when he admires a pocket watch in a store window. Laughton's approach is so tender that none of this seems forced or heavy-handed, but a natural part of the weave of a fairy tale taken to essentials.

Long after the film's release, and well after its rediscovery as an essential American film, a collection of outtakes was assembled as a documentary called *Charles Laughton Directs "The Night of the Hunter"* (2002), directed by film restorer Robert Gitt. Because Laughton frequently kept the camera rolling between takes, we can hear him directing the actors, with special focus on the children. Laughton clearly had the entire film, and the performances, in his head, and he instructs the young actors on exactly how he wants them to play each moment: "Eyes wider . . . keep your head steady . . . a little louder." The children's performances are assembled practically line by line, which helps explain their stylized presence in the film. And Laughton's stray instruction to Robert Mitchum—"Don't forget yours is a routine, Mitch"—is a key to how Mitchum kept his performance so beautifully balanced between menace and barnstorming camp.

It's one thing to identify the film's themes or point out its influences. But this hardly captures *The Night of the Hunter*'s uncanny power. The way paper dolls are swept away in an eerie wind, the use of a D. W. Griffithian iris effect, the bright light off the water that shimmers across Harry's face as an innocuous picnic goes on behind him—these are the touches that create such a sustained sense of mystery and lyricism. One sideline scene deserves mention: Just after the offscreen execution of Ben Harper, we follow a prison guard as he goes home after the hanging, quietly greets his wife, washes his hands, and wonders about the wisdom of keeping his job. He looks in on the bedroom of his children, a boy and a girl, like Ben Harper's kids; they sleep, and glow. The guard is completely peripheral to the movie, with another brief appearance just at the end. Yet, the movie takes time for this unnecessary, vaguely disturbing moment.

Offhand, I can't think of anything else quite like it in American film.

Of course, the film flopped. United Artists threw its publicity money behind another Mitchum picture, *Not as a Stranger*, and didn't back *The Night of the Hunter*. The audience stayed away accordingly. ("It's a hard world for little things," as Rachel Cooper says.) Critics were bewildered but intrigued, if they noticed the film at all: "Often too busy being arty to be scary," noted *Life* magazine, which nevertheless recognized an "authentic American fable."[2] As the years went by, *The Night of the Hunter* grew in stature. When the German film magazine *Steadycam* surveyed international critics in 1995 for their favorite movies—not the dusty "best" of all time but faves—*The Night of the Hunter* came in at fourth place, ahead of *Citizen Kane* (1941), *Lawrence of Arabia* (1962), and *North by Northwest* (1959)—all of which was small consolation to the people who made it.

Mitchum returned to his laid-back ruggedness and evoked the preacher in at least two subsequent films: as the swamp-monster ex-convict in *Cape Fear* (1962) and as a defrocked priest in *The Wrath of God* (1972). Cortez went to erratic studio work and the low-budget dynamism of Samuel Fuller's *Shock Corridor* (1962) and *The Naked Kiss* (1964), and Agee was dead within the year, never having seen the film. Walter Schumann, who devised the fascinating music score, also died early, in 1958. The only film producer Paul Gregory made after *The Night of the Hunter* was an adaptation of Norman Mailer's *The Naked and the Dead* (1958), originally meant for Laughton to direct. *The Night of the Hunter* was remade as an irrelevant Richard Chamberlain TV-movie in 1991.

Laughton's status as an actor remained strong, but he never directed another film. And he died in 1962, before the movie's cult status began to form—the too-familiar price paid for being ahead of one's time. None of the disappointing production history of the film is reflected in the movie itself, however, which is never less than authoritative, assured, and confidently strange. For this one film, behind the camera, Laughton was a master.

———〰———

Careful What You Wish For: *The Red Shoes* (1948)
Sheila Benson

I think the real reason why *The Red Shoes* was such a success was that we had all been told for ten years to go out and die for freedom and democracy . . . and now that the war was over, *The Red Shoes* told us to go and die for art.—Michael Powell[3]

With *The Red Shoes*, filmmakers Michael Powell and Emeric Pressburger cemented the image of a ballet company so firmly—the god-like impresario, his ravishing young star, that cozy family of like-minded artists—that it became the template for any story about the life of a dancer: You dance, you bleed, you die, more or less in that order.

The story is classic: A talented unknown rises in an international ballet company whose director offers her a great future so long as dance is her entire life. When she falls in love with the composer of *The Red Shoes* ballet score, her career-making role, his expectation that she give up dancing for him clashes with the impresario's rules. Torn between their implacable demands, she runs out of the theater in anguish and with one great leap throws herself down onto the path of an oncoming train under the vivid Monte Carlo sunshine.

The Red Shoes is now more than seventy years old. Yet, it's still the image of the world of ballet and a dancer's life. We know perfectly well that dancers today marry, and they have babies without sacrificing much more than their sleep. The art or life dilemma is . . . at least tranquil.

So, what is the power of *The Red Shoes*—beyond its almost shocking beauty? It's that each of its elements—camerawork, set design, music—seem to have been created full throttle, the better to sweep us, too, over that parapet in its fevered finale.

When they first meet, the film's famous question and response between the imperious head of Ballet Lermontov (Anton Walbrook) and Victoria Page (Moira Shearer), aspirant par excellence, sets up the film as high-stakes art (or pluperfect kitsch; your choice). He: "Why do you want to dance?". She: "Why do you want to live?"

Young dancers—or young athletes, or young actors—thrive on this attitude; it gets them though bad days, harsh teachers, times when their bodies let them down. So do filmmakers, of any age; it gets them through the small war that is the making of any film. Emeric Pressburger and especially Michael Powell were masterly at bringing audiences around to that point of view: That dedication to your career (or your vocation: Don't forget their 1947 film *Black Narcissus*, about nuns serving in the isolation of the Himalayas) is nothing less than a matter of life or death.

For extra voltage, *The Red Shoes'* cinematographer, Jack Cardiff, used color fearlessly (red hair flaming against chalk-white skin; a billowing sea-blue ball gown; white ballet tights streaked with blood) in a way we'd never seen before. And barely since. Upping the ante, the filmmakers created a fresh seventeen-minute ballet based on one of Hans Christian Andersen's more relentless fairy tales—beguiling shoes that dance their wearer to death. Then, as Lermontov, they cast Austria's great Anton Walbrook, an actor who could make his very intake of breath a hiss of danger, and whose purr of charm was just as intimidating.

You never doubt for a second that Ballet Lermontov exists and thrives, micromanaged with a level of taste that is, at the very least, the equal of Lermontov's own sumptuous embroidered robes de chambre. The directors turn this band of artists into one great creative family, each one stopping by to bid papa a brisk good night, with Albert Basserman as the soothing, bearlike set designer and Marius Goring as the high-strung young composer (the only irritating bit of casting).

Among the dancers there's no fighting, no biting, not even backstage back-biting between Robert Helpmann, who partners Shearer and choreographed *The Red Shoes* ballet, and Diaghilev veteran Léonide Massine, who insisted on getting separate choreographic credit for his creation of the diabolical Shoemaker. Whatever, gentlemen.

Ultimately, *The Red Shoes* lives or dies by our belief in—our love for—Moira Shearer's Vicky Page. We must believe her dedication, her elegance (not everyone can make a pearl and diamond tiara look right at home), and, most of all, her virtuosity. The gifts that made her a soloist at Britain's historic Sadler's Wells (alongside its reigning ballerina, Margot Fonteyn) make her indispensable on-screen, while her acting is as pure and natural as her dancing. She has another lovely plus: In front of a camera, she's clearly, innately a dancer, not only onstage, but also in the way she walks, even as she lies, exhausted, during rehearsal breaks.

And I promise you, the effect of the scene in which Vicky is the first dancer to appear at the sweat-stained barre, the morning after her triumphant debut, is not lost on any ballet student, anywhere.

Now, what is *The Red Shoes* doing in a discussion of films for children? You can start taking children to the ballet as soon as the seat-squirming, running-up-and-down-the-aisle impulse calms down (those are other people's children, of course). After all, there's a comforting distance between a theater seat and the stage, and when Giselle slips tragically into her grave, she's back soon enough for a live, very reassuring curtain call. And another. And another.

But movies get to you, one-on-one—you and those big images in the dark, with no help except to get under your seat. This Shoemaker, with his curlicue eyebrows, his curled leaps, his lightning-quick fingers and feet, is obviously trouble. Dangerous. Unpredictable. If our alter ego Vicky can put on this strange man's red toe slippers, ribbons and all, just by leaping into them en pointe, something is going on—and the surreal, genuinely scary ballet has just begun.

Then, of course, there's that matter of dying for art—or is it love?—at the end of the movie.

"Mr. Powell!" Moira Shearer asks, "Should I jump like a girl committing suicide or like a ballerina?"

"Like a ballerina."

Does grace really matter, when you're taking red toe shoes off poor, bloody feet? Dead is dead, and this crumpled young woman is very dead indeed, under the bright Monte Carlo sunshine.

Ballet-mad or not, you might want to hold off on *The Red Shoes* until your very young interested party can take it. Eleven? Fourteen? Thirty-five?

(That we have this film in its pristine and electrifying form is thanks to the great 2009 Criterion restoration and subsequent Blu-ray. It's the work of Robert Gitt at UCLA's Film and Television Archive, with the help of Martin Scorsese's Film Foundation, among others: Two and a half years of almost unbelievable retrieval and renewal.)

Between the Fantastic and the Mundane: *The Curse of the Cat People* (1944) and *Poltergeist* (1982)
David Sterritt

You can't judge a book by its cover or a person by appearances. So why judge movies by their titles? It can be misleading, to say the least.

Exhibit A is *The Curse of the Cat People* (1944). The title makes it sound like a hard-hitting horror film, involving some kind of curse—an angry, offensive word or a spell causing evil or bad luck, plus a monster with both human and feline traits. In fact, however, this 1944 feature is an uncommonly gentle fantasy, not made specifically for children but centering on a child character and delicately evoking the world of childhood imagination.

Poltergeist has a more truthful title, taken from an impish and disruptive variety of ghost. The 1982 movie is a kid-friendly chiller blending a fairy-tale atmosphere with lively visual effects and an affectionate portrait of a modern suburban family. It might frighten very small children, a *New York Times* reviewer wrote, but it could almost have been "dictated by an exuberant twelve-year-old" spinning a supernatural yarn around a campfire long into the night.[4] That beautifully catches the movie's nature.

How did *The Curse of the Cat People* acquire its terrifying title? Movie producer Val Lewton ran a special unit making low-budget thrillers at the RKO studio, compensating for modest funding with ominous moods and unpredictable plot twists. They scored a smash hit in 1942, with *Cat People*, about Irena, a young Serbian woman whose marriage to Oliver, an engineer in New York, is undermined by her belief that physical intimacy will turn her into a deadly cat person like the demonic creatures thought to haunt her native country.

The studio wanted to capitalize on its success with a sequel, and this time Lewton turned to his own boyhood for inspiration, lacing the screenplay with memories from his early years (Gunther V. Fritsch and Robert Wise directed). Although the sequel is even more restrained and subtle than the first film, RKO insisted on horror-movie marketing, giving it the shocker-style moniker and promoting it with such wildly unsuitable lines as, "A tender tale of terror!" Fortunately, they didn't weaken the quiet sensitivity of the movie itself.

The main character is six-year-old Amy, the daughter of Oliver and his wife, Alice, who married him after Irena's death. Amy has an overactive fantasy life, striking a make-believe friendship with a beautiful woman whose picture she sees, not understanding that the woman is Irena, her father's first wife. She also befriends a real woman in her neighborhood—a crazy old actress with an adult daughter who's also crazy, and possibly violent to boot.

Feeling he must dampen down Amy's continual daydreaming, which reminds him of the superstition that ruined Irena's life, Oliver punishes the little girl when she claims to see her invisible companion in their garden. Soon thereafter, Irena tells Amy that their visits must end. Amy desperately searches for her, winding up at the actress's house, where the deranged daughter tries to kill her—stopping only when Amy reaches out and hugs her, realizing that Irena's good spirit dwells in the soul of even this tragic woman. Irena then vanishes permanently, bringing the tale to a happy ending.

The legendary film critic James Agee praised *The Curse of the Cat People* for expressing the "poetry and danger of childhood," and many others have felt the same. Moviegoers found it disappointing in 1944—the title and taglines promised a full-out horror movie, after all—but it's recognized today as the fantasy classic it is.

Poltergeist also centers on a little girl in a situation at once fantastic and perilous. Her name is Carol Anne, she's five years old, and she knows that ghosts have invaded the house when one of them erupts from the TV screen in the middle of the night. "They're here!" she announces, giving the film its most famous line.

The ghosts are just mischievous at first, rearranging furniture and bending forks. But soon they do scarier things and finally snatch Carol Anne and imprison her in the spirit realm. Three parapsychologists fail to rescue her, so her parents hire psychic Tangina Barrons, who explains that an evil Beast is using the girl's high-powered "life force" to combat the "spectral light" that gives peace and salvation to departed souls. Tangina exorcises the demons and brings Carol Anne back, but the household must face one more fiendish attack before their own peace will be assured.

As unlikely as it seems, *Poltergeist* was directed by Tobe Hooper, best known for *The Texas Chain Saw Massacre*, the notorious horror hit of 1974. But writer-producer Steven Spielberg was the presiding spirit (so to speak) of the film, doing a good deal of the creative work while simultaneously directing *E.T. the Extra-Terrestrial* (1982), the megahit that premiered a week later.

A number of Spielberg's films focus on children, parents, and the importance of family warmth and security, and these themes are at the heart of *Poltergeist*, along with Spielberg's fascination with the impact of unearthly experiences on ordinary people in everyday environments. Those interests are spelled out in the early scenes, making it clear that bedrock traditional values underlie the story's harrowing events. The fundamental subject of *Poltergeist* and *E.T.*, Spielberg told me in 1982, is the "battle between the fantastic and mundane," played out in the kind of place where most moviegoers feel completely at home.[5]

Some of the visual effects in *Poltergeist* are corny, as well as creepy; when mud-slathered corpses burst from the ground, for instance, they look like they escaped from a haunted-house fun ride. Other images are marvelously inventive, as when a clown doll comes to life in the dead of night, or when a room fills with ghost-powered playthings swirling through the air. Although no characters are killed or significantly harmed, *Poltergeist* might well scare young viewers who aren't used to high-octane fantasy, and if it were released in the United States today, its rating would surely not be PG but PG-13, a category not yet established in 1982.

Of course, it's hard to be traumatized by a movie that ends with a humdrum Holiday Inn symbolizing the sanity and safety that Carol Anne's family ultimately find. But most audiences find that *Poltergeist* does live up to its tagline: "It knows what scares you."

—m—

Fauny Girl: Innocence Finds a Way through *Pan's Labyrinth* (2006)

Peter Keough[6]

Guillermo del Toro starts *Pan's Labyrinth* (2006) by entering the mind of a child. The camera hovers over the bloody face of twelve-year-old Ofelia (Ivana Baquero) and eddies downward to her eyes and into the black void of a pupil, descending into the subterranean kingdom of the dead. "Once upon a time," a voiceover begins, and the camera rises up through a womblike cave into the sunshine of Spain, 1944, in the aftermath of the Civil War and near the end of World War II, where Ofelia is reading the fairy tale that's being told.

As in del Toro's previous two films, *The Devil's Backbone* (2001) and *Hellboy* (2004), the objective facts of history, the dates and places and events, can't contain the chthonic forces that shape them, the demons and fairies that lurk in a child's books and her imagination, and under her bed. But here the director succeeds, as he didn't before, in his fusion of innocence and evil, nightmare and delight, in a cinematically exuberant work that blurs the line between lucid fable and surreal enigma.

Fairy tales tend to be allegories about the consequences of disobedience, and this isn't an exception, although the answers to such questions as who is to be obeyed, and why, remain ambiguous. Certainly, Ofelia's martinet stepfather, Capitán Vidal (Sergi López), a sadistic Fascist officer assigned to wipe out the last vestiges of Republican resistance in a frontier outpost, doesn't qualify as a legitimate authority. When he meets Ofelia and her pregnant mother, Carmen (Ariadna Gil), after they first arrive at his post, his greeting is icy and sinister. His habit of tinkering with a pocket watch (shades of del Toro's 1993 *Cronos* and *Peter Pan*'s Captain Hook) exudes creepiness. And when he brutally murders two poachers suspected of subversion, he dispels the charm initially generated by López's arch, malignant performance.

Ofelia seeks refuge from this unpleasant domestic situation in fantasy. Actually, the fantasies seek her. A giant insect, although not as imposing as the ones in del Toro's horror film *Mimic* (1997), flitters up to her at bedtime and metamorphoses into a fairy; it's a cross between Jiminy Cricket and Tinker Bell. This envoy leads her to the labyrinth of the title, where a towering faun (Doug Jones), bent like a folding ruler, tells her she's the daughter of the King of the Underworld. To prove she has not gone over to the mortal side, however, she must fulfill the inevitable Three Tasks. Should she obey? And what are these tasks testing?

Meanwhile, spies and guerrillas and Fascists clash, crises that indirectly intersect with Ofelia's encounters with a disgusting giant toad, a squirming mandrake root, and a cannibalistic monstrosity who looks like (among other things) Goya's painting of Saturn devouring his son. These are just a few of the stunning creations that are bound to get viewers searching through their volumes of Jung and Freud. Arresting though they may be, these mind-boggling effects, shot with limpid mystery by Guillermo Navarro and accompanied by chitinous whirs and crackles on the soundtrack, don't disrupt the double narrative but intensify it. When the two tales intersect, neither the nightmare of history nor the nightmare of childhood offers refuge from the other, but in one, at least, innocence proves triumphant.

Beauty and the Beast Within: Four Versions of *Beauty and the Beast*
Peter Keough

Like previous renditions of the ancient story, Bill Condon's 2017 live-action adaptation of the popular 1991 Disney animated musical *Beauty and the Beast* provided a new generation of children a chance to enjoy a kids' classic. It also gave the more academic-minded another opportunity to ponder the nature of Beauty, the story's doughty heroine.

Some Freudian analysts, for example, Bruno Bettelheim in his study of fairy tales, *The Uses of Enchantment* (1976), see the story of Beauty and the Beast as an allegory of a girl's overcoming her disgust with sexuality and redirecting her affections from an Oedipal attraction to a nonincestuous partner. Others with a more feminist bent argue that the story, especially as interpreted by the two Disney adaptations, depicts a woman's empowerment.

But what about the Beast? In the Disney films he is usually seen as little more than a foil for Beauty, but that has not been true in other versions. The beast took center stage in 1933, in *King Kong*, Merian C. Cooper and Ernest B. Schoedsack's variation on the template. That was the same year that another beast, Adolf Hitler, became chancellor of Germany. At the time, Nazism also had a growing number of followers in the United States, and maybe the potential for this barbarous ideology to infiltrate democracy is symbolized when Kong, a tyrant in his own realm of Skull Island, is shipped to Broadway by his ambitious kidnappers.

Chained to the stage and seemingly helpless, Kong is dazzled by the camera flashes of the paparazzi; however, instead of enjoying the limelight like a true star, he breaks free and goes on a rampage to protect Ann Darrow, the "Beauty" played by Fay Wray, who he clutches like a doll in his giant hand. Had he not succumbed to this absurd infatuation he might well have achieved show-biz success instead of taking a 102-story plunge from the top of the Empire State Building. And then—who knows—his celebrity and aura of strength (although in actuality, only a twenty-four-inch-tall stop-motion doll) could have translated into political power, if not for him, then for his keepers. Stranger things have happened: Who could have imagined that a reality show host might one day sit in the Oval Office?

After World War II, notions of Beauty and the bestial changed—especially in countries conquered by the Nazis, like France. In 1946, Jean Cocteau made *La Belle et la Bête*, an adaptation of the fairy tale that, like *King Kong*, was in part a product of its time. A year after the war, the beast that was Hitler had left the historical stage, but for the French the taint of Nazism remained. Vichy collaborators and those suspected of being such were prosecuted and sometimes imprisoned or executed. Cocteau, who was right-leaning and not unsympathetic to Hitler, was lucky to be spared.

Perhaps this film was an attempt at self-vindication. It reflects the historical circumstances while adhering to the story as set down in 1740, by Gabrielle-Suzanne Barbot de Villeneuve. In a stifling village, a combination of the town in Henri Georges Clouzot's *Le Corbeau* (1943) and a Dutch Renaissance painting, a harried father of three daughters and one wastrel son must go on a business trip. The father asks his daughters what gifts they want when he returns. It's a family like that in *Cinderella* or *King Lear*. Two of the daughters are vain, greedy, and ruthless. They ask for clothes and finery. But the youngest—self-sacrificing Belle

(Josette Day), whose paternal devotion Bettelheim might interpret in Freudian terms but who also might represent an idealized France menaced by Fascist invaders and turncoats—only wants a single rose.

An unfortunate request.

As the father returns home, he seeks shelter at a mysterious castle. Inside, animated arms on the walls hold torches, and the eyes of marble busts follow his movements. These dismembered body parts—regimented arms, bodiless heads—are reminders of the conquering armies and horrific carnage of the war that just ended.

Undaunted by the décor, Belle's father helps himself to a feast laid out on a table, and as he leaves, he plucks a rose for Belle. The Beast (Jean Marais) appears, furious. He tells the father that he will kill him unless one of his daughters agrees to take his place. Belle volunteers and, ever demure, is relieved when she is spared. She is grateful for the Beast's hospitality, but she rejects his proposal of marriage.

That is not the only proposal Belle has declined. She has also turned down boorish Avenant (also played by Jean Marais), an egotistical lout, giving as her excuse her need to care for her father. This rival suitor is Cocteau's ingenious, original contribution to the story. Although good-looking, he is amoral and willing to do anything to get his way—in short, a bully and brute like the Nazis and their French sympathizers. He is more of a beast than the Beast—who, as it turns out, is really a handsome prince transformed into a monster because, as he tells it, his parents "didn't believe in spirit"—a reference perhaps to the defeatism that doomed France in the war. Cocteau resolves this conflict between rivals who are also inverse images of one another, whose appearances belie their true nature, in a way that purges the wickedness and vindicates the spirit.

It should be a happy ending, but it is at best bittersweet. In part that is because of the nature of the Beast: He's more appealing when beastly than when in his vapidly handsome human form. In Cocteau's version, he elicits pathos when he suffers remorse for being a beast compelled to kill. After returning to Belle after a hunt, his hands smoking with innocent blood, he feels worthless and guilty. No wonder Belle feels sorry for him, and her pity turns to love for the suffering soul beneath the monstrous exterior.

There is no killing of forest creatures in the 1991 animated Disney version of the story. The Beast may have rage issues, but he mostly takes out his anger on the furniture. Some of the furniture, however, is alive. Unlike the silent heads and limbs in service to the Beast in the Cocteau version, here they won't shut up. They gab, joke, sing songs, and utter platitudes, and are the usual harmless Disney sidekicks.

Once again, the Beast meets his match in a village rival—an ox-like, conceited Adonis named Gaston. Gaston wants Belle for his bride, but she refuses—not because she suffers a Freudian attachment to her father, who is a buffoonish inventor more like an errant baby than a patriarchal presence. It's because Gaston is a jerk and she has higher ambitions than to live in a small-minded village chained to a dolt of a husband with smelly feet. This is an empowered, third-wave feminist Beauty, unwilling to accept a gender role imposed by the patriarchy.

The rose also takes on a new role in the Disney film. Belle (there are no siblings in this pared-down retelling) does not request one nor does her father steal one when he seeks refuge in the Beast's castle (the Beast imprisons him just because he's a bad host). Instead, the rose is a relic under a glass dome. The Beast had been a handsome prince who was also a cold-blooded oligarch representative of the Greed is Good generation of the late '80s. When a homeless old woman asks for shelter in his castle, he has her thrown out. She turns out to be an enchantress who puts a curse on him for his heartlessness and failure to see beyond appearances. Only when someone loves him despite his hideousness, she pronounces, will he regain his human form. If he fails to achieve this before the last rose petal falls, he will remain in beastly form forever.

As in Cocteau's film, Belle agrees to take the place of her father. Considering her other options—living in a backwater with a doddering dad and a lunkhead spouse—it might not be a bad deal. In the castle, the Beast is quickly smitten; he lavishes her with finery, food, books, and a magic mirror that will connect with anyone in the world—an eighteenth-century supernatural version of Skype by way of the Wicked Witch of the West.

It looks like things might work out. It would be the realization of King Kong's dream to possess his Beauty. But there remains the problem of Gaston. He may be dumb, but he's ruthless and sly, and has the charisma to muster a mob to destroy a monster who mirrors the citizens' fears. He raises an army to sweep the mismatched lovers away, but unlike in *King Kong*, Beauty doesn't kill the beast, she saves him.

Twenty-six years after the animated feature, now considered a classic, Disney remade it into the live-action version directed by Bill Condon (whose previous credits include the 2011–2012 *Part 1* and *Part 2* of *The Twilight Saga: Breaking Dawn*). It is lavish, star-studded, and, with a running time of two-plus hours, long.

It opens with a prologue featuring a lavish, louche ball in the style of Louis XIV. The pre-Beast Prince has been dolled up with a towering white wig, garish makeup, and a haughty attitude. As the voice-over narrative explains, the Prince has financed his decadent lifestyle by exploiting the townspeople with onerous taxes. He is vain, pitiless, and a snob. So, as in the 1991 film, when a crone shows up at his door at the height of one of his fabulous fêtes and offers him a rose, he laughs in her face and orders her thrown out.

Never laugh at a crone bearing a rose. As before, the old woman transforms into a glowing, golden, CGI enchantress reminiscent of Glinda from *The Wizard of Oz* (1939). The Prince begs for forgiveness. But she transforms him into the Beast; changes his household minions into knickknacks, furniture, and assorted chattel; and erases all memory of his existence from the world. As before, he is left with a slender hope of redemption and a seemingly impossible deadline.

Freed from this oppressive autocrat by supernatural intervention, do the townspeople's lives improve? Belle wouldn't think so. Played by Emma Watson, formerly the redoubtable Hermione of the Harry Potter series, she finds her neighbors dull, small-minded, intolerant, ignorant, and mean. They, in turn, ostracize her because she reads, teaches other girls to read, invents such labor-saving devices as a donkey-driven washing machine, and holds them in barely concealed contempt. They also mock her father, played with wry melancholy by Kevin Kline, regarding him as a kook because he is a failed Parisian artist who dabbles in making mechanical toys. Mostly, they can't understand why Belle doesn't accept the marriage proposal from Gaston, once again a macho dolt.

More than just a jerk, however, Gaston promotes an ugly mob mentality among the villagers, rousing them against scapegoats and perceived elites like Belle and her father, and later the Beast as well. He is the populist, revolutionary strongman challenging the aristocratic sovereignty represented by his alter ego, the Beast. Inevitably, as in previous cinema incarnations of the story, they must duel to the death. Once again, with Beauty's help, the Beast is triumphant.

His victory, however, is reactionary. It is a return to a benevolent version of the autocratic order of the opening—although in his gala wedding to Belle, now a princess, the common people do get to eat cake. But once again, the beautified Prince is a bore.

Asa Butterfield and Chloë Grace Moretz in *Hugo*

5

—⚂—

WELL ADAPTED
(OR MALADJUSTED)

Filmmakers adapt beloved books at their peril, especially childhood favorites, since, more than most readers, children vividly imagine the worlds and characters the words describe and have little patience with those who might cheapen or betray their visions. (Don't even mention the 2003 *The Cat in the Hat* with Mike Meyers to lovers of Dr. Seuss. His widow hated it so much she forbade any further live-action adaptations of her husband's books.)

Fans of Louisa May Alcott's perennial classic can therefore consider themselves lucky. As Carrie Rickey points out in her essay "The Three Ages of *Little Women*," they get not one but two outstanding adaptations, and one that's flawed but worth watching.

The weakest of the three *Women*, according to Rickey, is Mervyn LeRoy's 1949 version. Its condescension and sentimentality reflect the mood of the country at a time when the window of liberation that women enjoyed during World War II was about to slam shut with the conformist '50s. George Cukor's 1933 version, on the other hand, not only draws on the persevering spirit of the Depression era, but also benefits from the director's painterly compositions and graceful camerawork—not to mention a standout performance from Katharine Hepburn as Jo.

The best *Little Women*, however, is the one directed by a woman. "Released shortly after the '80s backlash against second-wave feminism," Rickey writes about the 1994 version, "Gillian Armstrong's *Little Women* considers female experience from a feminist perspective." But isn't that a bit anachronistic? "[It] may seem like 1990s political-correctness," Rickey acknowledges about the film's enlightened gender attitudes. "However, all of that, in fact, happens to be the actual beliefs and practices of the Alcott family." In short, Armstrong's version is the one most faithful to the book.

Those who love Charles Dickens's *A Christmas Carol* also have several adaptations to choose from. Michael Wilmington's nod for best goes to the 1951 version directed by Brian Desmond Hurst and starring Alastair Sim as Scrooge. It accomplishes something that seems simple and obvious but is nonetheless rarely achieved. "Hurst . . . and Sim's *Christmas Carol* . . . successfully avoids the usual sentimentality and the sugarplum visions and candy cane philosophy while telling us this story that a lot of us want so much to believe," explains Wilmington. "The fact that it's so scary and smart, as well as sweet, is part of what makes the 1951 *Christmas Carol* so powerful, and such a classic."

Sheila Benson also has good things to say about a film made from the works of another giant of British children's literature. Reginald Mills's *Tales of Beatrix Potter* (1971) does not aspire to realism or exacting fidelity to the text but embraces artifice—it's a ballet choreographed by Frederick Ashton. "Here dancers mime tiny mice, or a bratty Squirrel Nutkin, or a froggy fisherman leaping lily pad to lily pad," writes Benson. "Startling, perhaps," she adds, "but it takes no more than two minutes for this magnificent production to banish any disbelief."

Of the many movies made from Frances Hodgson Burnett's beloved novels, John Anderson singles out for praise Alfonso Cuarón's adaptation of the latter-day Cinderella story *A Little Princess* (1995). In it, Cuarón demonstrates an eye for period detail and skill, and shrewdly casts Liesel Matthews in the title role of Sara, a regal child persecuted in an orphanage when her father goes missing in the war. Although "photographed to look like a saint by Raphael," writes Anderson, Matthews "can be refreshingly blunt." The result, he concludes, is a "thoroughly enchanting children's film—which, like all thoroughly enchanting children's films, thoroughly seduces the grown-ups in the audience."

Brian Selznick's 2007 graphic novel *The Invention of Hugo Cabret* seems ready-made for a movie version with its hyperrealistic, cinematic illustrations. Such a style is appropriate because in the book, the orphaned hero of the title meets with the legendary pioneer of movies, Georges Méliès.

Martin Scorsese, a cinephile, as well as an auteur, proves well-adapted for such material. His *Hugo* (2011), as Emanuel Levy writes, "is one of his most personal and deeply felt works in a long time." Scorsese's version is a "children's adventure, aiming to appeal to younger viewers; however, at heart, *Hugo* is a film that can be enjoyed and appreciated by mature viewers savvy enough to revisit and learn more about the origins and magical powers of film as the dominant mass medium of the twentieth century."

Amy Heckerling updates Jane Austen by transforming her nineteenth-century masterpiece *Emma* into a smart contemporary teen comedy. "A wickedly funny teenage farce . . . that, like its heroine, turns out to have more to it than anyone could anticipate," Kenneth Turan writes in his review of *Clueless* (1995). "It manages to get more fun out of high school than most people had attending it."

Like *Clueless*, Scott McGehee and David Siegel's adaptation of Henry James's *What Maisie Knew* (2012) significantly alters the original, setting the late nineteenth-century story in well-to-do, modern-day New York. But as Gerald Peary writes in "Henry James's Dark Screwball Comedy," the film still re-creates James's uncanny insight into a child's point of view, with the six-year-old of the title innocently but acutely observing the shabby infidelities and spiritual bankruptcy of the adult world.

Peary credits the filmmakers' expert translation of James's dense prose into cinematic language but reserves his greatest praise for the performance of Onata Aprile as Maisie. She is, he writes, "such a find, a sweet, expressive little trouper. Adult actors come and go, enter and exit, but, fortunately, Onata is in every scene of the movie, its pint-sized, persuasive moral center."

The adult world observed in *What Maisie Knew* is also the reality inhabited by children's book writers—when they are not transported to worlds of their own creation. Reversing its usual process of turning reality into make-believe, Hollywood has often delved into the troubled lives of those who have created some the most beloved books for kids. In my essay "From *Neverland* to *Shadowlands*: Hollywood's Romance with Children's Book Authors," I examine this phenomenon and its possible origins. "Perhaps Hollywood feels drawn to the sources of some of their most lucrative franchises and wants to explore the mystery of their genius," I speculate. "Audiences, too, want to know more about those whose works enchanted their childhood. These writers made the myths that inspired so many movies, and so the movies make them into myths as well."

J. R. Jones follows up on the topics of biopics of children's book authors in his essay "*Mary Poppins Returns*, and She's Closer to the Feisty Original." Noting the fifty-four-year gap between Disney's original *Mary Poppins* (1964) and its "sequel," *Mary Poppins Returns* (2018), Jones discusses the interim feature *Saving Mr. Banks* (2013), which is about how the author of the Mary Poppins books, P. L. Travers, wrangled with Walt Disney about bringing the proper, caustic tone to the bumbershooted flying nanny of the title.

Travers would probably be pleased, he suggests, with the abrasiveness that Emily Blunt brings to the character in the 2018 movie compared to the more sugary portrayal by Julie Andrews in 1964. "Emily Blunt comes closer to capturing Mary's serrated edge," he writes. "Blunt brings more vinegar to the role with her eye-rolling and snarky head-cocking than Andrews could ever muster." Nonetheless, he concedes that in a contest between an author's original work and a movie adaptation, the latter invariably wins. "Travers always chafed at the idea of Mary Poppins being turned into a Disney character," he writes. "Now she's become one herself."

—⟨m⟩—

Three Ages of *Little Women*: 1933, 1949, and 1994
Carrie Rickey

Few American novels are as beloved as Louisa May Alcott's *Little Women*, an evergreen adapted for the big screen in 1933, 1949, and 1994. They have become family Christmas movies appealing to the religious and agnostic alike. (A fourth version, directed by Greta Gerwig, comes out December 25, 2019.)

As in the book, the movies purvey four very different types of teenagers who mature into mutually supportive young women. Meg, the eldest, is maternal and traditional. Jo, in part inspired by Alcott herself, is a tomboy and aspiring author who longs for the prerogatives enjoyed by boys and men. Beth is shy and musical, the family conscience. Amy, the youngest, is an artist longing for the wealth and ease possessed by her paternal aunt. Marmee, their mother, is the family glue.

Whether a literary adaptation or a historical drama, a period film tells as much about the era in which it is produced as it does about the era it reproduces. While the three Hollywood versions of Alcott's semiautobiography dramatize many of the same sequences, they differently frame the story of the four March sisters, their idealistic mother, and their moral (and mostly offscreen) father. For many Alcott readers, the matter of who plays Jo is as sensitive an issue as the feelings of comic-book fans on who plays Batman.

George Cukor's RKO film of 1933 stars Katharine Hepburn as Jo. From today's vantage point, it looks like a parable of how to survive the Great Depression, with the March family fallen from prosperity to working-class status during the Civil War—standing in for the economic downturn in the United States. Brought together by hard times, the Marches embody New Deal values of self-sacrifice to benefit the commonweal. They don't have much, but they give what they can to those less well off, like the Hummels, the immigrant family to whom they give their Christmas breakfast and whose sicknesses play a big part in Beth's death.

The screenplay by husband-and-wife scenarists Sarah Y. Mason and Victor Heerman enables Cukor to quickly establish the characters of his principals. Meg (Frances Dee), a governess, kisses her charges. Jo (Katharine Hepburn), companion to a cranky relative, hungrily devours a book while Aunt March nods off. Homebody Beth (Jean Parker) plays the piano in the living room. Schoolgirl Amy (Joan Bennett) gets in trouble for sketching caricatures on her slate. The effect is one of flipping through color plates of a Currier and Ives, and getting the immediate sense of place and personality.

Cukor draws on other illustrators in addition to Currier and Ives for the film's look and imagery. Those fascinated by the iconography of *Little Women*, which in literary circles is parsed as deeply as images of the Virgin Mary are in the religious and art-historical realms, will note that Cukor's compositions replicate those in illustrator Jessie Willcox Smith's 1915 edition of the novel. (*Little Women* has never been out of print.) Smith's watercolors of the March daughters clustered around their seated mother boast the warmth and emotional bond of Mary Cassatt's canvases of mother and child. But the filmmaker doesn't film his characters like still tableaux. They move—and so does his graceful camera, connecting and opposing the characters.

Interestingly, in Cukor's compositional arrangements, Hepburn's Jo always stands apart from the others in the frame. It's as if to say that three of the sisters are interchangeable, but Jo is unique. While her father is away at war, she is the man of the house, "scribbling" stories to make money to support her financially challenged family.

Yet, composer Max Steiner's buoyant musical cues have the effect of suggesting her optimism despite difficulty. The uplift of his score has the warmth and intimacy of a FDR "Fireside Chat."

Hepburn's athletic stride and booming voice illustrate a famous Alcott journal entry, "I am more than half-persuaded that I am a man's soul, put by some freak of nature into a woman's body." Whether exclaiming, "Christopher Columbus! What richness!" when invited into the Laurence mansion or shearing her hair to earn the money to pay Marmee's train fare, Hepburn accentuates Jo's androgyny in her signature role as America's perennial tomboy.

One of the film's nicer touches that bridges the Civil War era with that of the Depression is that Meg and Jo's dresses (designed by Walter Plunkett) are handed down to younger sisters Beth and Amy.

So, how can Mervyn LeRoy's MGM remake of *Little Women* (1949)—based on the 1933 Mason and Heerman script and likewise purveying Walter Plunkett costumes and Steiner music (reorchestrated by Adolph Deutsch)—differ so much from Cukor's version?

For one, June Allyson's Jo is a tomgirl with a raspy voice and lacks the physicality of Hepburn's athletic androgyne. For another, the Technicolor movie seems less an adaptation of *Little Women* than a companion piece to Vincente Minnelli's *Meet Me in St. Louis* (1944). Sally Benson, on whose holiday vignettes *St. Louis* is based, is credited with story construction of LeRoy's *Little Women*, and the finished movie highlights the seasons in the lives of the March family. Likewise, as in that popular MGM musical, LeRoy's movie boasts Mary Astor and Leon Ames as the parents.

Released in 1949, *Little Women* mirrored the post–World War II mass migration of women working outside the home to happy domesticity inside it. Meg and Amy are more obviously marriage-minded than in the film's previous iteration (perhaps because they're played by the luscious Janet Leigh and Elizabeth Taylor). The conflict between Jo and Laurie (the boy-next-door played by languid Peter Lawford) seems less 1865 than 1945. He proposes to her, condescendingly noting that if she'll accept his marriage proposal, she won't have to work. But she wants to work. "You hate my scribbling," retorts Jo, obviously stung. In the book and other film iterations Laurie's proposal isn't received because Jo's primary relationship is with her family and/or she is presexual, and/or she regards Laurie as a brother, not a lover.

LeRoy milks the film for nostalgia rather than emotion. Where Cukor's visual references are Mary Cassatt and Jessie Willcox Smith, LeRoy's is needlepoint. His actors, best of whom is the tremulous Margaret O'Brien as Beth, are sewn to cambric-like figures in a sampler. They do not move; neither does the camera, fixed as if framing the action under a proscenium arch.

In Gillian Armstrong's cinematic 1994 version of *Little Women*, camera and characters are alive with movement. Working from an imaginative screenplay by Robin Swicord, who laces the dialogue with entries from Alcott's personal journal, Armstrong opens the windows and brings fresh air, as well as the bracing winds of contemporary relevance, to the movie.

Armstrong works on locations instead of in the studio and with faster film (which doesn't require as much illumination) than did Cukor and LeRoy. Thus, she can re-create the gaslight, candlelight, and available light familiar from nineteenth-century paintings and photographs, which gives the film a historic credibility.

Released shortly after the '80s backlash against second-wave feminism, Armstrong's *Little Women* considers female experience from a feminist perspective. With one or two exceptions, Armstrong doesn't quote visual source material, as do Cukor and LeRoy. The interiors and costumes of her film are shabbier and more obviously worn than in the prior versions.

Susan Sarandon's Marmee says to the husband-hunting Meg (Trini Alvarado), who frets about her hair and gowns, "If you feel your value lies in being merely decorative, I worry that you'll think that's all you are." Many scenes in Armstrong's movie show women performing domestic or socially useful work: folding laundry, making bread, rolling bandages for the war effort, taking care of the needy. But it also honors the women pursuing their own creative work: Beth (Claire Danes) takes solace in her music, Amy (Kirsten Dunst as the preteen, Samantha Mathis as the teenage Amy) in her art, and Jo (Winona Ryder, casting her own special light) in her writing.

These little women (and their mother) challenge the status quo. When Amy's male teacher tells her, "It's as useful to educate a woman as to educate a female cat," Marmee promptly withdraws her from the school. Jo is bitterly envious of her best friend, Laurie (Christian Bale), as she helps ready him to go to Harvard, telling him that it's unfair that women are barred from institutions of higher education.

This may seem like 1990s political-correctness, as does Marmee railing against how corsets constrain girls and speaking out for how important temperance is, how girls need exercise as much as boys, and how to heal scarlet fever homeopathically; however, all of that, in fact, happens to be the beliefs and practices of the Alcott family.

In one scene, Jo (Winona Ryder) works as a governess in New York and accompanies her friend, Professor Bhaer, to the parlor of his progressive friends. One of them tells her that a "lady has no need of suffrage if she has a husband" whose vote she can influence because women are among the better angels.

"I find it poor logic to say that because women are good, women should vote," replies Jo. "Men do not vote because they are good; they vote because they are male. Women should vote, not because we are angels and men are animals, but because we are human beings and citizens of this country."

Armstrong's *Little Women* is not as Jo-centric as its predecessors. Jo's sisters are much more dimensional, the men who love her more tactful. Christian Bale's Laurie doesn't imagine himself Jo's financial savior. If she marries him, he says, "You won't have to write . . . unless you want to." Professor Bhaer (a swoony Gabriel Byrne) doesn't tell Jo that she's writing commercial junk. He tells her that her Gothic stories lack the spirit of the woman he knows.

By mastering a series of challenges, each March girl crosses the treacherous rope bridge between girlhood and womanhood. Dispensing wisdom while darning socks—and, by the way, earning the family's livelihood—Marmee neither judges her daughters nor solves their problems. She hands them the tools to solve the problems themselves—and to respect one another's very different choices.

When moviegoers argue which *Little Women* is best, I think, is there such a thing as a bad *Little Women*? When they ask me who my favorite movie Jo is, I answer that Hepburn and Ryder are the most satisfying because Hepburn best captures Jo's physicality, while Ryder best captures her spirit.

That moviegoers continue to have these conversations almost 150 years after the publication of *Little Women* shows what a hold Louisa May Alcott's book has on successive generations.

—⁓—

A Consummate *Christmas Carol* (1951)
Michael Wilmington[1]

Almost everyone's favorite nominee for best of all the many film adaptations of Charles Dickens's Yuletide evergreen *A Christmas Carol* is this 1951 cinematic gem, sometimes called *Scrooge*, sometimes called *A Christmas Carol*, directed by the underrated Brian Desmond Hurst and scripted by the underrated Noel Langley.

This *Carol* stars juicily eloquent comic actor Alastair Sim as the pathologically stingy Ebenezer Scrooge—the mean, miserly London businessman who considers Christmas a humbug. And Sim is supported by an excellent cast: the fantastic Michael Hordern as Jacob Marley, the touching Mervyn Johns and Hermione Baddeley as Mr. and Mrs. Bob Cratchit, George Cole as young Ebenezer, Patrick Macnee as the young Marley, Brian Worth as Scrooge's ebullient nephew Fred, and Peter Bull (who played the Russian ambassador Alexi de Sadesky in Stanley Kubrick's 1964 *Dr. Strangelove*) as both the film's narrator and one of the nastier businessmen in a film full of them. In fact, Scrooge's cold-blooded antipoverty program ("Are there no jails? Are there no workhouses?") suggests he might have been a popular candidate for certain contemporary ideological persuasions.

Why, however, is *this* film so well-loved—especially since it's a story we all know, and have seen or heard or maybe even dreamed up from the gut after an "indigestible bit of beef" ourselves? For one thing, this is a *Christmas Carol* made by first-rate filmmakers who obviously loved doing it, and loved both Dickens and his work. Hurst and Langley truly respect their source, and they capture a lot of Dickens's comic-dramatic-fantastic virtuosity, his unrivaled flair for character and his storytelling genius, with skill and relish. Both these filmmakers were highly literate: Hurst closed his career with a splendid 1962 adaptation of J. M.

Synge's *The Playboy of the Western World*, shot in Ireland, and Langley, aside from supplying witty lines for the Judy Garland *Wizard of Oz* (1939), wrote and directed another (more neglected) classic Dickens film, 1952's *The Pickwick Papers*.

Both *Playboy* and *Pickwick* are undervalued, and they deserve revivals. But neither will ever be as loved as much as this *Carol*. Perhaps critics and movie lovers like it so much because they can see how deftly Hurst and Langley have resisted the obvious temptations of the material. This is one of the most faithful of all *Carol* adaptations and one of the least sentimental, one of the most stylishly crafted, and one of the more psychologically acute. It's beyond question a film for adults and one that respects the discernment of children, which is almost never how *A Christmas Carol* is played. When the Ghost of Christmas Past (Michael Dolan) and the Ghost of Christmas Present (Francis De Wolff, decked out like a plum pudding) show up on a horrific, dark Christmas Eve (it's black as pitch outside even when it should be afternoon) to escort Scrooge though his sad, frustrated past and his greedy, cheerless present, they're almost like a team of Freudian (Jungian? Scroogian?) psychiatrists covered with mistletoe, digging into the roots of Scrooge's neuroses and compulsions.

The movie was shot by neglected near-genius cinematographer (later a prolific director), C. M. Pennington-Richards, whose other great photographic job was for documentarian Humphrey Jennings in his 1943 World War II masterpiece *Fires Were Started*. Pennington-Richards's crystalline blacks and whites, and his chilling angles, often remind you irresistibly of Gregg Toland's deep focus marvels in *Citizen Kane* (1941) or the gorgeous monochromes of the 1940s David Lean Dickens adaptations *Great Expectations* (1946) and *Oliver Twist* (1948). *A Christmas Carol* looks stunning throughout, and it also has a near-symphonic score by Richard Addinsell, who wrote the famous "Warsaw Concerto" for another Hurst film (1941's *Dangerous Moonlight*) and who here makes great, emotion-drenching use of the poignant Christmas hymn "Silent Night" and the dark, blood-chilling folk ballad "Barbara Allen." (If Scrooge could have listened to this soundtrack, he would have known immediately that his hard, cold heart didn't stand a chance.)

A Christmas Carol, shot at the height of the prime film noir period, looks like noir and feels like noir (so, at the end, does that other great Christmas movie inspired by *A Christmas Carol*, Frank Capra's 1946 *It's a Wonderful Life*). And it has what are usually film noir politics: unabashedly Labor Party and New Deal (as Dickens probably would have been, had he lived in those times). The acting is expert, deliciously British, and delightfully (but never annoyingly) exaggerated. The good and morally decent characters, like the Cratchits, or the youthful Scrooge's big-hearted boss, Fezziwig (Roddy Hughes), are mild or jovial but never saccharine (not even Tiny Tim, as played by the frighteningly named child actor Glyn Tearman).

The bad characters, like Sim's Scrooge (giggling and sneering, and casting sinister looks), Hordern as Marley (with his doleful warnings and magnificently agonized and deranged wails), and narrator Bull (an even colder-blooded financier than Scrooge), are devilish, mean, icy, keenly melodramatic, and sometimes deservedly tormented. Indeed, both Sim and Hordern became so identified with the parts of Scrooge and Marley that they both repeated them as voice actors for the Oscar-winning 1971 cartoon *A Christmas Carol* by Richard Williams.

Alastair Sim was an academic and an elocution expert, and he had melancholy eyes and an evil smile, and a gift for playing men who know too much and are rather annoyed at the silliness of the world. His diction was shatteringly perfect, and it's the foundation of his comic style, along with those baleful eyes. (I've always thought Alec Guinness, who won Sim's spot in the early '50s as Britain's leading comic movie actor, was sending Sim up a little as the Professor in the 1955 *The Ladykillers*.)

As Scrooge, Sim seems at first to be the smartest man in any room, even when he's putting down and insulting good people, even in his awful cynicism and his sickening greediness. That intelligence and some hints of humanity are among the reasons the movie affects us so deeply, especially after we see the young Scrooge, who loved good, selfless women—like his sister Fan (Carol Marsh) and his fiancée Alice (Rona Anderson)—and appreciated kind bosses, like the eventually ruined Fezziwig, but who decided that the world was itself so mean and grasping that it would screw him unless he screwed it first.

When Sim's Scrooge wakes up on Christmas morning to discover that he still has a chance, that he can still be a good human being and help instead of hurt people, he dissolves into wild capering jigs and cascades of loony giggles that are the exact opposite of the cold money-grubbing snake of a man we saw at first, the cynic who thought Christmas and Christmas-lovers were humbugs. And this new man is, the movie is clear in telling us, the true Scrooge—who has been buried under false creeds of greed and exploitation all these years. (The Christmas visitations were *his* dreams after all.) The fact that Hurst and Langley and Sim's *Christmas Carol* so avoids the usual sentimentality and the sugarplum visions and candy cane philosophy, while telling us this story that a lot of us want so much to believe, the fact that it's so scary and smart, as well as sweet, is part of what makes the 1951 *Christmas Carol* so powerful and such a classic.

Sim's transcendence in this role, and the movie's transcendence in the Dickens cinema canon, are not without irony. Lionel Barrymore, in many ways, owned the part of Scrooge for all his many years of annual radio performances of *A Christmas Carol*. (They went on through the '50s, and I heard them as a child.) But he missed out on MGM's mediocre movie version because, in 1938, his legs had already given out on him, and he needed a wheelchair. Reginald Owen played the film part, decently but not memorably.

So it was Sim, otherwise best known for the World War II home-front thriller *Green for Danger* (1946) and various tart comedies (from 1954's *The Belles of St. Trinian's* to 1972's *The Ruling Class*), who became the Scrooge of all Scrooges, just as the film is deservedly ranked as the *Christmas Carol* of all *Christmas Carols*. If you've never seen it on Christmas, it's a bit like never having seen *It's a Wonderful Life* (1946) or *Meet Me in St. Louis* (1944). But this time the eggnog is spiked, the tale a little darker. And more truthful, more penetrating. It's amazing, in fact, how modern this story and its message, and particularly Scrooge's philosophy, now seem. Greed? Business? Save the rich? Eat the poor? Are there no jails? Are there no workhouses? *Bah, humbug!*

—⟋ℳ⟍—

Dancers Bring to Life *Tales of Beatrix Potter* (1971)
Sheila Benson

Tales of Beatrix Potter tracks down some of the artist's most cherished creations—Peter Rabbit, Mrs. Tiggy-Winkle, Jeremy Fisher, the Two (exceedingly) Bad Mice, even that complete ninny Jemima Puddleduck—and finds them in the vivid green hills of the English Lake Country, where Beatrix Potter herself came to live and work.

What's new here is that these familiar animals (and frog) are now the central characters of a live-action ballet based on Potter's stories. The choreography is by the great Frederick Ashton, and entirely disappearing under their animal disguises are soloists of Britain's Royal Ballet. It's not necessary to know the enduring, palm-sized Beatrix Potter books to love the film, but it certainly adds to the fun. But parents of the very young might want to gauge their children's attention span the same way they would a trip to the theater to see the ballet.

Dancers miming tiny mice, or a bratty Squirrel Nutkin, or a froggy fisherman leaping lily pad to lily pad? Two minutes into this magnificent production and disbelief vanishes, as soon as Mrs. Tiggy-Winkle (Ashton), laundress extraordinaire, sets the scale and style of the film.

At first, she's only a white dot in the sunny distance, making her way down the rolling hills to her cottage. As she gets closer, the spines poking through her mob-cap prove that she's the dear little hedgehog herself, looking the very image of Potter's watercolor illustrations. And between the slight hitch in her step and the banjo underlining the orchestration, it's clear that all hands will know exactly how to characterize each mouse, frog, fowl, owl, and foxy-whiskered gentleman.

Inserted between their stories is a short, wordless introduction to the young Beatrix, seen absorbedly sketching one of the pet mice she keeps in a wooden cage on her desk at home. Then the camera travels downstairs, through a half-opened door, into a parlor where six of the perfectly costumed mice she's been drawing engage in a sprightly waltz—using their tails like jump ropes or twirling them rakishly to John Lanchbery's lilting original score.

It's a tribute to the film's costuming (by the 1987 *Little Dorrit* director Christine Edzard) and its animal designer, the great Rotislav Doboujinsky, that the transformation of dancers into Potter's creatures is not only seamless but allows them the kind of agility you see in the gasp-inducing leaps of Jeremy Fisher (Michael R. Coleman), the very essence of ballet *and* froggyness.

Fans of *Fantastic Mr. Fox* (2009) may be startled at the remarkably close resemblance of *Beatrix Potter's* suave, waist-coated Fox to *their* stop-motion Mr. Fox. Yes, *well*, as the English say.

Bear in mind that Doboujinsky's Foxy Whiskered Gentleman, circa 1971, didn't have George Clooney as a front man and was created to move in character with even the most bravura steps. So game, set, and match to the *Potter* team, and to director Reginald Mills (editor of *The Red Shoes*, among other Powell–Pressburger films).[2]

—⚋⚋—

Enchantingly Blunt: *A Little Princess* (1995)
John Anderson

The intersection of Harry Potter and Shirley Temple can be located somewhere in the vicinity of *A Little Princess*, Alfonso Cuarón's 1995 adaptation-with-liberties of the Frances Hodgson Burnett novel, which, in fact, predates Cuarón's contribution to the Potter universe, i.e., *The Prisoner of Azkaban* (2004), considered by many the best of the series. But it also predates *Y Tu Mamá También* (2001), which established the director as an incipient force in international art film. And it came before *Great Expectations* (1998), or *Children of Men* (2006), or, of course, the Oscar-winning films *Gravity* (2013) and *Roma* (2018). In 1995, you might say, Cuarón had less to live up to. So he made a thoroughly enchanting children's film—which, like all thoroughly enchanting children's films, thoroughly seduces the grown-ups in the audience.

Cuarón's version, with a screenplay by Richard LaGravenese and Elizabeth Chandler, is closer to the Shirley Temple film released in the fabled year of 1939, than it is to the Burnett book, although what the book and Cuarón have in common is definitive—namely, their indefinite article. The Walter Lang–directed movie of 1939, which was both Temple's last big hit and her first all-Technicolor film, was titled *THE Little Princess*, Shirley apparently having no equals. Both Cuarón's film and the book are titled *A Little Princess*—all little girls being princesses, as we're informed by the enchanting Sara Crewe (Liesel Matthews), the princess who happens to own this story.

Cuarón's Sara is a special princess, of course, and Matthews is much of the reason. The actress and heiress (to the Hyatt hotel fortune) was a particularly beautiful child, with large, mournful-when-necessary eyes and a crushed rosebud of a mouth. She made only three movies but is the furthest thing imaginable from the perky/petulant Temple. Photographed to look like a Raphael saint—by Cuarón's longtime DP, Emmanuel Lubezki—Matthews is also consistently dramatically convincing. Sara's parting from her father after they arrive from the "mystical land of India" in 1914 New York—and from which Captain Crewe must immediately return to fight the Huns—is genuinely moving; her later misery is tangible, likewise her joy. She never expends any obvious effort to win over her audience. She simply does.

In many ways, the two films follow the same arc: motherless child, deposited in a girl's school, treated royally if begrudgingly by a hard-hearted schoolmistress, until such time as her father and her money disappear, and she is put into rags and service as a scullery maid. In *A Little Princess*, the principal locale is New York, rather than London; Queen Victoria makes no appearance, as she did with Shirley Temple. But the pathos is earned by the same faithful fairy-tale devices, poverty, and orphanhood.

The despair we share concerning what Sara sees as her hopeless, fatherless future—her father has actually been gassed in the trenches of France, leaving him blind and amnesiac—is ameliorated by the production design of Bo Welch, who surrounds Miss Minchin's School for Girls with a city that certainly *suggests* ragtime-era Manhattan but is so enveloped in artifice, scrubbed surfaces, and purposeful gloss that it wraps itself around Sara—and the viewer too—reassuringly: How much real tragedy could occur in a place so enchanted? Cuarón makes free with fantastical elements in *A Little Princess*—the story that Sara tells her schoolmates (at least before the financial ceiling collapses) is dramatized, in the far-off "mystical land of India," by the Princess Sita (Alison Moir) and the blue-skinned Rama, who are seen enacting the great Hindu epic *The Ramayana*. (Rama is played by Liam Cunningham, who also plays Sara's father, albeit to no obvious Freudian objective.) But there's no shortage of the magical in Cuarón's New York, either, despite the ever-imminent threat to Sara's well-being.

Key to *A Little Princess* are the equal parts dread and charm that underlie its verdant surfaces—green dominates the movie's palette, from the paint job on Miss Minchin's castle-like school, to the girls' school uniforms, all the way to Minchin herself, who in her crueler moments is costumed in a color close to that of two-day-old, unrefrigerated guacamole. Eleanor Bron certainly makes Minchin a heavy, a dose of the Grand Guignol in Cuarón's modernist movie. But she gives a technically deft performance: Minchin, although a sour soul, puts on polished airs and plummy speech when addressing her betters. But despite her transparent efforts to affect a cultured manner, she can never escape her working-class inflections, especially when riled. The clash of gesture and tone are like ground glass, and mark her as particularly phony, more so than even the LaGravenese–Chandler dialogue.

Minchin's hatred of Sara, in whom she sees everything she envies and therefore despises, is only partly about class. How in the world she ever came to educate girls whose parents could afford her school is left to one's imagination, but there's a clue to her malformed character provided in a scene in which she sneers at Sara's resilience and unquenchable self-esteem.

"Don't tell me you still think you're a princess!?" she sputters, to which Sara replies, with considerable nerve, "I AM a princess! All girls are! Didn't your father ever tell you that?" Quite evidently, he did not.

Frances Hodgson Burnett killed off Captain Crewe early, and Sara's wealth was restored only after she was located at her school/prison by his business partner. In both movies discussed here (there were TV productions in the '70s and '80s, and a 1917 silent starring Mary Pickford, with a screenplay by Frances Marion), he survives as a war hero—of the Boer War in 1939 and World War I in 1995. Coincidence plays an outsized part in how both films resolve themselves, but in Cuarón's, it's beyond uncanny.

Next door to Miss Minchin's lives Charles Randolph (Arthur Malet), whose son is seen leaving for the front as Sara and the Captain are arriving in New York (as this is only 1914, it's unusual that a New Yorker would be leaving to fight in the war, but it's not explained). When Captain Crewe is found, blind and delirious in France, he is mistaken for Randolph's son and transported to New York—as previously noted, to the house immediately next door to where his daughter is being mistreated.

Randolph is disappointed, of course, but Ram Dass (Errol Sitahal), his mysterious Indian major domo, encourages him to care for Crewe, because he may, when his memory returns, be able to tell Randolph what happened to his son. This all occurs, but only after Sara and her father keep missing one another with maddening regularity. In the meantime, Ram Dass delivers a roomful of food and silk finery to the attic room inhabited by Sara and her fellow orphan and serving girl Becky (Vanessa Lee Chester), who in the Temple film is cockney but here is African American. (She is also taken home from Minchin's by Crewe at the end, presumably to be adopted, while Minchin herself becomes an ill-tempered chimney sweep, rather than an educational terrorist.)

Beyond the happy endings all around, *A Little Princess* is a film that encourages young girls' self-esteem and independent thinking. ("You can be anything you want," Crewe tells Sara, "as long as you believe.") It's also a movie whose heroine can be refreshingly blunt: All girls are princesses, Sara says to her nemesis, the loathsome Lavinia (Taylor Fry), "even snotty two-faced bullies." Shirley Temple would never speak that way. But *A Little Princess*, for all its magic, also carries a satisfying edge, which along with its many other qualities makes it a rare thing among children's films.

Martin Scorsese Pays Tribute to Cinema and Childhood in *Hugo* (2011)
Emanuel Levy

A must-see fable for movie lovers of all ages, Martin Scorsese's *Hugo* (2011) is one of his most technologically determined pictures (among other distinctions, it's the director's first foray into 3D), but it's also one of his most personal and deeply felt works in a long time.

The PG rating of *Hugo* emphasizes that, nominally, it is a children's adventure, aiming to appeal to younger viewers; however, at heart, *Hugo* is a film that can be enjoyed and appreciated by mature viewers savvy enough to revisit and find out more about the origins and magical powers of film as the dominant mass medium of the twentieth century.

In the past decade or so, Scorsese has struggled to find material suitable for his considerable talents. Except for *The Departed* (2006), which won him his first, long overdue Best Director Oscar, Scorsese, prior to *Hugo*, had made a series of subpar films, including *Gangs of New York* (2002), a compromised historical epic, *The Aviator* (2004), a glitzy but conventional biopic, and *Shutter Island* (2010), a trashy thriller-horror that divided critics.

The aforementioned titles have all starred Leonardo DiCaprio, and except for *Gangs of New York*, all found an appreciative audience; they were commercial hits, grossing north of $100 million at the box office. Yet, something was missing—call it a personal signature, a unique vision, an emotional affinity between the filmmaker and his texts. Many directors—Brian De Palma, Roman Polanski—could have made those pictures, perhaps even more effectively (and less expensively) than Scorsese.

Thus, *Hugo* represents Scorsese at the top of his form, functioning as a movie-magician himself, in complete control of the story's machinery and toys, as well as the technical properties of the movie medium. Visually, this big-budget, special effects film, courtesy of British producer Graham King, is ultra-polished, at times even dazzling.

It's hard to think of another director who has shown such passion for film history as Scorsese, and not just because of his Film Preservation Foundation, which is now globally oriented. Although based on Brian Selznick's award-winning 2007 cinematically illustrated children's best seller *The Invention of Hugo Cabret*, *Hugo* is a quintessential Scorsese film, one that displays some of the most recurrent themes in his rich oeuvre—in particular his love of cinema itself.

The movie is replete with ironies, contradictions, and paradoxes, and richly dense in cinematic allusions. For starters, *Hugo* begins as a classic Charles Dickens tale, about an orphan boy who lives in a train station. It then becomes a mystery-adventure, about the bond (and first love) between two teenagers, both parentless. And it concludes on a highly exuberant note, with Scorsese's paying homage to pioneering and revolutionary filmmaker Georges Méliès (1861–1938), showing on-screen images from his best-known work, the 1902 fantasy (and fantastical) *A Trip to the Moon* (*Le Voyage dans la Lune*).

Like Scorsese's best films, *Hugo* has a slender plot, based on a simple premise. A wily, resourceful boy, who lost his loving father in a fire, embarks on a long and arduous quest to unlock a secret that his father had left for him.

Adapted to the big screen by John Logan, the story is set in Paris in 1931, but a heightened version of that time and place. Although the details are particular, there's something about the film's conceptual and visual design that lends it a more abstract and universal quality.

Visually, this quality is evident from the opening sequence, a fast, dazzling, forward-tracking shot of a busy train station, with the camera sweeping along until it lands with a close-up of a twelve-year-old boy, Hugo, hiding behind the station's big clock. He provides the film's center, a link between the various secondary characters and subplots. Blessed with good looks and big, wide blue eyes, Asa Butterfield (who had appeared in 2008's *The Boy in the Striped Pajamas*) is well cast for the part.

The script is sketchy in providing specific characteristics about Hugo. In a flashback, we observe his close bond with his father (Jude Law), as they work together on a robotic figure (an extremely elaborate automaton that can write). After his father's death, Hugo ends up living with his coarse uncle (Ray Winstone) in the train station, where, in disguise, he's doing the man's job. When the uncle leaves, never to come back, Hugo is left to his own devices.

In the first chapters, we see how Hugo survives by stealing bread and milk, hiding behind the big clock, chased by a nasty cop (Sacha Baron Cohen) who hunts down orphans. Hugo's life changes when he meets Isabelle (Chloë Grace Moretz, one of the few Americans in the cast), a bright and resourceful girl, who becomes his reliable companion and ultimately helps him get out of his emotional shell.

While living more comfortably, Isabelle is also parentless—she resides with her godparents, "Papa Georges" and "Mama Jeanne." The friendship of Hugo and Isabelle is mutually rewarding. An intellectually curious, avid reader, Isabelle uses a complex and sophisticated vocabulary that Hugo doesn't fully comprehend. More importantly, she introduces Hugo to the station's bookstore owner (Christopher Lee), who, despite his forbidding looks, turns out to be a benevolent figure, giving Hugo special editions of *Robin Hood*, *David Copperfield*, and other classic literature. In return, Hugo takes Isabelle to the movies, where time and again we see his favorite silent comedian, Harold Lloyd, hanging from a giant clock. Quite masterfully, Scorsese later re-creates this iconic image with Hugo replacing Lloyd.

Scorsese doesn't neglect the story's elements of mystery—in line with the curiosity common to young teenagers. Hugo and Isabelle are always poking and prying into the lives of the people they meet, trying to figure out what's going on around them or how an object or machine works.

Perhaps the biggest mystery is represented by "Papa Georges" (Ben Kingsley), a bitter, ornery man in rapid decline. He is, in fact, Georges Méliès, who in real life made 500 films, at times shooting three films a week during the day while performing magic shows in the evening. Scorsese identifies completely with this genius who gave his all to the movies, a visionary who created a new art form but after a sudden loss of his fortune, his audience, and his luck decides to burn his remaining films. This explains how he ends up sitting behind the counter of a toy store in a quiet part of the Gare Montparnasse.

Hugo is a charming movie, a classy and classic fable, a bold adventure taken by Scorsese, who shapes existing material to his own vision. Although looking back on the past with fond nostalgia, *Hugo* is not sentimental. Instead it may be one of Scorsese's most upbeat and genuinely optimistic features, reaffirming the institution of the family as a warm, protective, and loving place, one that Hugo can finally belong to and call home.

—⟨⟨⟨—

Smart Times at Beverly Hills High in *Clueless* (1995)

Kenneth Turan[3]

To hear almost-sixteen Cher Horowitz tell it, "I actually have a way normal life." True, her mom died during "routine liposuction," but she now lives happily with her fierce litigator father ("He gets paid $500 an hour to fight with people") in great Beverly Hills style. "Isn't my house classic?" she enthuses. "Its columns date back to 1972."

Effervescent, unflappable, and supremely pleased with herself, Cher (delightfully played by Alicia Silverstone in arguably her best role) is the comic centerpiece of *Clueless* (1995), a wickedly funny teenage farce from writer-director Amy Heckerling that, like its heroine, turns out to have more to it than anyone could anticipate.

Heckerling, of course, has been to high school before. In 1982, she directed Sean Penn, Jennifer Jason Leigh, and Phoebe Cates in the hip *Fast Times at Ridgemont High* (1982). *Clueless* is just as clever and amusing, and this time around Heckerling has the advantage of a heroine even Jane Austen could love. In fact, she had a hand in creating her.

Even though Paramount did not exactly base its ad campaign on the fact, *Clueless* is a shrewd modern reworking of some of the themes and plotlines of Austen's beloved 1815 novel *Emma*, another story of a self-confident, socially prominent young woman who was surprised to find out how much she had to learn. Heckerling has even borrowed the name of one of the book's young men (it's Elton) for use by his corresponding number in the film.

The Austen connection points out the unexpected smartness of *Clueless*, which may be about high school but depends on familiarity with Billie Holiday and *Hamlet* for its laughs. Put together with verve and style, *Clueless* is a sweet-natured satire of LA's overpampered youth that manages to get more fun out of high school than most people had attending it.

Named, like her best friend, Dionne (Stacey Dash), after "great singers of the past who now do infomercials," Cher is absolutely the most popular girl at Bronson Alcott (Beverly Hills High under another name—that of the father of Louisa May Alcott, author of *Little Women*), an institution overrun with nose jobs and teen attitude.

Convinced that "searching for a boy in high school is as useless as searching for meaning in a Pauly Shore movie," Cher is also a self-assured virgin who blithely explains, "You see how picky I am about my shoes, and they only go on my feet."

Still, even for Cher, life does present problems. Like her serious ex-stepbrother Josh (Paul Rudd), a future environmental lawyer who wears Amnesty International T-shirts, listens to "complaint rock," and takes a certain pleasure in observing the superficiality of Cher's life while helping her dad (Dan Hedaya) with some legal chores.

Then debate teacher Mr. Hall (Wallace Shawn) gives her a C, a grade she considers "way harsh" given that her oral presentation on the Haitian refugee crisis concluded with a stirring "it does not say RSVP on the Statue of Liberty."

But when she spots Tai (Brittany Murphy), a sloppy, flannel shirt–wearing transfer student from New York, Cher's essentially sunny nature asserts itself. Determined to transform this "clueless" creature, Cher and Dionne change everything from the way she dresses to her taste in boys. But makeovers can be riskier than they seem. Just ask Emma Woodhouse.

Even though it makes extensive use of voice-over, always a dicey choice, *Clueless*'s script is a treat. And because Heckerling knows just where the jokes are, her direction is dead-on as well, with every actor in the extensive cast both understanding and responding admirably to the material.

Responding best of all is Silverstone, who gives a performance as flawless as Cher's complexion. A giddy mall queen who worships at the Westside Pavilion and uses "as if," "totally," and "whatever" as conversation building blocks, Cher can sound off-putting and manipulative. But Silverstone emphasizes Cher's good-hearted guilelessness until we have no choice but to embrace her, maxed-out credit cards and all.

—ɯ—

Henry James's Dark Screwball Comedy: *What Maisie Knew* (2012)

Gerald Peary[4]

What Maisie Knew, the 2012 film, is based on Henry James's 1897 novel, said to be among the first fictional works concerned with how divorce can adversely affect the young. According to a later 1909 preface to his book, James was motivated in his creation by a sad conversation at a dinner party about "some luckless child of a divorced couple" whose parents had been granted something new and liberal at the time: joint custody. Said James, "The wretched infant was . . . to find itself practically disowned, rebounding from racquet to racquet like a tennis ball or a shuttlecock." James's narrative is a dark domestic farce of marital chaos and failure, and, juxtaposed, the tale of a sterling little girl holding her ground amid the feuding, self-absorbed adults. Our Maisie. Perhaps James's most sympathetic protagonist.

What she "knows" is, at first, very little, as the cagey older folks hide from her what bad they are doing, including, a bit unusual for Henry James, a heck of a lot of bed-hopping. But as the novel progresses, the perceptive Maisie grasps more and more. The indulgent adults can't help but weigh the child down with their ugly secrets and reveal to her other people's gross deeds. And by the end of the book, which floats through a half-dozen years, a now-adolescent Maisie really does know far more than the deluded, emotionally infantile ensemble of the grown.

How to make a movie out of *What Maisie Knew*? Eighteen years prior to the shoot, Carroll Cartwright composed a screenplay with his neighbor, Nancy Doyne. He was an avid Jamesian, but he also was influenced in the writing, as he said in a 2013 interview, by his involvement in an ugly custody suit. He raised a young daughter by himself, taking her everywhere he went in the adult world. "She had to think on her feet," Cartwright remembered. So does little Maisie, whose part Cartwright wrote with great affection. "She does not complain, she does not whine, she stands up to all with great grace," he said describing his on-paper heroine when interviewed.

For Cartwright and Coyne, a sort of miracle happened. Their script from almost two decades before was given to actress Julianne Moore, and she decided quickly that she wanted to appear in it. A production was green-lighted, to be codirected by the astute team of Scott McGehee and David Siegel, filmmakers of indie favorites *Suture* (1993) and *The Deep End* (2001). Involving Cartwright and Doyne in the rewrites, the directors simplified James's formidable prose and compressed the half-dozen years of the tale into a single year. Wisely, they got rid of Maisie's cumbersome governess, Mrs. Wix, who sits like a hen on the second half of James's novel, overheating the story with her one-note carping.

A most significant change was placing *What Maisie Knew* in a contemporary setting—today's yuppified New York. McGehee and Siegel grasped that James's 1890s saga of selfish, arguing marrieds getting quickie divorces; taking up with anyone and everyone; and ignoring their child is amazingly prescient. What was problematic, if you seek an audience's favor, is that all four of the principal adults in the book turn out fairly rotten. Maisie's embattled parents, Beale and Ida, are, from start to divorce, useless raising a child. Our hope for Maisie's well-being shifts to her parents' second spouses, Miss Overmore and Sir Claude. Unlike her biological mom and dad, they sympathize with Maisie. But both prove disappointing as caregivers and, ultimately, are lacking in character and backbone. Maisie sensibly rejects all claimants as her parents but then, by default, sticks herself with the grating Mrs. Wix. The end!

Should the film take a more audience-friendly route?

McGehee and Siegel offer an unapologetic house cleaning of the novel. They give three of the four adult protagonists new names—the dad remains Beale—and three of them up-to-date professions. Only Miss Overmore, a governess in the book, is barely changed to Margo (Joanna Vanderham), a nanny. Maisie's father (Steve Coogan) is an international businessman, always flying away somewhere. Maisie's mother (Moore), renamed Susanna, is a once-famous pop singer now attempting a comeback, although committed to a dreary repertoire of '80s school-of-Pat Benatar. Maisie fits into neither's concerns.

When Beale and Susanna divorce, they speedily remarry. Beale weds Margo, so she will watch over Maisie while he traverses the globe with his cell phone. Susanna gets tied to Lincoln (Alexander Skarsgård), a mellow bartender, because—who knows why? Her insatiable neediness?

As with the book, Maisie's parents are just as awful a husband and wife in their second marriages. As in the book, their abused partners meet and, no surprise, fall for one another. Better, they seem to actually care about Maisie. And—I should stop here and not reveal if McGehee and Siegel remain with Henry James's melancholy conclusion or go feel-good and rescue dear Maisie from her childhood of neglect.

Onata Aprile as Maisie is such a find—a sweet, expressive little trouper, who, at age six for the shooting, did seem "to know." When she says of her mom's new man, Lincoln, "I love him!" Onata's sincerity—and wisdom—melts your heart.

Adult actors come and go, enter and exit, but, fortunately, Onata is in every scene of the movie, its pint-sized, persuasive moral center.

—⚊⚊—

From *Neverland* to *Shadowlands*: Hollywood's Romance with Children's Book Authors
Peter Keough[5]

As demonstrated by the success of Rob Marshall's *Mary Poppins Returns* (2018), a sequel (of sorts) to the perennial favorite *Mary Poppins* (1964), the no-nonsense flying nanny continues to delight audiences. But what about the person behind Poppins, children's author P. L. Travers? Played by Emma Thompson in John Lee Hancock's biopic *Saving Mr. Banks* (2013), she is as prickly as her creation—if not as magical. Focusing on Travers's thorny negotiations with Walt Disney on how her book would be presented on the screen, the film also delves into the traumatic events that inspired Travers to invent her indomitable, miracle-working au pair.

The life of a children's book author might seem an odd subject for a major motion picture, but *Banks* is no rarity. Other biopics about children's authors include *Dreamchild* (1985), about Lewis Carroll; *Finding Neverland* (2004), about J. M. Barrie; *Miss Potter* (2006), about Beatrix Potter; and *Shadowlands* (1993), about C. S. Lewis.

Why the interest? Perhaps Hollywood feels drawn to the sources of some of their most lucrative franchises and wants to explore the mystery of their genius. Audiences, too, want to know more about those whose works enchanted their childhood and their children. These writers made the myths that inspired so many movies, and so perhaps the movies want to make them into myths as well.

Or maybe stereotypes. The film versions of the aforementioned authors share common traits. They are all British, and Victorian in sensibility. All are childless, if not unmarried. All have tales of woe, often involving the death of family members. And they all suffer from social awkwardness, bordering at times on the pathological.

Take, for example, Lewis Carroll, the pen name for Charles L. Dodgson, author of the oft-adapted *Alice in Wonderland*, who appears in Gavin Millar's *Dreamchild*. The film intriguingly takes the point of view not of the author, but of the girl who inspired the book.

In 1932, the now-eighty-year-old Alice is in New York to be honored at an event celebrating Carroll's centenary. At first Alice is annoyed and bewildered by the fuss, but then she is visited by flashbacks and fantasies.

The flashbacks, at first, are more or less benign. She remembers listening to Dodgson (depicted in a creepy performance by Ian Holm) tell his stories and posing for his controversial photographs. The fantasies, however, are unambiguously horrible re-creations of scenes from the book. As conceived by Jim Henson's Creature Shop, the late Muppeteer's design studio, the Mad Hatter, the March Hare, and the other zany denizens of Wonderland have here been transformed into malignant grotesques. They mock the now-octogenarian Alice for her stupidity, senility, and impending death. Worst of all, Alice begins to remember something she has tried to forget.

Is it a repressed memory of sexual abuse? The filmmakers stop short of suggesting that Dodgson was a pedophile. Instead, what Alice has forgotten proves not to be traumatic, but tragic. She realizes that the magic and innocence of Wonderland is doomed to wither and die, like herself. All that remains are the stories.

Almost forty years after *Alice* was published in 1865, Scottish writer J. M. Barrie confronted similar themes in his 1904 play *Peter Pan*. It features Neverland, which, like Carroll's Wonderland, provides an imaginary refuge for those dissatisfied with the world of adults. With five-foot-ten Johnny Depp as the wizened, five-foot Barrie, Marc Forster's *Finding Neverland* from the start suggests that its version of the playwright might be somewhat imaginary as well.

It begins with Barrie trapped in an unhappy marriage and troubled by a faltering career. While taking a break romping with his dog in the park he bumps into the recently widowed Sylvia Llewelyn Davies (Kate Winslet) and her four (five in real life) sons. Smitten by the clan, Barrie soon becomes part of the family, joining in the kids' fantasies about pirates and Indians, stories that inspire his creativity and get him to jot down ideas in a notebook.

Meanwhile, feeling abandoned, his wife leaves him. Gossip spreads about Barrie spending so much time with a lonely widow—not to mention her four boys. But it's all innocent fun (although not according to Piers Dudgeon's 2009 biography)—make-believe that Barrie will eventually turn into the play *Peter Pan*, which revives his career and reaffirms his faith in incorruptible innocence and eternal youth. If you believe hard enough, so Barrie and the film imply, the disillusionment of growing up and the specter of mortality will fade before the childish wonders of Neverland.

No such sentimental nonsense for Beatrix Potter, however. *The Tale of Peter Rabbit*, her first book, published in 1902, begins with the title hero's father baked in a pie.

A model of normality compared to Dodgson and Barrie, the writer (Renée Zellweger) in Chris Noonan's *Miss Potter* nonetheless challenges the norms of her day and serves as a proto-feminist role model. Instead of becoming a respectable wife in accordance with her parvenu mother's ambitions, Potter rejects all suitors and revels in the animal characters she draws and which come to life on the screen via animation. An insightful publisher, Norman Warne (Ewan McGregor), falls in love with Potter's anthropomorphized menagerie. He puts the tales into print, and they become among the most popular children's books of all time.

Having achieved this, Potter foregoes her vow never to marry and becomes engaged to Warne, a move that draws her back into the real world of transience and loss. Unlike Carroll and Barrie, however, she does not respond by retreating deeper into fantasy. Instead, she vindicates her wonderland in a more concrete way, turning her grief into action by buying up thousands of acres of unspoiled farmland, preserving it from developers.

In these films, fantasy sequences illustrate the authors' fancies. But not in *Shadowlands*, Richard Attenborough's biopic of the literary lion C. S. Lewis (Anthony Hopkins), author of the Narnia series of books, beginning in 1950, with *The Lion, the Witch, and the Wardrobe*, three of which to date have been adapted to the screen. But in this movie a ten-year-old fan, imitating the book, opens a wardrobe in the author's attic and finds—nothing.

The boy is Douglas, son of Joy Gresham (Debra Winger), an American poet who sent Lewis a fan letter and became a close friend. Like Barrie with Llewelyn Davies, the confirmed bachelor Lewis's relationship with the brash American divorcée is a source of gossip. But unlike Barrie, Lewis is drawn not to the regressive innocence represented by the woman's son, but to the reality principle insisted on by the tough-minded mother.

Accustomed to lecturing captive audiences about the Christian justification for the existence of pain, Lewis learns from Joy that he can't really speak about pain because he has insulated himself from experiencing it. He has thus resisted the experience of love—until, like Potter, he is smitten, and . . . let's just say that falling in love with a children's book writer can be hazardous to your health.

As these movies demonstrate, Dodgson, Barrie, Potter, and Lewis are like everyone else—flawed and broken and not always nice. But unlike everyone else, they have preserved enough of their childhood to bring it to life and delight the child in us all.

—ɯ—

Mary Poppins Returns, and She's Closer to the Feisty Original
J. R. Jones

Mary Poppins Returns (2018) holds a record for longest wait between a movie and its sequel, arriving fifty-four years after Julie Andrews and Dick Van Dyke sang and danced their way through the live-action Disney classic of 1964. The sequel has been so long coming, in fact, that Walt Disney Pictures has already released a drama about the making of the original film. Released just before Christmas 2013, and relentlessly flogged by the studio as an Oscar contender, *Saving Mr. Banks* chronicles the struggle between Walt Disney (a genial Tom Hanks) and British writer P. L. Travers (a dyspeptic Emma Thompson) about how her characters would be portrayed on-screen, a struggle that ends only when the world-famous producer heals the author's wounded inner child and she succumbs at last to the studio's particular brand of stardust.

Saving Mr. Banks may not have won Walt Disney Pictures a boatload of Oscars (only Best Original Score), but it's an inspired piece of corporate storytelling, putting the studio's spin on a long-standing public relations headache. Five years later, as if to seal the deal, *Mary Poppins Returns* replicates Disney's vision as faithfully as possible. Like *Mary Poppins*, it's a grand, sprawling entertainment, full of color, music, dancing, and song. Almost every special-effects sequence or musical showstopper harks back to one from the original. The studio's only accommodation to Travers, really, was casting Emily Blunt in the title role. With her scornful eyes and cruel smile, Blunt is a more acerbic presence than Julie Andrews, and more in keeping with the character Travers created. In the books, Mary could be a little scary.

Then again, so could Pamela Travers. Disney first approached her for the rights to Mary Poppins after his two young daughters introduced him to the books in 1944, but she found his movies obvious and saccharine, and held out until the late 1950s, when dwindling royalties forced her hand. In April 1961, she flew from London to Los Angeles to serve as a consultant on the film and, during her ten-day visit, clashed with Disney and his production team, notably screenwriter Don DaGradi and songwriting brothers Richard and Robert Sherman (who had shown up with such gems as "A Spoonful of Sugar" and "Chim Chim Cheree"). Audiotape of their work sessions, dug out of the Disney archives by Travers biographer Valerie Lawson, showed the writer faulting everything from the dialogue to the set details to the treatment of Mary Poppins and Mr. Banks, the London banker whose children she agrees to mind after dropping out of the sky on an umbrella.

The Disney team, needing a credible story arc on which to hang the books' fanciful, unconnected episodes, had constructed a narrative in which Mary Poppins straightens out the father, a smug, self-assured businessman who wants his children to grow up faster. "What wand was waved to turn Mr. Banks . . . from an anxious, ever-loving father into a man who could cheerfully tear into pieces a poem that his children had written?" Travers later complained in a letter to a friend. Her model for Mr. Banks had been her beloved father, a branch manager with the Australian Joint Stock Bank in Maryborough whose drinking had gotten him demoted to clerk, and who died of his addiction when Pamela was seven years old. The only moment in *Mary Poppins* that rang true for Travers was the last scene, in which a reformed Mr. Banks heads out to gambol with his children to the Sherman brothers' lilting "Let's Go Fly a Kite."

Travers had a more complicated relationship with Andrews, who brought Mary to life on-screen. "Well, you've got the nose for it," the author observed when they met during preproduction. Andrews returned the author's anxious letters during the shoot, when Disney had cut off communications with her, and has spoken well of Travers, who died in 1996. Yet, the two women seem to have disagreed about how Mary should be played. "Why was Mary Poppins, already beloved for what she was—plain, vain, and incorruptible—transmogrified into a soubrette?" Travers later wrote, referring to the coquettish sopranos of light opera. Andrews, for her part, thought Mary could be verbally cruel with the children. "Sometimes . . . when I read the books, I got the feeling that Mary Poppins was thoughtless, or just a little unkind once in a while," she remarked in a DVD audio commentary. "So I had to . . . try to make it seem like I was doing it as a joke or with a smile or something like that."

Andrews was a spoonful of sugar indeed, but on the page Mary Poppins could be more like a spoonful of castor oil. With the children she is brusque, easily offended, and quick to anger, a dispenser of "terrible" glances and subtle put-downs, especially where the vexing Michael is concerned. She "sniffs," "snaps," and "scoffs," her manner "scornful," "haughty," or "disgusted." She keeps the children entirely in line; as Michael observes in the inaugural book, "You could not look at Mary Poppins and disobey her. There was something strange and extraordinary about her—something that was frightening and at the same time exciting." When Mary denies that one of their magical adventures ever took place, the children fall silent, "for they had learnt that it was better not to argue with Mary Poppins, no matter how odd anything seemed." Yet, they snuggle closer to her on the bus and fall asleep.

Emily Blunt comes closer to capturing Mary's serrated edge. After all, Blunt enjoyed one of her biggest hits with Denis Villeneuve's *Sicario* (2015), playing a tough-as-nails FBI agent who goes head to head with a Mexican drug cartel. If anything, Mary Poppins has been sanded down even further for the sequel, but Blunt brings more vinegar to the role with her eye-rolling and snarky head-cocking than Andrews could ever muster. "Sit up straight, you're not a flour bag," Mary snaps at young John Banks (Nathanael Saleh), one of her three charges. When his sister, Anabel (Pixie Davies), appears in a dirty dress, the nanny observes, "You could grow a garden in that much soil." If the real Mary Poppins showed up today, helicopter parents would be phoning 911 to rat her out. They miss the appeal of such a woman: The children wouldn't feel nearly as safe with her if they didn't find her so fearsome.

Watching *Mary Poppins Returns*, one can't help but remember that Disney made the character his own. Travers never forgave him for it: After the great showman died in 1966, she began venting her spleen in private remarks to journalists, just to remind them who had created Mary and who knew her real mind. In this context, *Saving Mr. Banks* seems like both the ultimate spin control and the true sequel to *Mary Poppins*, with Walt Disney, that champion of whimsy and wonder, in the role of Mary, and Travers, with her sour complaints and stiff upper lip, as the female Mr. Banks. Travers always chafed at the idea of Mary Poppins being turned into a Disney character; now she's become one herself.

Brigitte Fossey and Georges Poujouly in *Forbidden Games*

6

—ɱ—

MATTERS OF LIFE AND DEATH

Most kids can't wait to grow up, but the process includes some dismaying revelations. Learning the truth about Santa Claus and the Easter Bunny is just the beginning. Luckily, movies can serve as a buffer or training ground for some of the worst life has to offer.

Take war, for example. Some video games, TV shows, and movies make it look like fun. Maybe that's one way for young people to cope with the reality. But other films confront the truth with an artfulness, detachment, and compassion that allow some comprehension of the enormity.

Morris Dickstein considers two such films in his essay "Children of War." "Because modern warfare has so often been directed at civilians," he writes, "children have been among the most horrendous casualties." For confirmation of this, one need only look at the conflicts in Syria, Iraq, Nigeria, Somalia, and a dozen other war zones, the news reports of which flare up in the media and are as quickly forgotten.

The children in Roberto Rossellini's *Germany Year Zero* (1948)—about a boy in the ruins of post–World War II Berlin—and René Clément's *Forbidden Games* (1952)—about a girl in the chaos of post-blitzkrieg France—are not so easily forgotten. "These stories are trained more on survival than on violent combat," Dickstein writes. "Yet, death is ever present in them. Both are peopled with adults who are hapless or hopeless, enabling children to construct their own world"—a world that anyone sharing it will find hard to shake.

In Fred Zinnemann's *The Search* (1948), discussed by Emanuel Levy in his essay "A Search for Hope in the Ruins," the adults are not all hapless or hopeless, but they still can't help all the children damaged by the war. Set like *Germany Year Zero* in a devastated Germany under Allied occupation, *The Search* focuses on one refugee boy, an Auschwitz survivor who is separated from his mother, and a GI, played by Montgomery Clift, who befriends him. "One of the first

American films to deal with the Holocaust and its impact." Levy writes. It was also the first American feature film shot in the defeated country, and the location adds to the film's immediacy and pathos. "Shooting the picture in bombed-out German cities, Zinnemann achieved a more authentic, semidocumentary look," Levy explains. "[That] style was enhanced by mixing professional actors with nonprofessionals. Zinnemann always delighted in the fact that many ... assumed that Montgomery Clift ... had been a real GI."

Sometimes the travails of so-called peacetime present children with life-or-death challenges as traumatic as those faced in war. In his essay "Innocent Bystanders: Five Films about Kids Growing Up in an Unforgiving World," Jay Carr covers both scenarios.

In *Hope and Glory* (1987), John Boorman looks back at his childhood during the blitz with ambivalent nostalgia. "For some Britons," writes Carr, "war wasn't all hell. It was liberating."

Not so for those trying to survive in the wasteland of "liberated" Rome in Vittorio De Sica's *Bicycle Thieves* (1948), the neorealist masterpiece about a father and son searching for the bicycle without which they may not survive. As in *Germany Year Zero*, the adults come up short, and in the end the "son almost switches father–son roles."

The Spanish Civil War was ending when the events in Víctor Erice's *Spirit of the Beehive* (1973) begin, but the sharp-eyed little heroine sees all. As with the children in *Forbidden Games*, a secret ritual offers refuge. "When nothing but horror swamps a child's world," writes Carr, "he or she retreats inside, searching for a bearable reality."

Nor do all horrors occur in wartime, as is seen in Kazakhstan filmmaker Gulshat Omarova's *Schizo* (2004) and the Belgian Dardenne brothers' *Rosetta* (1999). In both films, teenagers must go to extremes to support themselves and their families in a society ruled by cruelty, greed, and exploitation. Can they survive? "Kids cope," Carr believes. "Assuming, that is, that they escape death or trauma ... and other savage follies rained down upon them by adults."

A chaotic and perilous political landscape provides the setting for Chris Menges's *A World Apart* (1988), which takes place in South Africa during the apartheid era. Thirteen-year-old Molly's parents are antiapartheid activists hunted and persecuted by the government. Her father flees the country and her mother is imprisoned, and so both sacrifice their responsibilities as parents for the good of the cause. As Peter Rainer writes in his essay "Politics Makes for Poor Parenting in *A World Apart*," the film "describes the horrors of apartheid, but it's also about the horrors exacted on the children of those who devote their lives to its destruction."

Iran may be run by a regime in some ways as oppressive as apartheid South Africa, but because Iranian filmmakers often feature kids as characters to address adult issues that otherwise might be censored, they have made some of the world's most compelling children's films. In his essay "Iran's Child-Centered Films," Godfrey Cheshire examines this phenomenon and discusses how this feature of Iranian cinema might help Western audiences better understand a society usually regarded with suspicion and hostility.

But will American kids and their parents get past the subtitles and the different customs and clothes? "The audience was enraptured," Cheshire writes about a screening of Iranian director Majid Majidi's *Children of Heaven* (1997). "This remains the most spectacular instance I've seen of cinema's power to overcome cultural barriers and preconceptions."

—〰—

Children of War: *Germany Year Zero* (1948) and *Forbidden Games* (1952)
Morris Dickstein

One test of any society is how it treats its most vulnerable members, especially the way it protects or abuses its children. Because modern warfare has so often been directed at civilians, children have been among the most horrendous casualties. The weapons of advanced technology help distance the warring parties from the cities they destroy and the people they kill, maim, or render homeless and hungry. In World War II, combat between professional soldiers or conscripts gave way to toxic forms of total warfare, while fierce civil wars and terror campaigns, fueled by radical hatred, have long targeted ordinary people as a tactic of intimidation or revenge. In trying to wipe out entire populations, the Nazis turned children into deliberate prey, not simply collateral damage.

Movies have often weighed the costs of war by gauging its impact on children. Two of the strongest works, both made in the wake of the last world war, were Roberto Rossellini's *Germany Year Zero* (1948), the third and least-known film in his war trilogy, and René Clément's *Forbidden Games* (1952). After being rejected at Cannes, Clément's film became an arthouse favorite when it won the Golden Lion award at the Venice Film Festival. Both movies are brought to life by the incandescent performances of astonishingly poised child actors, whose eyes become our window into the world around them. These stories are trained more on survival than violent combat. Yet, death is ever present in them. Both are peopled with adults who are hapless or hopeless, enabling children to construct their own world. But they develop their subjects in strikingly different ways.

René Clément had begun his career as a documentary filmmaker, an approach that carried over into his first feature film, *The Battle of the Rails* (1946), dealing with resistance and sabotage among French railway workers during the German occupation; however, *Forbidden Games* feels at times like a Russian feature film of the 1920s or 1930s, with sharp editing, striking camera angles, idyllic intervals, and the often stagy acting that separates the adults from the child performers.

Rossellini, on the other hand, although he had honed his craft in the "white telephone" school of middle-class movies during the war, gave a powerful documentary feeling to all three works of his war trilogy, starting with *Rome, Open City* (1945) and *Paisan* (1946). *Germany Year Zero* is built upon haunting location footage surveying the wreckage that was Berlin in the summer of 1947. Its people live like cave-dwellers, scrounging to survive in half-ruined structures within a postapocalyptic landscape, although the interiors were filmed later in Rome. For all the extremity of the setting, Rossellini's nonprofessional actors give the film an understated, "dedramatized" tone (to use the late critic Peter Brunette's term) that paradoxically makes the action feel real and immediate.

Despite the studio work, *Germany Year Zero* seems like a documentary about the ravages of the war. We first see thirteen-year-old Edmund (Edmund Moeschke) working as a gravedigger to support his desperate family, but he is driven off because he's underage. The family shares a flat with four other tenants in a damaged building. Edmund's father is ill and bedridden and demoralized, seeing himself as a burden to others, someone "condemned to live." His sister survives as a hostess and bar girl for Allied soldiers, just barely holding back from having to sell her body so that the family can eat. Edmund's older brother, a Wehrmacht fighter to the bitter end, is in hiding with them, without a ration card, out of fear that he'll be imprisoned if he registers. "I was a soldier," he says, but now "I'm a nobody."

Surrounded by these dysfunctional adults, including nasty neighbors in their crowded flat, the resourceful Edmund, ever busy and hopeful, is almost the sole support of his struggling family. But he has grown up too soon, encountered death too early, and taken on more responsibility than any kid his age should need to assume. A former teacher seems to care about him, but he's a pederast and still a Nazi; his Darwinist view that the strong must look out for themselves, not care for the weak, has a baleful effect on Edmund. "You must have the courage to let the weak die," he tells the boy.

Edmund has heard his brother threaten to kill himself, heard his dispirited father long for death, heard their landlord talk about the old man as a useless encumbrance. In a strangely undramatic turn, Edmund takes this literally and, as if in kindness, poisons his father. Walking through the ruined city one last time, his face pensive, his bright-eyed look now troubled, he realizes the enormity of what he's done and takes his own life, jumping from the upper floor of a ruined building. It would be hard to imagine a more potent theme. Yet, the adolescent parricide and suicide are carried off without melodrama, as if Edmund were just one more victim of an entire nation's moral suicide.

The parallels are driven home in two scenes. First is when Edmund's old teacher uses him to sell a record player to some British GIs near the Chancellery where Hitler himself died. He plays for them a recording of one of Hitler's speeches, promising ultimate victory, while the camera pans through the consequences of the Führer's megalomania all around them. Later, as Edmund is putting poison into the drink he's prepared for his father, we hear the old man lamenting the craven folly of the German people in going along with the Nazis. For Rossellini, the deep-dyed innocence of the young highlights the insidious corruption of the adults, from Hitler to the boy's own brother, teachers, and neighbors, a world in which everything is for sale and everyone is barely getting by.

Forbidden Games is set squarely in the middle of the war but on rural farmland that feels remote from it. It begins with a powerful scene of civilians in chaotic flight under German aerial bombardment, centering on five-year-old Paulette (Brigitte Fossey), her parents, and their dog. When the dog runs away, she chases after him; her mother and father come after her and are killed. Pursuing the dog, now dead and tossed into a river, she meets an eleven-year-old farm boy, Michel (Georges Poujouly), who convinces his peasant family to take her in.

The family is caught up in an endless feud with one its neighbors, a pointless quarrel that serves as a farcical counterpoint to the war itself. One of their older sons, kicked by a horse, gradually wastes away. The adults seem insensitive about death, just as the two children, for all their innocence, grow mesmerized by it. Together they have buried Paulette's dog and, to keep it from being lonely, created a secret graveyard around it for other small creatures. They steal crosses as markers for these tiny graves, and this eventually exposes what they've done, which also echoes the war around them. But what really matters is the tender relationship that develops between them, at once protective and loving, and the private world, insulated from adult meanness and violence, that they have woven around them. Paulette's luminous face and golden hair make her appear at once angelic and innocently feminine, while Michel (like Edmund) is more the little man than any child should be forced to be.

The film was criticized for portraying French peasants as rustic fools, but what they really represent is the quarrelsome foolishness, the insensitivity, of the adult world, not so different from the selfishness and corruption surrounding Edmund in the Rossellini film. Just as Edmund is repeatedly swindled and manipulated, even by older kids who've formed a thieving little gang, Paulette is cared for by no one but Michel. He takes her under his wing, although he himself, treated like a hired hand by his capricious father, has little power. His family agrees not to send her away if he returns all the crosses he's removed, but they're lying to him and they allow the police to come collect her. He responds by uprooting these Christian symbols and throwing them in the river, as if to show that the ethical ideal they represent has been grossly violated.

The movie's infinitely touching final scene kept me in tears. It reminded me of the forced separation of the long-married old couple in Leo McCarey's poignant drama *Make Way for Tomorrow* (1937), when their distracted children decide they can no longer live on their own. They put a brave face on it and, in a heartbreaking moment, say good-bye in a busy railroad station. Here we see Paulette, looking as inscrutably beatific as ever, sitting alone in a crowded refugee center. A kindly nun puts a label around her neck, telling her she'll be placed somewhere. She's become a parcel to be deposited on someone's doorstep.

As the movie ends, she is running through the crowd shouting "Michel, Michel," cut off from the only real humanity she has encountered since losing her parents. Their secret world together, forbidden or ignored by adults who oversee them, has proven to be as fragile as that larger world. As Roger Ebert wrote, "The film is so powerful because it does not compromise on two things: the horror of war and the innocence of childhood. Fossey's face becomes a mirror that refuses to reflect what she must see and feel." Her impassive look is an accusation; her vulnerability, like Edmund's, indicts the world of war that has so embroiled her.

—◈—

A Search for Hope in the Ruins: *The Search* (1948)
Emanuel Levy

One of the first American films to deal with the Holocaust and its impact, Fred Zinnemann's *The Search* (1948) is an emotionally moving, visually astute tale of a young Auschwitz survivor (Ivan Jandl) desperately searching for his mother in post–World War II Europe.

Jandl, who was discovered while singing with a choir in Prague, won a Special Oscar Award for the "outstanding juvenile performance of 1948," a well-deserved recognition for a heartbreaking rendition of a boy who has lost his entire world—including his identity, name (which he cannot remember), and ability for interpersonal communication.

Jandl was not allowed to attend the Oscar ceremonies, although it is not clear whether it was a result of his parents and/or the authorities' decision; Czechoslovakia was under a strict communist regime. There were hopes that he would become a child star, but, according to my 1982 interview with Zinnemann, who kept in touch with Jandl for several years, he made one or two Czech films before disappearing into anonymity; Jandl died in Prague in 1987, at fifty.

The Search is notable for other reasons. The film established actor Montgomery Clift as a major talent. Having just shot Howard Hawks's epic western *Red River* (1948), opposite John Wayne, Clift became the brightest male star to conquer Hollywood and promote method acting in the film industry, two years before Marlon Brando made a splash with his stunning debut in *The Men*, which was also helmed by Zinnemann. Although *The Search* was Clift's second film, it was theatrically released before *Red River*.

The first film to be made in Europe after World War II with an American director and crew members, *The Search* was partially inspired by *Europe's Children*, the 1943 book of photographs by Therese Bonney that chronicled war orphans. While based on rigorous research of actual footage, the tale is largely fictionalized, written by Richard Schweizer and David Wechsler (Paul Jarrico also contributed to the script), who were Oscar-nominated for Best Writing, Screenplay and Best Writing, Motion Picture Story, the latter of which they won.

Roughly divided into three parts—each lasting a reel or so—the narrative is uneven, reflecting a series of anxieties on the part of the filmmakers and some compromises made in trying to make the admittedly tough and risky movie more accessible to the mass public. As a result, the film gets increasingly more conventional, and the "happy ending" feels contrived and tacked onto what, for the most part, is a realistic, semidocumentary picture.

The tale's first part is the most authentic and touching, depicting trains bringing in homeless children, labeled displaced persons (DP), who are taken by Mrs. Murray (Aline MacMahon) and other United Nations Relief and Rehabilitation Administration (UNRRA) workers to a nearby transit camp. Following procedures, the children are interviewed by UNRRA officials, whose goal is to identify them and reunite them—if possible—with their immediate families or relatives. The children, who speak various languages, are scared, damaged, insecure, and highly suspicious, not knowing what to expect. Some kids perceive the benevolent workers as strict authoritarian figures—not unlike the Nazi officers who had imprisoned and tortured them.

The story soon centers on its protagonist, a nine-year-old traumatized boy named Karel (Jandl). Interrogated about his past, he responds to every question with the same brief and impersonal phrase—"Ich weiß nicht" ("I don't know")— avoiding eye contact with the officers and other children.

Through flashbacks, we learn that Karel grew up in a wealthy and happy Czech family that spent evenings together playing classical music and singing. The Nazis had deported Karel's sister and father, a doctor, while he and his mother were sent to a concentration camp.

As happened with countless other families, mother and son are painfully separated. Karel remembers in a moving flashback watching across a fence the last time he saw his beloved mother, a sight that has left an open wound and has made him fearfully suspicious of any fence, wall, door, or closed space.

After the war, Karel barely survives by scavenging for food with other homeless children. At the main camp, the children are divided into groups and loaded into trucks and ambulances, which transfer them to other camps. The children are terrified, and some try to resist, as they remember how Nazis often used similar ambulances to take away and gas their victims. Moreover, during the journey, the smell of exhaust fumes causes some of the children to panic.

Karel's new friend Raoul manages to open the back door, and the children begin to scatter. Karel and Raoul try to swim across a river to escape from the UNRRA employees. Sadly and ironically, Raoul, who knows how to swim, drowns, and Karel, who doesn't know, survives by hiding in the reeds from the chasing officers. For several days, he lives like a frightened animal in burnt-out houses of the city, foraging for food in trash cans.

The film's second part (and main story) concerns the bond that evolves between Karel and an ultra-kind and sensitive U.S. Army engineer named Ralph Stevenson, known as Steve (Montgomery Clift). Steve finds the almost starved Karel by the road, feeds the reluctant boy, and then forcefully takes him to his home, which he shares with another soldier (Wendell Corey). Hostile, scared, and suspicious, Karel tries to escape until Steve convinces him (by leaving the doors open) of his genuine intention to take care of him. Steve assigns the boy the name Jim, because Karel cannot recall his real name.

When Karel/Jim sees another boy with his mother, he begins to remember his own mother near a fence in the concentration camp. He runs away one evening thinking that the fence is nearby. When he finds a fence at a factory, he looks desperately—and, of course, in vain—for his mom among the workers.

Once again, Steve searches and finds Jim. To lessen his suffering, Steve lies, telling Jim that his mother is dead, hoping that with this knowledge he will stop searching for her and start building a new existence and a new identity. He also promises Jim that he will try to adopt him and take him to the United States to begin a new life there.

Meanwhile, through cross-cutting, the film switches to Karel's mother, Hanna Malik (Jarmila Novotná). It turns out that she is alive, and that she, too, has been searching for her son. By chance—and this is the major contrived element in an otherwise realistic narrative—she begins working for Mrs. Murray at the same UNRRA camp where her son had been processed.

After a while, she decides to leave the camp. At the same time, Steve takes Karel to the UNRRA camp before leaving for the States, hoping to send for him once the bureaucratic paperwork is completed. Mrs. Murray remembers the boy's appearance and, suspecting that Jim is Karel, hurries to the train station to bring Mrs. Malik back just as it pulls out of the station. But she sighs with relief (and disbelief) when she spots Mrs. Malik on the train platform; she had changed her mind and decided to stay.

Taking her back to the UNRRA camp, Mrs. Murray asks Mrs. Malik to greet the newest group of children. Steve tells Jim to join the new arrivals as Mrs. Malik begins to organize them and bids them to follow her. Jim walks past without recognizing her. Mrs. Malik almost makes the same mistake but then turns and calls, "Karel!" The boy and his mother are finally reunited.

Many of the scenes were shot amid the actual ruins of postwar German cities, for example, Ingolstadt, Nuremberg, and Würzburg. The film also used a Zurich studio and UNRRA camps in the U.S.-occupied zone of Germany, thus capturing the terrors of refugees right after World War II. By shooting the picture in bombed-out German cities, Zinnemann achieved a more authentic, semidocumentary look.

The film's quasi-documentary style was enhanced by mixing professional actors with nonprofessionals. Zinnemann always delighted in the fact that many reviewers and moviegoers assumed that Montgomery Clift, who didn't look like a star in this picture, had been a real GI without any previous acting experience.

Zinnemann, whose parents died in the Holocaust, had been working in Hollywood since 1930, directing shorts. But many people assumed that *The Search* was his American debut since it was the first time he had received major recognition. That included an award from the Directors Guild of America, an Oscar nomination, and a citation from the British Film Academy deeming it the "best film embodying the principles of the United Nations Charter."

Zinnemann would maintain his A-list status as a director throughout the 1950s, with such films as the 1952 Gary Cooper western *High Noon* and especially *From Here to Eternity*, which swept most of the 1953 Oscars, including Best Picture, Best Director, and Best Screenplay. The film's five acting nominations included a second Best Actor nod for Montgomery Clift, again playing a sensitive soldier.

—⟋⟍—

Innocent Bystanders: Five Films about Kids Growing Up in an Unforgiving World
Jay Carr

Kids cope, assuming, that is, that they escape death or crippling trauma from war and other savage follies rained down upon them by adults. They live in the moment, they adapt, and they roll with whatever's happening on the ground—even when the ground has been blasted to rubble.

A case in point is John Boorman's *Hope and Glory* (1987), an improbably larky World War II film, in which schoolkids (Boorman was one) turned Blitz-transformed London into playgrounds. England's bravery when they were down but not out has been amply depicted in film. But the country's surprising nostalgia for the ordeal suggests that for some Britons, war wasn't all hell. It was liberating. The release of constraints, the drafting of women to do absent men's jobs, giving them opportunities and authority they never had known, meant many never looked back.

And the kids! Living in dread by night, not knowing where a Luftwaffe bomb might land, their anarchic impulses were given full vent by day. Unsupervised, they gleefully jumped onto bombsites, whacking away with scraps of lumber to complete the destruction while the adults were busy practicing their own more genteel forms of anarchy. Time and again, Boorman finds images to express these kids' versions of the war they lived, where a jackpot consisted of finding an undetonated cartridge, clamping it into a vise, and detonating it by hammering a nail into it while staying clear of the bullet. When he and his mother and older sister watch a newsreel of the war, Bill Rowan (Sebastian Rice-Edwards), the young Boorman stand-in, cries, "It's not the same."

The boy, knowing better, doesn't buy the glamorized myth about the war depicted on movie screens, with their seductive patriotism and the stirring music

of Elgar on the soundtrack. The subversive message in *Hope and Glory* is unmis-
takable. War can not only bring unexpected fun, but also be a mass prison break.
This beguiling family scrapbook radiantly and lovingly turns the war into the
kind of myth that movies of the time never would have. Yes, it's scary when the
bombs are dropping, especially if you didn't live anywhere near one of London's
Underground stations, where many would huddle throughout the night. But
after each bombing, something wonderful rushes in and changes the world forever, especially for women and children, and not just the deepening sense of a
"we're-all-in-this-together" community. Wise, funny, humane, and life-affirming
despite the flames, *Hope and Glory* is personal myth-making, as opposed to the
official factory-made myths produced on demand by the movies of the time. It
brings together, and then releases, the right kinds of energies.

Belgium's Dardenne brothers—Luc and Jean-Pierre—are the most spiritual and
compassionate of filmmakers. In film after film, they plunge to the bottom of
Europe's socioeconomic ladder, not to find victims or advance a political agenda,
but to assert that these people have value and deserve dignity. In *Rosetta* (1999),
Émilie Dequenne, in the title role of a beleaguered seventeen-year-old, is as
proud as she is fierce. When she's fired from her factory job, she locks herself in a
bathroom and refuses to leave until she's rehired. It doesn't work. Only a job will
break her out of the dilapidated trailer park where she lives with her alcoholic
mother. She won't take charity or handouts. Her life is a day-to-day struggle to
survive. If she had a job, she could climb the first rung on the ladder to stability.

Except that it's not that simple. Without many spoken lines, Dequenne plays
Rosetta mostly with the stubborn set of her jaw. Her cravings for stability take
the tiniest, almost pathetic forms: little rituals. Each day she enters the trailer
park through the same hole in a chain-link fence. To navigate its muddy ground,
she keeps a pair of rubber boots stored in the same hollow log. What elevates
Rosetta into the extraordinary film it is, apart from its determination to give voice
to the disenfranchised without ever patronizing or sentimentalizing them, is that
part of Rosetta's energies involves keeping her goodness intact in a world that
makes war upon it every day. Rosetta doesn't just want to survive. She insists on
doing it with a good conscience.

Rosetta is more than intimate; it's claustrophobic by design because Rosetta's
world is. Life always seems about to close in on her, much like the boy she hopes
will lead her to a job but instead buzzes around her on his motorbike, trying to
get something going with her. The bleakness and inhospitableness of Rosetta's
world is not for all viewers, but to present her in any other context would be
dishonest, and the Dardennes are about nothing but integrity. This also means no

happy endings. But neither does *Rosetta* end tragically. We're left feeling that in a capitalist society where poverty is all but a crime, there's a wisp of a chance that Rosetta and her idealistic warrior's nature might beat the odds and drag herself and her mother up to that first rung.

When nothing but horror swamps a child's world, he or she retreats inside, searching for a bearable reality. This idea, applied to the aftermath of the bloody Spanish Civil War, animates Víctor Erice's *The Spirit of the Beehive* (1973) in biting, dreamlike ways, with drenching colors and a claustrophobic feeling despite the film being shot on the broad Castilian plain.

At its center is six-year-old Ana (Ana Torrent), although part of the film's point is that its world has no center. Ana's family—her mother, an older sister, and a much older father who keeps bees—is never seen together. They are a fractured family in a fractured country. The year is 1940, and Francisco Franco's army is mopping up the last of the defeated Republican army. The link between these events is Frankenstein's monster, shown by a traveling cinema.

Ana, afraid of so much, feels a kinship to the screen monster who only wanted a friend, even though he inadvertently drowned the little girl who befriended him. When a fleeing Republican soldier hides on the family's property, Ana, driven by her attraction to the monster, helps him—with dire results that send Ana to a poison mushroom she may or may not eat.

The film was made two years before Franco's death, and his stranglehold on Spain had begun to loosen, but his censors were still on the job, and Erice loaded the film with symbolism no Spaniard (except literal-minded censors) could fail to note. Grave little Ana—she only smiles once—is unforgettable as she negotiates the little girl's escapist fantasy and the harsh consequences that arise from it. But by the end there's a hint of a promise that the family and the nation may once again reunite and breathe freely. Meanwhile, Torrent, who carries the film, delivers one of cinema's most mesmerizing performances by a child.

From the bleaker reaches of Kazakhstan comes Gulshat Omarova's assured and refreshing *Schizo* (2004). Far from being the cut-rate horror schlockfest it conjures up, it's that rarest of cinematic wonders—a film that keeps surprising you, driven by a young hero like none you've ever seen.

Discovered by Omarova in an orphanage to which he was returned after the shoot, Oldzhas Nusupbayev was, like most of the actors, a nonprofessional. His Mustafa, nicknamed "Shiza," or "Schizo" at school, is a fifteen-year-old who doesn't say much and wants to live the flashy life of his mother's live-in boyfriend, a mob gofer. But while he's not destined for the academic life, he's smart and observant. Although slow at some things, he's quick with others. Like a darting sardine, he's small and agile enough to swim with sharks.

There are plenty of the latter in his corner of the world. Close-ups of hands changing money, holding guns, hammering away at one another in illegal rigged boxing matches run by the local mafia are contrasted with panoramic long shots of inertia and decay—groups of idle unemployed men, buildings half-begun or abandoned, buildings crumbling and corroding into ruin. Desperation pushes the unemployed into bare-knuckle bouts for small purses, while the gangsters make their money from the betting. Schizo, given employment by his mother's boyfriend, likes the money he makes from recruiting suckers into stepping into the ring against the trained fighters in no-holds-barred contests. But when he's given a pittance to pass along to Zinka (Olga Landina), the widow of a fighter killed in the ring, something in him changes.

He bonds with the woman and her small boy, and feels in some way responsible for them. A stickup attempt, designed to get them money, backfires. So he comes up with plan B—in the form of a tough alcoholic uncle he persuades to fight the hitherto unbeaten mob juggernaut.

We are not talking *Fight Club* (1999) here. Not since Charles Bronson punched his way through the Depression in Walter Hill's *Hard Times* (1975) have we seen a bare-knuckle slugfest in which more was at stake. When *Schizo* snaps out of its soul-destroying lassitude and explodes, it does so in a big way, as the boy stumbles toward adulthood and regenerates the new nuclear family for which he had been searching, even though he, Zinka, and her small son are more like three orphans than two parents and a child. Your heart rises as you fear for where their naiveté might lead them. But it at least has given them a leg up on this small-scale but high-stakes journey.

Vittorio De Sica's *Bicycle Thieves* (1948) wasn't Italian neorealism's first masterpiece, nor its last. But its deceptively simple story of an impoverished Roman worker desperately scrambling to recover the stolen bicycle he needs to support his family, with his young son scurrying alongside in the frantic search, is the quintessential expression of its time and place, simultaneously poetic and pragmatic. Neorealism, shot in the streets using available light, cast mostly with nonprofessional actors, was Italian film struggling back to life. De Sica had one truck, one taxi, and one director's chair when he made *Bicycle Thieves*.

Why the plural? Betraying a lack of understanding, the U.S. release was titled *The Bicycle Thief*, as if the theft was an isolated incident. But the film resonates beyond one workman's plight. Nonetheless, for Antonio, the bike rescued from a pawnshop in exchange for the family's linens is essential to his job pasting posters of Rita Hayworth on Rome's walls. It's about the poor stealing from one another in a dog-eat-dog world and the brutalizing effects of poverty. Neither of the institutions vying for power—the Church and the Communist Party—offers a free lunch. Their charity means they corral you. The film, unfolding in a way that seems happenstance, was meticulously planned, its backdrop the impassive faces of ordinary Romans.

Because he liked the pearly light of dawn, De Sica did a lot of shooting at that time. Some of the esthetic strokes are breathtaking—the play of shadows against buildings, the flow of ladder-bearing workers on bikes suggesting schools of fish, parting to glide past bulkier buses, then closing ranks again.

Antonio was embodied by Lamberto Maggiorani, a real factory worker. But eight-year-old Enzo Staiola as his son Bruno is the film's soul. His melancholy clown's face says more than his few words do. But then no one says much in *Bicycle Thieves*. They don't have to. For all its picaresque motion, it's a quiet film, never more so than in the small moments between father and son. Bruno devotedly polishes his dad's bike, struggles to keep up with his father's hurtling through streets and plazas, then grows up a lot after his father decides he can only save his family from ruin by stealing a bike himself.

Bicycle Thieves is a sad film, with no cheap consolations. To see it now is to realize how much deeper it cuts than the political and ideological agendas of the day that some wanted to foist upon it. Just as the father realizes he's diminished his humanity and dignity by stealing the bike, his son almost switches father–son roles, clasping his father's hand, lovingly pulling him from harsh self-judgment back into the human race. Quiet as it is, the moment is one of film's great endings.

—⁓—

Politics Makes for Poor Parenting in *A World Apart* (1988)
Peter Rainer

The setting of *A World Apart* (1988) is a South Africa inflamed by apartheid, but coiled inside the film's epic consciousness is a powerfully intimate story. It's about thirteen-year-old Molly (Jodhi May), whose parents, Gus and Diana Roth (Jeroen Krabbé and Barbara Hershey), are antiapartheid crusaders. Directed by Chris Menges (it's the world-class cinematographer's first feature) and written by Shawn Slovo, the movie is based on her experiences growing up as the daughter of African National Congress (ANC) activists in South Africa. It describes the horrors of apartheid, but it's also about the horrors exacted on the children of those who devote their lives to its destruction.

Menges and Slovo are such intelligent, sympathetic artists that this dramatic approach comes across as anything but reactionary. They recognize the gravity in Molly Roth's story. They acknowledge that even saints and martyrs owe their loved ones love.

Unlike, say, *Cry Freedom* (1987), where Richard Attenborough laid out the awfulness of apartheid for us as if it were his own personal revelation, *A World Apart*, set in 1963, assumes an audience sophisticated enough to have outlived the first blush of outrage. The film's cycle of surveillance, detention, and torture has a nauseating familiarity, and because the racism is still entrenched, the distancing of twenty-five years only compounds the sorrow.

Molly's father flees South Africa to go into hiding at the start of the film, leaving her and her two younger sisters in the care of her mother and grandmother. Molly's woes with her mother are not presented as a child's rant against the ungratefulness of her parents (the usual Hollywood approach). She's highly intelligent and not unaware of what brave and necessary risks her mother is taking. But she also senses that her mother is only fully alive when she is challenging her country's injustices.

Diana Roth is willfully blind to the injustices in her own home. She's an admirable woman but not a likable one, and her masklike rectitude covers a complex of evasions. When she's jailed without a trial under the infamous ninety-day detention act, her interrogator (David Suchet) rasps that her heroism is "nothing but an excuse for being a terrible mother," and the accusation hits home. A look of misery crosses her face: She's denatured by her righteousness.

Except for Diana's scenes in prison, and a few others, the movie is told entirely from Molly's point of view. This may account for a certain remoteness in the way we view Diana. We can't quite get a fix on her, or her politics. She's apparently a communist, but what that means in terms of the antiapartheid movement is glossed over. (Slovo's father, Joe Slovo, is a communist and the only white member of the ANC; her mother, Ruth First, was killed by a letter bomb in London, where she was exiled with her children in 1982.)

A fuller characterization might have enabled us to see Diana in ways her daughter couldn't—as, politically, something less than a saint—but it also would have politicized the story to no real purpose. Molly's story is, rightfully, the heart of this movie. Besides, *A World Apart* is informed with a retrospective sense of outrage. Shawn Slovo must be aware of what her mother, and women like her mother, were attempting to do in South Africa. Yet, she's still trying to come to terms with her mother's legacy. She's still trying to forgive. The movie has its wish-fulfillment side. Molly's demand for love matches her mother's righteousness, and it's the toughness of that demand that finally brings them together. Diana recognizes in her daughter a kindred spirit.

The entire movie is a prelude to Molly's final plea: "What about *me*?" (It's a plea worthy of Frankie in Carson McCullers's 1946 novel *The Member of the Wedding*.) The unfolding of events is crisp and lyrical but also a little nightmarish. It's not just that Diana finds herself increasingly entrapped; it's that Molly can find no way to share in her mother's entrapment—which would at least make her feel wanted.

When Molly and her little sisters and grandmother are finally allowed to visit Diana in prison, they discover she's been transferred to another cell in Pretoria. And when they visit her there weeks later, Diana tells Molly not to cry in front of the guards. Despite Diana's radicalism, her sense of decorum has a bizarre, upper-crusty British propriety. She doesn't want her daughter to show fear and weakness in front of her captors—or in private.

When Menges and Slovo attempt to show how communal and spiritual the lives of the black South Africans are, in contrast to Molly's alienation, the film falters. The Roth's housekeeper, Elsie (Linda Mvusi), teaches Molly liberation anthems; she brings her along to visit her extended family in a squalid township. Elsie's firebrand cousin, Solomon (Albee Lesotho), recently released from prison, is all smiles with Molly; he gives her a symbolic, multicolored ribbon as a keepsake of the struggle.

Wherever Molly goes, the black South Africans treat her with bemused dignity; they remind her that she is the daughter of a great woman. This is a world where the most oppressed are, spiritually, the least benighted, and it's a bit too much of a fantasyland. It doesn't jibe with the stringent, antisentimental tone of Molly's story. If the filmmakers had shown at least one black who resented what Diana was trying to do—who, perhaps, viewed her crusade as a form of communistic self-aggrandizement—the movie might have forged a powerful link between Molly's anger and historical circumstance. She might not have seemed so alone in her mounting, half-admitted rage. (As it is, her only alliance in rage is with her mother's captors.)

Molly's aloneness is, of course, the film's guiding light, but her solitude does seem a bit rigged. There's an and-then-there-were-none quality to the scenario: We know her best friend (Nadine Chalmers) will reject her, just as we know that Solomon will fall, and so on.

Some of the anticipated scenes are still amazing. Elsie's wailing at Solomon's fate is unspeakably tragic. This woman, with her great capacity for joy, is perhaps the most intuitive character in the movie; she has the empathy for Molly that Diana lacks, and that empathy seems to exist effortlessly, and for all things. When she breaks down, it's as if the world had suddenly gone mad. Inconsolable, she staggers away from solace.

Menges worked as a documentary filmmaker in South Africa in the early 1960s, and this may explain why he's able to create sequences like this with the immediacy and flush of real life. It's unusual for a cinematographer-turned-director to make a movie that looks this good and yet is still so resonant and psychologically rich.

It's also rare to see a movie by a "visual" director with such fine performances. Barbara Hershey doesn't make a false play for sympathy; she shows us Diana's rectitude in all its flinty unpleasantness. Jodhi May, who never before acted professionally, draws you into her helplessness and rage. By the end, her plain-Jane looks have turned soulful. Linda Mvusi fills out her scenes with a richness out of all proportion to their brief time on-screen. (All three women shared the Best Actress prize at the 1988 Cannes Film Festival.)

If *A World Apart* doesn't seem like any other movie, that could be not only because Menges, himself a father, and Slovo are working out of their own experience, but also because the film gets into areas we usually associate with writers like Nadine Gordimer, Vincent Crapanzano, and Breyten Breytenbach—writers who show us how whites, too, are devastated by apartheid.

The filmmakers try for an upbeat rallying cry at the end, but the tragedy of the story is that the Roths are destroyed even as they triumph. Their moral consciousness is not enough to redeem their lives, just their struggle.

Iran's Child-Centered Films
Godfrey Cheshire[1]

Halfway through *The Mirror*, a 1997 Iranian film by Jafar Panahi, the audience finds itself at a startling juncture. We have been following a little girl named Mina, whose arm is in a cast and who wears a backpack, as well as the head scarf that women and girls must wear in Iran, as she makes her way across Tehran. The first-grader's problem is that her mom didn't arrive to pick her up after school, as usually happens, so she elected to find her own way home.

Thus began a journey that however slight the dramatic premise may sound is fascinating to follow, alternately hilarious, suspenseful, and rich in offhanded observational insights. Mina first hitches a ride with a motorcyclist who's a friend of her teacher. Soon, she tries other modes of transport. The streets are awash with grown-ups, some who notice her and try to help, others who remain preoccupied with their own dramas. Mina, however, boards a crowded bus (males in the front, females in the rear) and seems determined to reach her destination, until the startling moment when she announces that she's had it: She's fed up with filming.

Mina Mohammad-Khani, the little girl playing Mina the fictional little girl, is staging her own work stoppage. She's sick of making the movie, she declares, and rather than shooting another scene, she's going home—her real home. She rips off the fake cast and her costume, and bounds off the bus. As we watch through what seems the lens of a documentary camera observing the shooting of *The Mirror*, director Panahi and his crew look on, flummoxed, as their young actress spurns their pleas to continue, then dashes off into traffic. The rest of the movie—a delightful, transparent conceit—depicts the supposed documentary camera's pell-mell pursuit of the "real" Mina as she zigzags across Tehran.

This scene, the pivotal moment in a film that invites us to see cinema as an Alice-in-Wonderland looking glass, could alone serve as a crash course in certain acclaimed Iranian movies of recent decades, since it contains several of their hallmarks. It takes filmmaking itself as one of its subjects. It purposefully, wittily blurs the line between fiction and documentary. It features captivatingly natural performances by nonactors. It's as much allegorical as conventionally dramatic. Above all, it centers on a child.

Iranian films, which are known for a distinctive combination of simplicity and sophistication, narrative directness and poetic allusiveness, don't all concern children on idiosyncratic quests. But the motif is so prevalent that it has become something of a trademark, and it informs a number of the films that put Iranian cinema on the map for filmgoers in the United States and other countries beginning in the 1990s.

For Americans and other non-Iranians both young and old, these movies can still be a revelation—and an education. When this critic began studying Iranian movies in 1991, he had a view of that distant country that was perhaps typical of people whose knowledge came largely from superficial media images. In 1979, Iran had a revolution that brought to power a theocracy that viewed the United States as the "Great Satan" and sanctioned the holding of American hostages for 444 days. "America Held Hostage" shouted the TV news coverage during that time, and for a long time thereafter typical news images coming from Iran showed angry demonstrators burning American flags and Uncle Sam effigies.

Such images created a widely shared impression of Iranians as simple-minded fanatics burning with venomous anti-American zeal. (Prior to the rise of ISIS, aka the Islamic State, in mid-2014, polls showed that Americans viewed Iran as their greatest enemy.) The very different reality behind that misleading, media-generated impression is indicated by polls in Iran that show its populace (as opposed to the regime that governs them) as the most pro-American in the Middle East, and indeed more so than most European countries. It's also indicated by the beauty and accomplishment of Iran's most distinguished movies, which, drawing on a 3,000-year-old cosmopolitan culture, have won top prizes at virtually every international film festival in the world.

Iranian films concerning children are at the center of that achievement, and it should be noted for prospective viewers that the kind of films discussed here fall into two groups. Some, like *The Mirror*, are best suited for older adolescents and adults. Others, however, are suitable for some children and younger adolescents. (Most are available on DVD in subtitled form; to this writer's knowledge, none are offered in English-dubbed versions.)

One film in the latter category brings to mind a day that I've often called my most memorable experience in a movie theater, ever. In the spring of 2000, the late critic Roger Ebert invited me to participate in a screening of the 1997 Iranian film *Children of Heaven* at an event he had founded in Champaign, Illinois, called the Overlooked Film Festival (later renamed Ebertfest). Ebert not only wanted to screen the film, which he thought had received less attention than it deserved, but also proposed showing it to an audience ranging in age from seven to fourteen.

Before the show began in the packed 1,500-seat Virginia Theater, Ebert explained to the expectant viewers that they would need to read some subtitles (the film is relatively light in dialogue) and that, if need be, older kids should share what they read with the younger ones. No doubt this was the first foreign film most of these kids had ever seen, and an Iranian film at that. Would they sit still for it or bolt the theater in boredom? I couldn't help but wonder—and worry.

I needn't have, because from the first moments onward, the audience was enraptured. Written and directed by Majid Majidi, *Children of Heaven* (1997) tells a simple, affecting story that's mainly seen from the point of view of two grade-school kids, a boy named Ali and his younger sister, Zahra. In the film's opening screen, the girl's just-repaired pink shoes are lost, and since the siblings know their parents are too poor to buy new ones, they devise a ruse whereby Zahra will wear Ali's sneakers to school in the morning, then return them in time for him to wear them to afternoon classes. The scheme works for a while, but when they are found out, Ali has to come up with another way to help the family.

One reason the movie works so well with young audiences, even American kids, is that its storytelling is primarily visual and emotionally immediate: One sibling's look at another as they try to hide something from their parents speaks the universal language of childhood. But there's also the fact that the love between brother and sister, and within the family, is so palpable. As Ebert said in his review of the film, it "glows with a kind of good-hearted purity." Beyond that, it climaxes with a viscerally exciting foot race that offers Ali the chance to win a new pair of shoes. In the final moments of the story, the young audience in the Virginia was completely engrossed, cheering and clapping.

This remains the most spectacular instance I've seen of cinema's power to overcome cultural barriers and preconceptions. These young viewers were not only transported inside a nation that the U.S. media rarely presents up close and thoughtfully, but also they got a strong taste of the profound humanism—a concern for kids, families, and the poor—that, as a core value of Iranian cinema, makes it so surprising to American viewers when they first encounter it. When the lights came up, the kids were obviously excited and amazed by what they had seen, and Ebert invited anyone with questions to come up on stage and discuss the film with him, his wife Chaz, and myself. More than twenty young viewers took the invitation, and their questions were smart, perceptive, and engaged. When one girl asked why the film's final shot showed Ali's blistered feet in a pool surrounded by goldfish, Chaz offered, "Someone said to me, it's like God is kissing the boy's feet through the goldfish"—a remark that aptly summarizes both this film's aura of spiritual generosity and the impact it had on an unsuspecting group of Illinois grade-schoolers.

Children of Heaven was the first Iranian film nominated for the Oscar for Best Foreign Language Film (a prize eventually won by Asghar Farhadi's *A Separation* in 2012). Two years prior to its arrival, Iranian cinema saw the launch of its first international art house hit when *The White Balloon* by Jafar Panahi, whose sophomore effort would be *The Mirror*, won the Camera d'Or prize (for best first feature) at the Cannes Film Festival. In some ways, the two films still stand as the best examples of the child-centered films that helped bring global attention to Iranian cinema in the 1990s.

Scripted by the late Abbas Kiarostami, Iran's most celebrated filmmaker, *The White Balloon* also involves a child, goldfish, and a quest. It's the afternoon of New Year's (a major holiday that, in Iran, takes place at the spring equinox), and seven-year-old Razieh (played by Aida Mohammad-Khani, the older sister of *The Mirror's* Mina) is determined to buy a goldfish for the Persian rituals that are part of the holiday. Although her harried mother objects that they already have a pool full of the fish, she surrenders to Razieh's nagging persistence and gives her a large bill that she can use to obtain her objective. Thus begins a desultory journey that's as charmingly engrossing as it is, often, drolly hilarious.

Told in real time, the eighty-five-minute tale first follows Razieh to an outdoor market, where she stops to watch the show of a snake-charmer and soon finds her money in the reptile's mouth. Once that difficulty is overcome, she resumes an odyssey that entails one obstacle after another, as well as encounters with distracted merchants, a concerned matron, an off-duty soldier, and a young balloon seller. While these interactions have elements of drama and comedy, the film in some ways exerts the appeal of a closely observed documentary, showing us the lives of an array of Iranians in a complex urban environment. And all these impressions are filtered through the perceptions of a little girl who is literally at the mercy of the city and the adults who control its operations.

Mercy, in fact, is key to the film's mood and resonance. Like other Iranian filmmakers, Panahi and Kiarostami here aren't just telling a story. They're creating a sensory/dramatic world in which aesthetic and ethical concerns intertwine. In both, ideas of balance and wholeness dominate, warding off their opposites. In the aesthetic realm, the film evokes the poetry of the everyday, the quotidian, even as Panahi's lyrical camera style and Kiarostami's narrative both seem designed to trace arcs that will ultimately lead Razieh, whether or not she achieves her objective, back to point zero: home.

The ethical dimension may be more important still. The remarkable humanism of postrevolutionary Iranian films is founded on an ideal of compassion: of caring for other people, even (or especially) those who can't adequately care for themselves. In *Children of Heaven*, young Ali goes to great lengths to care for both his little sister and his impoverished, beleaguered father. In *The White Balloon*, while some adults appear oblivious to little Razieh and her concerns, her safety and eventual return home are guaranteed by countless small acts of kindness and help—as if the whole of Iranian (or human?) society operates on an unspoken compact of mutual compassion and assistance. In the film's final moments, Panahi and Kiarostami shift attention away from Razieh and her goldfish onto another, minor character, wittily making the point that even the peripheral people in our worlds (real or cinematic) deserve our attention and concern.

While the compassionate regard of many post-1979 Iranian films reflects deliberate content initiatives undertaken by the cultural authorities of the Islamic Republic, it deserves noting that Iran's cinematic focus on children dates back further. In 1969, under the last shah's regime, a government organization known as the Center for the Intellectual Development of Children and Young Adults—called Kanoon by Iranians—created a filmmaking division and put Abbas Kiarostami, then a young artist and aspiring filmmaker, in charge. Kiarostami used the post in a way that not only addressed children as subjects, but also allowed him and various filmmaker friends to make novel, sometimes experimental films away from both commercial and ideological pressures. The result was a notable set of shorts and a few features that were, as Kiarostami put it in an interview with me, "films about, but not always for, children"—a distinction that would continue after the Iranian Revolution.

Kiarostami's own first feature, *The Traveler* (1974; available in the United States as part of the Criterion Collection DVD of the 1990 Kiarostami masterpiece *Close-Up*), a strikingly accomplished work, belongs among those films that are about but not aimed at children. It concerns a boy in a provincial town so determined to see a soccer match in Tehran that he cons friends and acquaintances into giving him money (his karmic punishment is that he reaches Tehran but falls asleep and misses the match). Filmed in stark black and white, and suffused with the caustic mood of many Iranian films of the 1970s, the film offered the effective opposite of the compassionate vision that would come after the Revolution; its hero is a heel who simply exploits the kindness of others. Yet, the movie also established the narrative paradigm of a child's quest.

After the Ayatollah Khomeini gave his blessing to the continuation of cinema following the Iranian Revolution, a group of young intellectuals in the government set about rebuilding the country's film infrastructure and aiding movies they saw as conveying the new regime's Islamic values. Perhaps surprisingly, explicitly religious themes were avoided in favor of a kind of generalized humanistic concern. Meanwhile, Kanoon was allowed to continue, and a number of filmmakers realized that making films centered on children was a way of skirting the many new content restrictions the Islamic Republic had placed on films representing adults. Out of this situation in the late 1980s came several notable child-centered films, including three masterpieces that laid the groundwork for the international breakthroughs of the following decade.

Amir Naderi's autobiographical *The Runner* (1985) set the pattern for many future films by focusing on the hardships endured by a poor boy scavenging for a living in a war-torn coastal city. Yet, as in the Italian neorealist and French new wave films that inspired many Iranian directors, its sincere social concern was balanced by the intense and exhilarating lyricism of Naderi's bravura visual approach (including color film, which became standard in the postrevolutionary period). *Where Is the Friend's House?* (1987), Kiarostami's first post-1979 feature, brought a poetic sensitivity and an anticipation of *The White Balloon*'s concern with adult–child interactions to the tale of a little boy trying to find a pal's residence to exchange notebooks they accidentally swapped at school. And Bahram Beyzai's *Bashu, the Little Stranger* (1989), about a dark-skinned boy who has trouble fitting in with the residents of a small village after a farm wife grudgingly gives him shelter during the Iran–Iraq War, tackled both the hardships of war and the pressures of prejudice and poverty in rural areas; the film's lead performances are considered among the best in Iranian cinema.

By the 1990s, such films as *The White Balloon*, *Children of Heaven*, and *The Mirror*, while winning accolades worldwide and bringing Iranian movies into the West's art houses, were also just the tip of a larger phenomenon. Child-centered films had become a staple in Iran's commercial movie and TV industries too, popular with all classes and with enough international reach that Japan, for example, imported them regularly.

Meanwhile, in Iran's artistic cinema, the genre also spanned filmmaking generations. One of the most lauded of late 1990s films, *The Apple* (1998), a fascinating semidocumentary about two young sisters kept captive in their parents' house from birth until being discovered by social workers, was made by Samira Makhmalbaf, the daughter of celebrated director Mohsen Makhmalbaf. Samira was seventeen when she directed the film, and Iranians smiled at a rumor that she made it partly out of a sense of competition with her younger sister, who'd already made a film. When her short *The Day My Aunt Was Ill* premiered at Switzerland's prestigious Locarno Film Festival in 1997, Hana Makhmalbaf was all of eight years old—an Iranian child, like the heroine of *The Mirror*, evidently determined not to let the cinematic agenda be set only by adults.

Thomasin Harcourt McKenzie in *Leave No Trace*

7

ORDINARY HEROES

All kids (and critics too) watch movies for three reasons: a hero to root for; a villain to hate; and that tricky in-between character, someone who could turn out to be either bad or good, or a little of both, or hasn't quite figured it out, or doesn't really know who he or she is—or even whether they are a he *or* a she. That's the kind of hero that most people are, especially when you're just growing up.

This is the case for a trio of thirteen-year-old girls in 1982 Stockholm who rock out in Lukas Moodysson's *We Are the Best!* (2013). They are as rough around the edges as the punk music they play in the ad hoc band of the title, but they don't take any guff from the heavy metal guys, who tell them punk is dead and girls can't do rock and roll anyway. Their defiant, if musically challenged, ensemble doesn't solve all the problems posed by adolescence, but it teaches them self-assertion, solidarity, and even the value of tolerance. The film inspires not only kids, but also adults. Sheila Benson, in her review, recommends it to "anyone in despair about "kids these days." Moodysson leaves no doubt that they'll get to the other side of thirteen, safely and together."

If the punk rockers in *We Are the Best!* ever get discouraged, they can look to the aging hoofer played by Fred Astaire in Vincente Minnelli's *The Band Wagon* (1953) for inspiration. He seems washed up at the beginning of the film when he arrives in New York to jump-start his career. Although demoralized, he doesn't give up. In her essay "Dancing 'By Myself' in *The Band Wagon* (1953)," Stephanie Zacharek explains what keeps him going. "Because this is Fred Astaire he has the tools to turn strange and unwelcome feelings of personal inadequacy and insecurity into the song-and-dance number 'By Myself.'" She describes it as "one of the finest musical numbers about loneliness ever produced. It treats loneliness as a portal to a world of possibilities, reachable only when you step—or dance— toward the future."

Will kids relate to the fifty-four-year-old star of a film six decades old? "If childhood is a dry run for the long stretch of road we call adulthood," Zacharek writes, "then some loneliness . . . is unavoidable." They should find inspiration in this "modestly scaled anthem of self-determination, a bit of alchemy that spins gold from self-pity." And if they don't, then there is also the wacky novelty number "Triplets." "Kids find it funny," Zacharek writes, "because why wouldn't they?"

Astaire had the advantage of his gender; even three decades after the challenges faced in *We Are the Best!* teenage girls still resist the identity society imposes on them. In "Growing Up Female in *Lady Bird* (2017), *The Fits* (2015), and *Leave No Trace* (2018)," Robert Horton singles out three films—each directed by women—that portray that conflict with humor, pathos, and utter authenticity. "It took decades," he writes, "but with the surge of women entering the directing profession, the mid-2010s proved to be a golden age for female takes on the transition from innocence to experience. . . . Here are three of the most distinctive examples, each in an utterly different key."

Being true to oneself or even figuring out who that self might be poses more of a challenge if adult authorities try to change one's sexuality. Horton praises *The Miseducation of Cameron Post* (2018), which is about adolescents subjected to religious gay-conversion therapy, for its "quietly complete takedown of an ignorant practice." One of the techniques of the practice is for the subjects to write down all the bad things that made them gay. Horton relates this to his own experience as a young Catholic when he had to "come up with two or three credible transgressions I could offer up in the confessional every week to sound believably sinful."

No conversion therapy is offered to the seven-year-old Belgian boy Ludovic in Alain Berliner's *Ma Vie en Rose* (1997), and if people don't accept his identification as a girl, that's their problem. As Nathan Lee points out in "Boys Will Be Girls in *Ma Vie en Rose* (1997)," the film celebrates the joy of self-realization. "Ludo is blissfully unburdened by any sense of impropriety," he writes. "Dressing up, playing with dolls, imagining the day when s/he will marry the boy next door; all of this is a met with delight and the excitement of discovering how *fun* it is to become who you are."

Like Ludovic, the title twelve-year-old in Philippine director Auraeus Solito's *The Blossoming of Maximo Oliveros* (2005) has embraced his nontraditional sexual identity without a second thought. In the Manila slum of Sampaloc, the unabashedly gay Maxi stands out like an exotically beautiful flower. Such a fragile specimen, one assumes, cannot survive such a brutal, macho environment.

Nonetheless, he thrives, and his family and community love him. "For viewers living in the privileged cultures of the West," writes Godfrey Cheshire, "[this] reality offers a useful challenge to the unthinking assumption that tolerance is more natural to 'us' than to 'them,' and to rich rather than to poor. And when it comes to sexual assumptions, [it] proves even more illuminating and thought-provoking."

The Native American youths in Chloé Zhao's *The Rider* (2017) are pretty macho; they don't play with dolls, they ride horses. Their problem is not with gender, but with human frailty and mortality; as rodeo riders, their careers, and lives, are just one disastrous fall away. Young Brady has already suffered a brain injury that might kill him if he falls again, but he sees no other choice than to persevere. "He's achieved celebrity on the rodeo circuit," I write in my review. "It's part of his identity, the basis of his self-esteem. As he points out, a horse is put down when it's so damaged it can no longer run or jump or do the things that horses do. 'But I'm a person,' he says, 'and I've got to live.'"

—⁓—

Punk Heroines in *We Are the Best!* (2013)
Sheila Benson

The rowdy, insightful *We Are the Best!* (2013) brings back with a rush the loneliness that comes from holding passionate, contrary opinions in high school, especially if you're a thirteen-year old girl championing punk music in docile, middle-class Stockholm in 1982, a city oozing self-satisfaction.

Fortunately, Bobo (Mira Barkhammar) is not alone. She has Klara (Mira Grosin), also thirteen, her best friend and counterbalance. Where Bobo hangs back, Klara rushes pell-mell; where Bobo is cautious, Klara is dogmatic. But where it counts, Klara is equally punk, with her mini-Mohawk and her nervy confidence in her convictions. *Their* convictions.

The film's director, Lukas Moodysson, has a history of works with uncommon generosity, toward young women (the heartbreaking 2002 film *Lilya 4-Ever*) and those outside the mainstream (*Together* from 2000). He adapted *We Are the Best!* from his wife Coco's 2008 autobiographical graphic novel *Never Goodnight*. Just for fun, Google it—it won't take more than two clicks—and there is Coco at Bobo's age, all earnest intensity, in her John Lennon glasses and fiercely back-combed hair. It's little wonder *We Are the Best!* moves through the entire landscape of adolescent friendship—staunchness, jealousy, longing, loneliness, bruised feelings, envy, and steadfastness—so knowledgably.

When Bobo and Klara's classmates sneeringly declare that punk is dead and that heavy metal rules, Klara's response is immediate: She and Bobo are forming a punk band. That neither one of them plays so much as the triangle is immaterial. Commandeering a rehearsal room at the youth center, they set about to drown out Iron Fist, the center's posturing boy-band. Klara, of course, claims the bass, leaving Bobo grumpily to the drums, and while nothing they create in that first joyful mess could ever be confused with music, the very act is heady. Still, the band could sound . . . fuller.

At the school talent show (wickedly hilarious), they spot tall, quiet Hedvig (Liv LeMoyne), a classical guitarist. To Klara, recruiting Hedvig—as piously religious as Klara and Bobo are determinedly rebellious—into the band isn't self-serving. It's a "political act" to befriend another outcast, even an unsmiling Christian like Hedvig. Bobo sees it as an act of punk—"We can get her to think more clearly—like us."

Warily, surprisingly, Hedvig becomes the band's linchpin. She introduces them to a few fundamentals: chords, keys, rhythm. Together they shape the band's anti-gym-class anthem: "Hate the sport! Hate the sport! People everywhere die and scream. All you care about is your soccer team!"

The giddiness of this new shared friendship carries them right up to—and past—Klara's peak of inspiration: chopping off Hedvig's long blond hair (on camera and for real), inadvertently creating a stunning punk icon. The fallout from *that* bit of impetuousness underlines director Moodysson's evenhandedness. Hedvig's mother could, as she points out to both quaking girls, have them arrested for their rashness. What she offers instead isn't simply Christian, it's one of the film's gentle deadpan highlights.

The other adults in *We Are the Best!* are a mixed bag, well-meaning but muddled and appalling to their offspring—and possibly to us. Bobo has the job of seeing her single mother Lena through the collapse of yet another love affair; "It's important to eat," she coaxes her mother, "or you'll be weary, tired, and sick." No wonder Bobo is silently on the sidelines of her mother's birthday party, watching as the current boyfriend toasts, "To Lena! Forty years old and still horny as a teenager."

Klara's family of five looks great to Bobo, even as she amusedly watches them wrangle over the change in men's and women's roles (it *is* the early '80s). But both girls draw the line at having Klara's well-meaning, clarinet-playing father extend family togetherness by tootling through their band meetings.

Too much family, too little Life!

It is the band—now defiantly called *We Are the Best!* after a savagely ironic song about Sweden's smothering Motherland—that steadies both girls through low spots, bad patches, even romantic betrayal. And it's Klara and (especially) Bobo who are absolutely essential to anyone in despair about "kids these days." Moodysson leaves no doubt that they'll get to the other side of thirteen, safely and together.

—∽∾∽—

Dancing "By Myself" in *The Band Wagon* (1953)
Stephanie Zacharek

Adults don't like to think about the loneliness of children. Whether we consider our own childhood happy or otherwise, to think of a child *today* feeling lost and alone in the world is simply too sad to bear. But if childhood is a dry run for the long stretch of road we call adulthood, then some loneliness—in the sense that all human beings feel detached and adrift from our compatriots at one time or another—is unavoidable.

Luckily, there is a song (if not many songs) for every occasion, and Vincente Minnelli's glorious, Crayola-box 1953 musical *The Band Wagon* features one of the finest musical numbers about loneliness ever produced. When Fred Astaire, as semi-washed-up middle-aged musical star Tony Hunter, rolls into New York by train, there's no one to greet him—no photographers, no special lady friend. But because this is Fred Astaire, he has the tools to turn strange and unwelcome feelings of personal inadequacy and insecurity into a song-and-dance number. He tip-taps and glides through Central Station—everything he does looks like walking, only airier. "I'll face the unknown, I'll build a world of my own," he sings in his extraordinary non-singer's voice, downy and buoyant, a voice that hangs, light as a cumulus cloud, comfortingly close to earth.

"By Myself," written by Arthur Schwartz and Howard Dietz, and particularly as sung by Astaire, is a modestly scaled anthem of self-determination, a bit of alchemy that spins gold from self-pity: It treats loneliness as a portal to a world of possibilities, reachable only when you step—or dance—toward the future. And it sets the tone for *The Band Wagon*, one of the great movie musicals but one that, in its willingness to charge right up to fear and insecurity, isn't always the easiest to immediately love. When Astaire's Tony Hunter arrives in New York from Los Angeles, it's a kind of homecoming: He's an old-time

Broadway hoofer who made it big in Hollywood, only to reach that inevitable, middle-age point when he feels forgotten. (Astaire himself was fifty-four at the time.) But Tony still has friends, two close ones, in particular, Lily and Lester Marton, played by Nanette Fabray and deadpan genius Oscar Levant. They're a husband-and-wife writing team (movie-mirror images, in fact, of the duo who wrote *The Band Wagon*, Betty Comden and Adolph Green), and they have an idea for a new musical, a surefire hit. They have a director lined up, a bag of hot air in an ascot with the suitably pretentious name of Jeffrey Cordova (played, with a just-broad-enough wink, by Scottish-born song-and-dance man Jack Buchanan), and they hope to cast a leggy ballerina, Cyd Charisse's Gabrielle Gerard, as Tony's costar.

Tony balks: Cordova wants to turn Lily and Lester's straightforward, crackling idea into a remodeling of *Faust*; Gabrielle is too tall, too haughty, too *ballet* for him. He has his doubts about the whole thing, and when those misgivings turn out to be accurate, he spearheads a new version of the show, with Gabrielle, the Martons, and even a loosened-up Cordova all on board.

The "new" show-within-a-show makes up a hefty chunk of *The Band Wagon*'s musical numbers, including the movie's elaborate "Girl Hunt Ballet" centerpiece, in which Astaire and Charisse—the former appearing as an unusually dapper hard-boiled detective, the latter playing both a blond naïf and a sultry, raven-haired bad gal—glide through a film noir dream. The show-within-a-show structure allows for a crazy patchwork of musical numbers, some more successful than others: Fabray, in a gingham dress, her hair festooned with daisies, flounces through one of the sillier ones, "Louisiana Hayride," but at least it's lively. And the "Triplets" novelty number—in which Astaire, Fabray, and Buchanan play grouchy identical triplets—has a compelling, surreal energy about it. And kids find it funny—because why wouldn't they?

But the best numbers, and the best moments, in *The Band Wagon* are those that give Astaire the opportunity to be the most Astaire he can be. *The Band Wagon* may not be the "best" Fred Astaire movie—that honor might go to the glorious 1935 *Top Hat*, costarring Ginger Rogers, his finest partner. But *The Band Wagon* might be the most concentrated, unadulterated Astairean of all Astaire movies: As Tony, a man in the midst of a personal reinvention, he's a dream vision of how to look, how to move, how to present yourself to the world with unerring confidence even if, like Tony, you aren't quite sure of your place in that world. *The Band Wagon* was shot in Technicolor, but even if it hadn't been, Tony Hunter would still have favored royal-blue socks worn with a violet tie or a lanky, dark suit whose lines are defined by creamy chalk stripes. These are clothes that enhance the wearer and his movements, bold announcements of a man who knows his own heart even if, as with all human beings, the state of knowing one's heart is ever shifting.

Tony Hunter is a man at a crossroads: The only option is to choose a direction and keep moving. Tony is moving from the minute he gets off that train, going his own way, "by himself, alone." When he's greeted by his friends, Lily and Lester, they whisk him off to Times Square, a place he hardly recognizes: Theaters he played in the old days are gone, giving way to garish hot-dog joints and penny arcades. (It's a half-jarring, half-comforting reminder that the reinvention of Times Square is perpetual.) Tony is both put off by the cheap showiness of that penny arcade and enticed by it: He wends his way through, sampling the best and possibly the worst it has to offer—a machine that tests his love appeal, a funhouse mirror that distorts anything it reflects. And it's here, at a shoeshine stand, that Tony finds his most magnificent dance partner—a man who is, in fact, a much better partner for Astaire than Charisse is. Charisse is graceful, but she's also cool and muscular in a way that's at odds with Astaire's lightness, the inherent springiness of his limbs and joints.

Tony stops to have his shoes shined, and while he's at it, he sings a song: "A Shine on Your Shoes" is a kind of follow-up to "By Myself," a paean to the simple things that make you look and feel better. He begins dancing with the man who wields the rag and brushes. In the movie, he doesn't have a name, but in real life, he was Leroy Daniels, a real-life Los Angeles bootblack. In the film, Daniels wears a vibrant orange Hawaiian shirt and a pair of loose tan trousers that allow him to move freely as he works and dances. (His pink socks are a counterpoint to Astaire's blue ones.) He kneels at Tony's feet, whisking his polishing rag to and fro as glancingly and gracefully as a set of brushes on a drumhead. He circles Tony like a planet circling the sun, but here's the thing: Although Astaire is the professional dancer, the one we came to see, it's almost impossible to keep our attention from drifting to Daniels, a comet of color, movement, and joy. Together, the two are a wonder—Astaire is the star, but the dance is unimaginable without Daniels.

"A Shine on Your Shoes" tends to make contemporary audiences uncomfortable because it shows the shoeshine man, a gentleman of color, as the stereotypical subservient, preternaturally happy Negro. But to read the sequence so narrowly is to miss the point, as well as the magic of the dance. If only we could erase all the uncomfortable bits of our history as Americans, movie history included! We'd all feel so much better. But there's no moving forward if we don't know where we've come from. As film critic Stuart Klawans put it, "To me, Leroy's performance shone like the dawn of the civil rights movement, whose glory had been about to burst over the horizon. Here was a demonstration of what could be done by overlooked people once their creative powers were set free, if only for a day, if only in a make-believe setting."[1]

The dance belongs as much to Daniels as it does to Astaire; they're partners in the truest sense, not least because "A Shine on Your Shoes" is chiefly a song about possibility, about the future that might unfold from one small gesture. "When there's a shine on your shoes, there's a melody in your heart," Astaire sings, at one point exclaiming from the top of his shoeshine-chair world, "Wonderful!" Just minutes before, he was wondering how he was going to get by, all by himself, alone. Now, in the reflection of his freshly shined shoes, he has at least a window into the answer. Our best ideas often spring from loneliness, a kind of listening and seeing. Sometimes, it can even feel like dancing.

—⧑—

Growing Up Female in *Lady Bird* (2017), *The Fits* (2015), and *Leave No Trace* (2018)
Robert Horton[2]

When Pauline Kael reviewed *American Graffiti* (1973), she took pointed issue with the film's bittersweet coda, in which we learn what became of the teenage boys whose adventures we'd been watching. *The boys.* Not the girls, as Kael noted; not a word about the lovely, vibrant, urgent characters played by Candy Clark, Mackenzie Phillips, and Cindy Williams.

Mind you, *American Graffiti* is pretty terrific, and its coming-of-age material is more thoughtful than many examples of the Hollywood bildungsroman. It was cowritten by Gloria Katz, and its female characters are just as vivid as the men, the end-credits gaffe notwithstanding. But that last-minute oversight served as a reminder that having more such stories told by female filmmakers could only be a good thing.

It took decades, but with the surge of women entering the directing profession, the mid-2010s proved to be a golden age for female takes on the transition from innocence to experience. In movies as disparate as Céline Sciamma's *Bande de filles* (*Girlhood*, 2014), Andrea Arnold's *American Honey* (2016), and Marielle Heller's *Diary of a Teenage Girl* (2015), the visions are definite, gnarly, and without condescension. The declarative nature of those titles suggests a movement marking its territory. Here are three of the most distinctive examples, each in an utterly different key.

LADY BIRD (2017)

On Lady Bird's eighteenth birthday, she goes to the local convenience store and purchases three items: cigarettes, a scratch card, and a copy of *Playgirl*. These are things she could not legally buy before today, so the sense of ritual is strong. Whether she really wants any of these items is not the point; she's eighteen, and if you live (literally, as pointed out to her) on the wrong side of the tracks in Sacramento, you take your grown-up initiation rites where you can get them.

Greta Gerwig's *Lady Bird* is peppered with details that ring true—in fact, the film sometimes seems to consist entirely of such observations, strung together along the familiar lines of the final-year-in-high-school structure. Some of these observations are generic, for example, the solitary yelp of satisfaction after a promising romantic encounter or the disappointing quickness of the heroine's loss of virginity. But a big part of the appeal of *Lady Bird* is its girl's-eye view of these conventions, instead of the umpteenth iteration of boys peeping into the girls' locker room, sifting through the stash of *Playboys*, or crushing hard on the unobtainable prom queen.

Lady Bird (the peerless Saoirse Ronan), whose real name is Christine, crushes hard on the prom queen, too, but in this case, it's not romance that fuels the attraction. This urge is all about class—Jenna (Odeya Rush) is from a nice neighborhood, so nice that Lady Bird wouldn't even consider having her over to her own humble home. Gerwig takes care to locate Lady Bird's family life in economic reality, too; with her father (Tracy Letts) out of work in middle age, there's an underlying panic that hangs around the house like a ghost. Lady Bird falls for boys (Lucas Hedges and Timothée Chalamet), but these passing flings are not more important than her connection with her mother (Laurie Metcalf), a difficult and disappointed woman.

The film is shot through with tiny incidents and lovely turns of phrase, but its most distinctive feature may be its absolutely sure-footed feeling for pace. Mostly constructed around short scenes, *Lady Bird* skips along with the impatient energy of its heroine. If anything, the film's shortcoming is the way it rarely pauses to let a wound sink in or a thoughtless remark draw blood. The film gets great comedy from awkwardness, but there's absolutely nothing awkward about its confident forward motion.

I'm not one to insist that male artists can't tell women's stories; countless novels, movies, and songs provide the eloquent evidence on that score. But there is something exhilarating in *Lady Bird*'s female-centric view of high school, a view that very much includes Gerwig's empathetic and witty portraits of male characters. Maybe a man might have written the moment where Lady Bird decries her position during what she thought was a mutual deflowering ("Who the fuck is on top their first time?"), but it feels like something original and, obviously, overdue.

THE FITS (2015)

One of the ways you can spot a strong new movie director is by listening to what she does with the soundtrack—not the music, although that's part of it, but the whole sonic enchilada. I like a lot of things about *The Fits*, and the first thing that got me was the way it sounds.

As the film evokes one Cincinnati girl's bumpy journey into the mysteries of adolescence, the soundtrack ripples with densely layered noise: the slap of feet on a hardwood floor during dance practice; the rhythmic meeting of boxing gloves in the workout room; the exact way a song echoes in a big, empty school gym. The noises are realistic enough, but when they're piled on top of one another, it sounds like a dream.

The Fits was written and directed by Anna Rose Holmer, who developed the story with editor Saela Davis and producer Lisa Kjerulff. But "story" isn't the right word, because *The Fits* is more an immersion into one girl's point of view as she tries to figure out her identity during a peculiar time at school.

When we first meet Toni (Royalty Hightower), she's working out in the school gym, emulating her hardworking older brother. But Toni isn't entirely a jock yet; she gazes through a school doorway (there are a lot of people looking through doorways in this movie) in the direction of dance practice, where the school's glamorous "Lionesses" are holding rehearsal. Toni tries out for the squad, and although she can't get the rhythm at first—her body is still attuned to the grim routine of exercise rather than dance—she eventually finds the beat. This breakthrough happens in a great sequence done in a single shot, of Toni dancing alone on a freeway overpass, as though shouting her skills to the world.

Toni is otherwise quiet, a cautious observer (the film is practically a visual poem on the topic of introversion). This is in marked contrast to her classmate, Beezy, who tries out for the squad at the same time. The irrepressible Beezy is played by Alexis Neblett, a girl with a lot of pepper—someone's probably developing a sitcom for her right now.

But something else is going on at school. The older Lionesses are suffering from fainting spells or seizures or . . . something. Maybe the drinking water is bad, school officials say, or maybe it's the power of suggestion. Whatever it is—and don't expect an answer—Holmer clearly sees it as deeply connected to the experience of teenage girldom. The girls who have had fits carry with them the aura of having been somewhere special; girls who haven't had spells are longing to join the club. After Beezy faints one day and Toni says something to her later on the subject, Beezy snaps, "What would you know about it?"

The film has no scenes of home life and almost no grown-ups present. This is all about the hothouse of youth. Cinematographer Paul Yee's camera is often low, at kid-level, reinforcing the idea that what we're looking at is Toni's way of seeing. To that end, Holmer makes ordinary places seem charged with possibility or strangeness: When Toni and Beezy break into the gym at night and try on the brand-new, sparkly dance costumes, it's a grand adventure; when Toni hops into the school's emptied swimming pool, the spot becomes a big, lonely cavern.

Back to that soundtrack. Along with the interesting ambient noises, there is music, maybe the most distinctive movie music since Mica Levi's score for *Under the Skin* (2013). Composed by Danny Bensi and Saunder Jurriaans (they did the cool scores for 2011's *Martha Marcy May Marlene* and *Enemy*), the music sounds a little like experimental jazz mixed with the hand-clapping rhythm of cheerleader chants. Like so much about *The Fits*, it takes the familiar and makes it into something new.

LEAVE NO TRACE (2018)

The first thing that strikes you in *Leave No Trace* is the density of the Pacific Northwest forest—all that enveloping greenness. People live in these woods, swallowed up by the choking undergrowth. And that's the way they want it. The movie's title, usually employed as an antilittering motto, refers to a main character's desire to vanish from society, to exist on his own terms, and then disappear.

The forest in question is actually a park just outside Portland, Oregon; it's close enough to walk into the city for supplies. The disappearing man is Will (Ben Foster), a veteran with some degree of PTSD. What complicates his retreat from the world is his fierce bond with his adolescent daughter, Tom (Thomasin Harcourt McKenzie, a New Zealander), who lives with him in the woods. They hunker down in their tent, build fires when they need to, and stay out of sight. The end of this idyll coincides with Tom's wistful desire to have a more normal, settled life—a life that would be unbearable for her father.

That's the gist of Debra Granik's first narrative feature since *Winter's Bone* (2010), the strikingly original American folk classic that brought little-known Jennifer Lawrence to prominence. Granik and producer Anne Rosellini adapted Peter Rock's 2009 novel *My Abandonment*, and while the story's outcome may never really be in doubt, the beautifully observed details of this heroine's journey are heartbreaking. For instance, a lesser movie would have created villains out of the Portland bureaucrats who process homeless people. But here, they're human beings doing their difficult jobs—decent people, actually. Everyone means well, and that makes the situation sadder.

When Will and Tom are "placed" at a prefab rural house, we're not meant to sneer at the situation. For Tom, it's a wonderfully stable, clean home. But Will can't hack it. The job handed him is honest work. Yet, he's cutting down Christmas trees at a farm. What could be more remote from his need to be swaddled by the forest than this industrial method of harvesting holiday decor? This pain is deep-set in Foster's performance, which—given his scarcity of dialogue— he expresses mostly through his eyes. In his high-pitched early work, Foster was a real Roman candle, but in recent years (2016's *Hell or High Water*, for instance), he's evolved into an effective underactor.

Leave No Trace is really about Tom, who wrestles with her loyalty to her father and her obvious need for a roof and walls. In McKenzie's wonderful performance, Tom is wary about expressing her wants, but you can see the little glimmers of hope and relief flash across her face when she thinks they might settle. It's a terrific portrait of how personality emerges in a young person; some of Tom's manner is clearly modeled after her father's stoicism. Yet, her own distinctiveness keeps trying to break out. At one point Tom tells her dad, "Same thing that's wrong with you isn't wrong with me," to which he answers simply but completely, "I know." This movie distills its purpose in small, precise helpings; like someone living off the land, it's terribly specific about its choices. Each one counts.

Perverse Conversion in *The Miseducation of Cameron Post* (2018)

Robert Horton[3]

Every kid at the gay-conversion therapy center must draw an iceberg. If they can fill in the huge, below-water section of the iceberg with the written reasons for their homosexual activity, they will better understand how they could have slipped from the straight path. And then they will be cured.

In *The Miseducation of Cameron Post* (2018), the iceberg is a running joke, born of despair. The teenagers trapped in the therapy center try to think of gay-causing explanations they can write on their icebergs—a childhood trauma? an overbearing parent?—and sometimes borrow other kids' scrawlings (how well I remember being a Catholic schoolboy and trying to come up with two or three credible transgressions I could offer up in the confessional every week to sound believably sinful). You have to wonder whether the organizers of the God's Promise school have really thought through this iceberg metaphor. Are the teenagers the icebergs, or are they the ships steaming toward a collision?

Such programs are not known for clear thinking, and *Miseducation*—a 2018 Sundance Grand Jury Prize winner—is devastating in its depiction of the fictional God's Promise. But what makes this film so memorable is the rounded view it takes toward its cast of characters and even the religious fanatics who run the place. Our title character, played by Chloë Grace Moretz, gets packed off to God's Promise after making out with a girl on prom night, 1993. Luckily, she falls in with a couple of inmates who share a sardonic view about all this: the one-legged Jane Fonda—that's her name, although there's no follow-up to the gag—played by *American Honey* (2016) marvel Sasha Lane, and a Native American teen named Adam (the sneakily funny Forrest Goodluck from 2015's *The Revenant*). The place has its share of true believers, one of whom is Cameron's spooky roommate (the convincingly odd Emily Skeggs), who exercise to Christian rock songs and air their guilt in group therapy.

But no one really belongs at God's Promise, except maybe fearsome head doctor Lydia Marsh, played with crocodile focus by Jennifer Ehle. Even Lydia's cheerleading brother, Reverend Rick (John Gallagher Jr.), betrays signs that his own happy-face conversion from a gay adolescence has perhaps not entirely jelled. Gallagher's deft performance is typical of this movie's approach: Director Desiree Akhavan, adapting (with cowriter Cecilia Frugiuele) Emily M. Danforth's 2012 young adult novel, resists the temptation to mock the more ludicrous aspects of this intrinsically ludicrous situation. Nor does she turn her reflective heroine into a proactive, fist-pumping warrior. Instead, she allows us to perceive the iceberg that sits beneath the surface of the story, the uncertainties, fears, and anger.

Akhavan here fulfills the promise of her 2014 film *Appropriate Behavior* (in which she also starred), a Brooklyn comedy of manners that proved that the now-ancient style of the classic Woody Allen picture can be deftly adapted to suit an Iranian American bisexual heroine. In both films, Akhavan demonstrates a gentle but passionate touch and a real gift with performers. The young actors in *Miseducation*—and we should add Owen Campbell, as a sincere Christian boy—have an offhand, intimate style of ensemble playing. A few conventional story beats in the last twenty minutes can't diminish this achievement or cloud the fact that Akhavan has executed a quietly complete takedown of an ignorant practice.

—⁓—

Boys Will Be Girls in *Ma Vie en Rose* (1997)
Nathan Lee

How do you make a film about a transgendered seven-year-old? To ask that question already presupposes another: How does a child, *any* child, understand and experience their own gender identity? We might start by remembering that childhood is a time when everything takes shape through play, when the line between reality and imagination, between who we are and who we pretend to be, is supple and elastic, a thing to be stretched like taffy, flown like a kite, tumbled down the stairs like a Slinky. The idea that gender is constructed, mutable, and open to experiment and invention becomes a theoretical or political proposition only when the categories of normative social roles have hardened. For the child, nothing could be more natural than playing with gender because all of "nature" is a playground. The little boy who knows he's really a little girl is no more scandalous than the fact that perfectly reasonable conversations may be held with teddy bears.

The problem, of course, is that grown-ups *are* scandalized by the gender play of children. *Ma Vie en Rose* ("My Life in Pink"), a groundbreaking movie about the joys and pains of childhood gender nonconformity, is organized entirely around this rift between the innocence of play and the discomfort it provokes in the adult world of shame, guilt, and the anxiety to maintain social standing. Directed by Alain Berliner from a script he coauthored with Chris Vander Stappen, the story unfolds in a candy-colored Belgian suburb as the Fabre family grapples—for the most part poorly—with the claims to girlhood made by their youngest son, Ludovic (Georges Du Fresne).[4]

The great charm of *Ma Vie en Rose* is also the source of its bruising poignancy: For Ludo, the curious fact that s/he seems to have been born a boy is not a cause for unhappiness but rather the canvas on which to bedazzle the portrait of a *garçon-fille* in bloom. Ludo is blissfully unburdened by any sense of impropriety. Dressing up, playing with dolls, imagining the day when s/he will marry the boy next door; all of this is a met with delight and the excitement of discovering how *fun* it is to become who you are. Mom (Michèle Laroque) and Dad (Jean-Phillipe Écoffey) already know who they are, or who they want people to think they are to maintain their social standing; one of the key insights of *Ma Vie en Rose* is how the enforcement of gender norms is related to such class anxiety.

With its brightly colored production design and literal flights of fancy (Ludo frequently escapes into the fantasy world of a beloved TV show), the movie is suffused with a tone of magic realism. By situating us in the world as Ludo sees it, Berliner renders the conflicts that arise all the more acute. *Ma Vie en Rose* has rightly come under criticism for its R rating, a punitive evaluation that has more to do with censorious discomfort about the exploration of childhood gender than any specific "adult" content that might trouble younger viewers.

At the same time, the psychic violence in the movie is not inconsiderable. Ludo's bullying at the hands of classmates, neighbors, and especially his parents is even more acute for the *tonal* dissonance it strikes in the film's whimsical setting. *Ma Vie en Rose* works on the ethical problem of childhood gender difference in part by turning it into a cinematic problem.

At a time when Laverne Cox and *Transparent* have become widely beloved mainstream cultural phenomena, *Ma Vie en Rose* remains singular in its treatment of transgender identity in the prepubescent imaginary. At the same time, there's nothing all that unusual about the story it tells and the ambiguities it leaves hanging about Ludo's happiness and sense of self. What's special about the movie is finally not the novelty (or controversy) of its treatment of a particular kind of subjectivity. By staging the tale of a rare bloom, *Ma Vie en Rose* lets flower a universal parable. Ludo, *c'est nous*. Or as RuPaul is fond of saying, "We're born naked and the rest is drag."

—⟋⟋⟋—

Flower Power: *The Blossoming of Maximo Oliveros* (2005)
Godfrey Cheshire[5]

Serving on the jury for debut films at the 2005 Montreal World Film Festival, I was reminded how often evaluating movies revolves around disagreement. Yet, while our small, intensely opinionated jury disagreed about most of the awards we had to decide, we were surprised to find that we were in instant accord about what should win first prize: a disarmingly revelatory Filipino film called *The Blossoming of Maximo Oliveros.*

When the prize was announced on the festival's closing night, Auraeus Solito, the film's young director, bounded onstage in tears, thanking the jury "on behalf of filmmakers across the Third World." As he did, we jurors witnessed an extraordinary ovation from the public that let us know we weren't alone: Everyone in Montreal, it seemed, was cheering for Solito's low-budget wonder to take the top award.

Audience passion for *Maximo Oliveros* has a lot do with its sweetness of spirit and emotional generosity, as well as its remarkable, self-evident cultural authenticity. The film concerns the denizens of a slum called Gulpit Street in the Sampaloc neighborhood of Manila, where some of the filmmakers live (they used their apartments for sets). The place is conjured with a specificity and a flavor that you almost never see this side of ethnographic filmmaking. Ten minutes in, you've entered not only a story, but also a world of indelible images, rituals, textures, and eccentricities.

At once gritty and lyrical, Solito's knowing depiction of this world introduces us to several vivid individual residents of Gulpit Street, most notably the film's unforgettable title character.

Maxi (Nathan Lopez), as he's called, is a lithe, bright-eyed, boundlessly personable twelve-year-old gay boy who no one would mistake for straight. Sashaying through the slums with his inimitable hip-swinging stride, he occasions a lot of passing smiles but nothing more negative than that. At home, he rules the roost, cooking and mending for a rough-hewn masculine household that, since the death of his mother, includes his father Paco (Solimon Cruz) and big brothers Boy (Neil Ryan Sese) and Bogs (Ping Medina).

The grown-ups in the Oliveros clan are all petty criminals, but that doesn't make Maxi an outcast within his own home. Although his dad and siblings kid his swishy ways, they clearly love him and depend on his ministrations as a kind of surrogate mom.

The film's portrayal of one very "out" gay kid is striking, largely because Maxi himself is such a vivid character (Solito did a remarkable job with young Nathan Lopez, a noneffeminate boy who imitated his sister's mannerisms in creating the character). Even more fascinating, however, is the degree of nonplussed acceptance with which Maxi is regarded by virtually everyone in his world, beginning with his own dodgy, macho family.

This tolerance doesn't reflect any kind of politically correct viewpoint on the filmmakers' part, I think. Rather, it's a snapshot of one culture that's valuable for its accuracy and currency: Anyone who's traveled in the developing world—especially, it sometimes seems, in Catholic cultures—knows that there are kids like Maxi (although not always quite so flamboyant) everywhere now and that they tend to be more easily woven into the social fabric in poor neighborhoods than in more well-off precincts.

For viewers living in the privileged cultures of the West, the reality just described offers a useful challenge to the unthinking assumption that tolerance is more natural to "us" than to "them," and to rich rather than to poor. And when it comes to sexual assumptions, the work of Solito and screenwriter Michiko Yamamoto proves even more illuminating and thought-provoking.

The crux of *Maximo Oliveros*'s drama comes when Maxi develops a crush on a young cop named Victor (a strong performance by J. R. Valentin), who has just started working the neighborhood. This is where the film's difference of cultural viewpoint really comes to the fore. American movies can't seem to deal with desire on the part of the young—who are generally assumed to be its objects rather than its subjects—in any fashion, and adding in the gay element would only invite a meltdown of hysteria among our more rigid cultural arbiters.

Solito and company succeed in this tricky area, however, not only because they are subtle and insightful, although they certainly are both: The unfolding pas de deux between the boy and the kindly, bemused policeman is played out with just the right notes of awkwardness, yearning, and solicitude. Yet, what's distinctive here is how skillfully and inexorably a tale of two individuals is woven into larger narratives of family, community, class, and culture.

In any case, what the filmmakers portray here are murmurs of the heart, not stirrings of the loins. The movie contains no explicitly sexual content, and its gentle, persuasive emphasis on positive—if sometimes challenging—emotions and personal growth make it an ideal film for parents seeking to discuss questions of adolescent sexuality and world culture with their children. Ultimately, the film's message is upbeat and embracing, and that's largely because we do indeed witness the blossoming of Maxi, who is able to grow and succeed in a world that accepts him as he is.

Like other great movies from the Third World, *Maximo Oliveros* is not the kind of film that impresses with its sleek flawlessness. It's a film of tremendous heart, spirit, and originality—the kind that wins awards in competitions where everything around it cost ten times as much to make.

—⚬⚬—

Uneasy *Rider*
Peter Keough[6]

Drawn from the lives of real people who portray themselves, Chloé Zhao's *The Rider* (2017) achieves what cinema is capable of at its best: It reproduces a world with such acuteness, fidelity, and empathy that it transcends the mundane and touches on the universal.

In one such glimpse of sublimity, a group of young Native American rodeo riders drink beer, roughhouse, and sing songs in the immensity of the Badlands surrounding the Pine Ridge Indian Reservation in South Dakota. When dusk lights the uncanny landscape they gather around a fire; talk about injuries and riding through the pain; and recall anecdotes about Lane (Lane Scott as himself), a fellow cowboy who is now a paraplegic after being thrown while bull-riding. Their memories and fears give way to a prayer—a rare instance of a film achieving a genuine religious moment.

One of the riders is Brady (Brady Jandreau, a nonactor playing a character based on himself), and Lane's fate resonates with him not only because they are close friends, but also because he too has suffered a devastating injury. His skull fractured when he was thrown from a horse in a rodeo event; he now has a metal plate in his head and has been warned by his doctors not to ride again. The next fall, they tell him, might paralyze or kill him.

Nonetheless, Brady climbs into the saddle again as soon as he has recovered sufficiently. He's determined to ride despite the advice of his widower father, Tim (Tim Jandreau, Brady's real-life father), who is a genial gambler, and his sister, Lilly (Brady's real-life sister), who has Asperger's syndrome and whose sunny, commonsense remarks serve as the voice of reason.

But even when his hand seizes up uncontrollably from his lingering brain injury, Brady sees no other choice but to persevere. He's achieved celebrity status on the rodeo circuit. It's part of his identity, the basis of his self-esteem. As he points out, a horse is put down when it's so damaged it can no longer run or jump or do the things that horses do. "But I'm a person," he says, "and I've got to live."

Zhao turns material that might have been treacly and simple-minded into an allegory of male identity—reminiscent of *Lonely Are the Brave* (1962) and

Brokeback Mountain (2005)—with the quality of myth. Her neorealist style allows for such astonishing, authentic sequences as when Brady tames a wild horse; or bonds with his sister; or visits his friend Lane at a rehab facility, where they communicate in sign-language. Such epiphanies might break your heart, but they affirm the human capacity to prevail.

Lupita Nyong'o, Chadwick Boseman, and Letitia Wright in *Black Panther*

8

———〰———

EXTRAORDINARY HEROES

For more than thirty years, probably starting when Tim Burton's *Batman* broke the box office in 1989 (although it got a head start in 1978, with *Superman*), superheroes and the kids who love them have dominated Hollywood. Tapping into the huge catalog of characters, plots, settings, and backstories built up throughout the decades by the staid DC Comics group (Superman, Batman, Wonder Woman, etc.) and the edgier Marvel (Spider-Man, Thor, Captain America, and many others), they have spun out alternative worlds in billion-dollar franchises and sequels.

Some say this phenomenon has been to the detriment of cinema, that superhero movies infantilize audiences, indulge in CGI at the expense of character and plot, and solidify the reign of the blockbuster and the bottom line. Others (sometimes the same people) note that like all movies about heroes, these films allow young audiences to fantasize about facing tough challenges and prevailing. They don't offer an escape from reality but a means of dealing with it.

In the case of Christopher Nolan's *Batman Begins* (2005), the harsh realities are internal as much as external. Nolan adds to the familiar origin story in which Bruce Wayne witnesses his parents gunned down in an alley a supplementary trauma that is more phobic and insidious. It leaves Wayne with an irrational fear that he can confront only by transforming it into a new identity, one that can fight evil, if it doesn't succumb to it.

Until recently, one thing all superheroes had in common with Batman besides being neurotic was that they were all white. As Peter Travers points out, Ryan Coogler's *Black Panther* (2018) changed all that. In it the Marvel superhero of the title rules a hidden African country boasting vast resources and dazzling technology when he's not battling bad guys in the guise of a panther.

The film is revolutionary, Travers argues, not only because it made a ton of money and probably will embolden studios to make similar movies, but also because it gives black children a hero that looks like them. "White children see themselves reflected constantly in the universe of comic books turned movies," writes Travers. "But for black kids, representation is something new, something energizing, something necessary."

Like *Black Panther*, *Wonder Woman* (2017) opened the white, male-dominated superhero club to a broader demographic and did so with equal aplomb and exuberance. Like Black Panther, the title Amazon lives in an idyllic, hidden realm but feels compelled to leave to help others: in this case the Allies in World War I. In his review, Michael Sragow extols the film's topical relevance and its empowerment of a young female audience. "Although it rightly shuns topical references," he writes, "it makes a tiara seem as revolutionary as a pussy hat with the message 'love trumps hate.'" More importantly, he thinks it's fun for all audiences because it combines a "superhero origin story with a combat film, an espionage caper, and an apocalyptic ultra-fighting championship . . . [it] recaptures the scintillating looseness comic books once had."

In these superhero movies young viewers vicariously exert power in an imaginary world that is within their control. But in a number of movies the adult heroes sometimes come up short when it comes to saving the world from some menace, and the kids have to do the job themselves. In "Children's Crusades," I analyze this phenomenon in movies ranging from *Invaders from Mars* (1953) to *Spider-Man: Into the Spider-Verse* (2018) and conclude that although they may be satisfying wish-fulfillment fantasies, they reflect a "real world where adults have . . . failed to fulfill their responsibilities."

If children can be superheroes, why not the entire family? That's the premise of Brad Bird's slyly comic animated adventures *The Incredibles* (2004) and *Incredibles 2* (2018). In an alternate reality much funnier than our own, the government has banned superheroes because they are too disruptive. Frustrated in his job as an office drone, the superpowered but out-of-shape Mr. Incredible puts his costume back on and resumes saving the world with the assistance of his similarly superpowered wife and children.

They're back at it again in the sequel, with a difference. "If *The Incredibles* was a pop epic, *Incredibles 2* is a mom-and-pop epic," writes Michael Sragow in "Superheroes Run in the Family in *Incredibles 2* (2018)." With its off-the-wall-absurdity, dazzling antics, and lacerating satire the film presents a funhouse reflection of today's world that every member of the family can recognize and enjoy.

—ᴍ—

Terror Tactics in *Batman Begins* (2005)
Peter Keough

What, exactly, is "terror?" In *Batman Begins*, it's a device, a means of manipulation. This *Batman* begins with terror, a flashback to a nightmarish event squirming with Freudian implications. Young Bruce Wayne (Gus Lewis) falls into an abandoned well on his millionaire father's estate and thousands of bats surge from the darkness, swarming over him. The scene itself is only mildly frightening, but director and screenwriter Christopher Nolan doesn't want to manipulate his audience, he wants us to understand how fear forms character and fate, and how when it's mastered it can be turned against others, used, like the Force, to cloud weak minds and make them do one's bidding.

It's a tricky balance, exercising a faculty while at the same time trying to comprehend—if not duplicate—it, as Nolan did with memory and identity in *Memento* (2000). He doesn't just respect the audience's intelligence, he demands we use it, something that the target adolescent demographic should find refreshing after being bombarded by the mindless CGI extravaganzas that Hollywood believes they crave. Anyone expecting from *Batman Begins* a lazy immersion in spectacle, thrills, and faux "terror" will be disappointed. For those looking for a thoughtful, poetic fable about how what's most frightening in our lives today is often a shadow of what scared us as kids, this is the movie for them.

Young Bruce doesn't adjust well to his trauma, despite the support of his philanthropic dad, who says things like, "We must fall in order to rise again." Such bromides don't help when Bruce and his mom and dad attend what looks like a Gotham City Opera House production of *Faust* (or is it a new Andrew Lloyd Webber production called *Bats?*) and the boy is terrified when the extras take leathery-winged flight. Bruce insists on leaving, and outside, in a sordid alley (Nolan's Gotham, unlike Tim Burton's, is clearly Chicago, with a few CGI additions and many more layers of trash and corruption), his parents are gunned down by a desperate mugger in the scene familiar to aficionados of the superhero. Thus, one primal scene of horror summons, with insidious logic, the next.

Add vigilante rage to guilt, dread, and unlimited wealth, and what is the shattered youth to do? The adult Bruce (Christian Bale) journeys to the heart of darkness, determined to confront evil to overcome it, a quest that takes him to the Himalayas and the lair of Ducard (Liam Neeson, in a variation of his

Jedi role), representative of the League of Shadows, an ancient ninja-like order dedicated to maintaining justice. At first, Ducard seduces Bruce and even the most lily-livered liberal viewer into his harsh worldview of good and evil, and his methods of using terror (induced handily by a locally grown drug) to defeat the terrifying. But he, it seems, is one more evil to confront and overcome.

So, after an exile of years, it's back to Gotham City, where Bruce takes on the role of a playboy indifferent to the suffering of his fellow citizens, much to the disgust of dedicated district attorney and former childhood sweetheart Rachel (Katie Holmes). But like Bale's yuppie creep in *American Psycho* (2000), Bruce has invented a lethal alter ego, one that takes on the identity of that which he fears most.

As with Peter Parker's Spider-Man in the first of those films, Bruce's Batman is a work in progress, put together with elements of his ninja training, bits of hardware from the Wayne Enterprises experimental applications warehouse (overseen by an avuncular Morgan Freeman), and TLC from family butler Alfred (Michael Caine earning a stipend). The enemy he challenges has many faces: a mobster with half the city under his control; a baby-faced psychiatrist working for a mysterious foreign agent; a system of entitlement that thrives on the misery of the masses. But the ultimate adversary is terror: illusory, ubiquitous, irrational. It's the ideal instrument for the cynical moviemaker or politician but one that Nolan regards with the cold eye of an artist.

Black Panther (2018) Makes Superhero History
Peter Travers[1]

This black superhero movie, arguably Marvel's best, was nominated for a Best Picture Oscar and is already in the record books as the third highest-grossing film of all time. and an Oscar contender as Best Picture. But that's only money and awards glitter. See it through the eyes of a child, especially a child of color, and *Black Panther* (2018) is nothing short of revolutionary. White children see themselves reflected constantly in the universe of comic books turned movies. But for black kids, representation is something new, something energizing, something necessary. For youth (and adults) of color who have longed forever to see a screen superhero who looks like them, Marvel's rousing Afrocentric adventure is an answered prayer.

But wait a minute: Hasn't *Black Panther* been around since the 1960s, when Stan Lee and Jack Kirby created him for the comics? Why did it take a half-century for Marvel to get him up on screen? The not-so-secret answer is that the suits didn't think a black epic would sell, mostly because there's never been one. The stellar Chadwick Boseman already played T'Challa, aka Black Panther, in 2016's *Captain America: Civil War*, but it was a supporting role in a Marvel Cinematic Universe best categorized as #AvengersSoWhite. *Black Panther* brings T'Challa front and center. He's no longer a sidekick or second banana to a Thor or a Captain America. In this stand-alone, solo outing, the spotlight is all his. Ever allergic to risk, Hollywood held its breath. Now it's counting the profits. Will it change things? Who knows? But screen history has been made.

The film's PG-13 level of violence would seem to restrict its availability to younger audiences. But that's only for parents who use films to mollify children rather than as a spark to share thoughts and feelings. I still treasure the moments my dad and mom talked me through Disney films that killed off parents with impunity (they're still doing that). Not just a correction for years of diversity neglect, *Black Panther* is a big-budget blockbuster that digs into the roots of blackness itself and creates a cultural impact that outweighs its mostly bloodless action.

T'Challa is royalty. He's the king of Wakanda—a fictional African country where he presents one image as a ruler and another as a crime-fighting superhero disguised as a panther. His costume is threaded with vibranium, a mineral with magical properties and a national resource that T'Challa keeps hidden, along with his cloistered country's other huge scientific discoveries. Perhaps the most inspiring decision made by director Ryan Coogler (*Fruitvale Station*, *Creed*) is to treat Wakanda as a character itself, a place that resonates with its own social structure and rules of government, including choosing its king through physical challenge.

It's T'Challa's isolationism that puts him in conflict with his cousin, Erik Killmonger (Michael B. Jordan), a former black-ops soldier who is the son of Prince N'Jobu and an American woman from Oakland, California. Killmonger believes that his father has been murdered by T'Challa's father, leaving this orphan from the streets of Oakland hungry for revenge.

Jordan is blazingly good in the role, playing this warrior (he notches scars onto his body to represent his kills) with such tormented morality and emotional intensity that Killmonger's humanity is never in doubt. Angry at T'Challa's refusal to use his country's resources to assist disenfranchised black people throughout the world, Killmonger challenges T'Challa for the throne of Wakanda. "The world is going to start over," Killmonger tells his cousin. "And this time we're on top."

A global race war sparked by two African men who share the same blood-line may seem like a lot to digest for young viewers. After all, how many movies aimed at families feature a character like Killmonger, a villain with a point? But Coogler, who wrote the script with Joe Robert Cole, never loses sight of *Black Panther* as a tale as elemental as *The Lion King* (1994) or the *Star Wars* franchise. *Black Panther* has not been constructed as something easy to digest and dismiss. Digital pablum is readily available via streaming services. *Black Panther* is the opposite. It's a film that not only encourages discussion between parents and children, but also rewards it.

And the explosion of stereotypes doesn't stop with race. Take gender. If you're thinking you're in for another Marvel macho power trip, forget it. The women are more than a match for the men in this game, from the iconic Angela Bassett as Ramonda, T'Challa's widowed mother, to the ready-to-rumble Lupita Nyong'o as Nakia, T'Challa's ex-love and a spy for Wakanda in the outside world. And wait until you see the dynamite Danai Gurira—Michonne on *The Walking Dead*—fire on all cylinders as Okoye, head of Wakanda's all-female Special Forces known as the Dora Milaje. Her head shaved, her eyes beaming likes lasers, and her weapons at the ready, she is the living definition of fierce. And there's no beating the smarts and sass of the wonderous Letitia Wright, who brings scene-stealing to the level of grand larceny as Princess Shuri, T'Challa's kid sister. "Did you freeze *again*?" Shuri asks her big brother, teasing his surprisingly slow reflexes in the heat of battle once he catches sight of true love. A scientist and tech-tinkerer, she's always the brainiest person in the room, giving Q from the James Bond series a run for his money by inventing the coolest gadgets. Wright is a star in the making, who makes damn sure that Shuri will be a role model to young girls for years to come.

What family audiences will find in *Black Panther* is a fantasy film rooted in the here and now. Unlike other Marvel superheroes, T'Challa is a king with a burden of responsibility. Does he keep Wakanda safe by hiding its technolog-ical advances or share them with volatile intruders eager to weaponize resources meant to strengthen and heal? In *Get Out* (2017), Jordan Peele satirized white appropriation of black culture. Here, Coogler makes black identity invincible but avoids simplification by turning Wakanda into a society of different tribes, each with its own customs, goals, and political agendas that reflect a conflicted world much like our own.

There aren't many superhero films that blow you away with thunderous ef-fects and also tackle ethnic and gender issues, crush racial stereotypes, celebrate women, *and* condemn Trump-era notions of exclusionism. It's less controversial and way more tactful to be oblivious. But that's not Coogler's style. Created by African Americans, who make up most of the cast, the film has taken flak from critics who believe that Marvel is hijacking African traditions to sell tickets, bemoaning the fact that the film was mostly shot in Atlanta instead of Africa. But the accusations ring hollow and ignore the mint-fresh inventiveness and passionate commitment to the black experience that's instilled in every frame.

Is *Black Panther* suitable for all ages? That's an issue parents will have to decide for themselves. But if you want a film that inspires your children to talk to you about who they are and how we all live in an exhilarating, sometimes scary, vastly changing world, *Black Panther* truly is for everyone and for the ages.

—⟨⟨⟨—

Wonder Woman (2017) Enters the Pantheon
Michael Sragow[2]

Wonder Woman is a spectacular delight, up until the obligatory and repetitive last-act combat of the gods. Sweet and funny but with a kick to it, this movie pulls off the rare pop culture feat of hitting the dead center of the zeitgeist, without breaking a sweat. Although it rightly shuns topical references, it makes a tiara seem as revolutionary as a pussy hat with the message "love trumps hate." Now "Amazon" does not immediately refer to an online retail giant but to the female warriors who inhabit an island kingdom. And "Princess Diana" will summon not only Britain's tragic "people's princess," but also this film's triumphant goddess (soulfully embodied by Gal Gadot), who leaves the Amazons' island with dashing American-flyer-turned-Allied-spy Steve Trevor (Chris Pine, having the time of his young life). She aims to conquer Ares, the God of War. Along the way, she brings World War I to its bitter end.

It might sound overly ambitious for a superhero film to transport the Great War into blockbuster American pop culture, but Wonder Woman does it deftly and movingly. (And, to our national shame, what other form of mass entertainment has marked this momentous centennial?) The original Wonder Woman fought the Nazis, but it's surprisingly pungent to depict her fighting the "war to end all wars." Ending war is what she thinks she's doing when she and Steve team up to stop the evil General Ludendorff (Danny Huston) from using a lethal gas devised by evil genius Dr. Maru, aka "Dr. Poison" (Elena Anaya).

Diana believes the general is Ares in disguise. Is she the one true heir of a special Olympian legacy? Does the God of War actually walk twentieth-century Earth? Suspense and magic meld in *Wonder Woman*. Combining a superhero origin story with a combat film, an espionage caper, and an apocalyptic ultra-fighting championship (the weakest link), the director, Patty Jenkins, recaptures the scintillating looseness comic books once had, before they became "graphic novels." Jenkins and screenwriter Allan Heinberg generally keep the tone supple and the narrative nimble, even while erecting a modern-day frame and navigating myths within myths (the movie is mostly one headlong flashback).

The filmmakers give us exactly what audiences want from a Wonder Woman movie—powerful women in classical armor training for breathtaking combat—then leaven it with the farcical sight of Diana as a tyke (Lilly Aspell) playing Amazon-see-Amazon-do with martial arts. They unveil their creation story in animation that resembles a pop art Sistine Chapel with 3-D figures and cartoon energy bolts. On her home island of Themyscira (known in older comic books as "Paradise Island"), Diana's mom, Queen Hippolyta (Connie Nielsen), tells her about Ares, who poisoned mankind and hates the Amazons because Zeus created the female warriors to redeem men via love.

Ares killed off the rest of the gods, but Zeus, himself critically wounded, severely weakened the God of War and, for the Amazons, created Themyscira as a haven, where they could prepare to defeat Ares if ever he were to rise again. Hippolyta tells Diana she sculpted her out of clay (she's the only baby on the island), but early on Jenkins teases an alternate birth narrative. When Hippolyta releases Diana to train with General Antiope (Robin Wright), Hippolyta's sister, she reveals matchless strengths, instincts, and extraordinary superpowers, for instance, the ability to create convulsive force fields when she slams two metallic cuffs together.

Jenkins lets each scene play out to the end. She gives you time to savor the fine-grained beauties of Matthew Jensen's supernal cinematography (this movie exploits the depth and range of actual film). And Aline Bonetto's swirling storybook production design, which includes harmonious Art Deco swirls and a woman-made rendition of Lake Powell's Rainbow Arch, is, in turn, glorious, poignant, and inspiring. Everything seems fresh, not overcalculated or worried into emotional oblivion. It's even kind of fun that Wright sounds more Scandinavian than Nielsen, who is Danish-born.

The movie's MacGuffin is Dr. Poison's manual of evil, with her handwritten array of coded formulae for WMDs. Steve has stolen it, and the German navy tails him for it. The ensuing shoreline battle between Hippolyta's warriors and the Kaiser's marines fulfills the comic-book fantasy in Hawkman comic books, as well as Wonder Woman—using weapons of the past to defeat modern firepower. Jenkins and her team employ variable speeds to keep the action credible, dynamic, and involving as they imbue their big Amazon set piece with choreographic glee.

It's exhilarating to see Wright, as General Antiope, launch herself like a catapult off a shield or release three arrows at once to bring down a trio of enemy fighters simultaneously.

Credit for Gadot and Pine's instant sexy-humorous rapport goes to these performers and the understated flirty comedy in Heinberg's script. (Heinberg shares story credit with Zack Snyder and Jason Fuchs.) Diana speaks nothing but the truth, but Trevor, a gung-ho espionage agent, can't help twisting himself into verbal knots. She treats him partly as a novelty, partly as a sidekick and instructor. She can be devastating when she's matter-of-fact. Espying him toweling off naked in an Amazonian hot tub, she asks whether he's a typical man. Rattled, he replies he's "above average." Even when he gets comfortable with her, he never fully shakes his disbelief about how lucky he was that he found her—or, rather, that she found him. Playing a second banana who's very close to the top banana liberates Pine's gifts for irony, abashment, and romantic comedy. Pine builds his performance with cunning. He's amiably mock-heroic, then stirringly heroic. He makes us see why Wonder Woman would fall in love with him.

Gadot is mind-bendingly good—naturally supernatural. The key to her performance is playing Diana as the protagonist in a delayed coming-of-age story. On her island she's constantly proving herself or discovering new and unexpected powers. In London, where she and Steve visit the War Office, or Belgium, where she blazes through the trenches and helps save a town from German terror, she keeps learning about human fashions, foibles, duplicities, and atrocities, without losing her belief in mankind's potential redemption. Her tragic experiences strengthen her faith in the healing power of love. Gadot creates a Wonder Woman for all ages, infusing childlike earnestness and idealism with adolescent intensity and adult heft. She's an acrobatic comedian when she tries on 1918 fashions and tests whether they allow her combat moves full sway. She's an offhand drop-dead gorgeous model when she sports a modified Brit uniform with slouch hat and specs. And she's a full-scale romantic heroine when she gives her all for love.

At no point does *Wonder Woman* become a one-woman show. In London, Steve reconnects with his cheerful can-do secretary Etta Candy (the uproarious Lucy Davis) and enlists the support of two trusted special ops, the fast-talking French Moroccan con-man and ex-actor Sameer (the charming, effusive Saïd Taghmaoui) and the PTSD-afflicted Scottish sharpshooter Charlie (played by Ewen Bremner with his usual boisterous lyricism, especially when he sings Robert Burns's "Green Grow the Rashes, O"). On the Continent, they join up with a Native American smuggler known as "The Chief" (Eugene Brave Rock, a massive presence), while Steve reports back to his silent partner in the Imperial War Cabinet (the marvelously elusive David Thewlis).

Along with Anaya's Dr. Poison, who draws out her best lines with sardonic menace, each gets a moment to shine in Bonetto's glittering showcase. The woman who designed one of my favorite movies of this millennium, Jean-Pierre Jeunet's *A Very Long Engagement* (2004), outdoes herself in *Wonder Woman*. Until the battering finale, she and Jenkins focus the action so that even in the ravages of no-man's-land, the sound and fury signify something. When we respond to Wonder Woman drawing German fire with her shield, we're reacting to the nobility behind the conception. When Steve and Diana dance in the snow at night outside a Belgian café, we feel their warmth slicing through the darkness.

So it's doubly deflating that the climactic confrontation between Wonder Woman and Ares plays like just one more cage match sadly plucked out of a cage. It's a noisy synthesis of every head-pounding clash between Good and Evil we've seen in the past two decades. How often can we watch a super-antagonist mold asphalt and metal like Silly Putty and push the protagonist to the breaking point? It's bizarre to think such a sight could be a bit ho-hum. After that gargantuan conflict, the denouement is blissfully quiet.

Earlier, when Diana and Steve amble through the streets around Selfridge's department store, they pass shop signs for "Bunbury of London." It must be a reference to Oscar Wilde's notion of "Bunburying" in *The Importance of Being Earnest*—using a fictional excuse to get out of doing something humdrum. Whether Bonetto, Jenkins, or a set decorator planted that homage, it speaks to this entire production's resistance to anything tedious—except, that is, for the last-god-standing climax.

Wonder Woman puts many of the comic book's gimmicks on full display, from her Lasso of Truth to her bullet-deflecting bracelets. Mostly, however, the movie's freshness derives from the purity of feeling that emanates from the core of its star. It has taken almost eight decades for "America's guardian angel" to swoop onto the big screen. Who knew DC Comics fans were really waiting for Gadot?

Children's Crusades
Peter Keough

It's hard enough for young people to manage their own lives. Now they're expected to save the world, too. The adults sure aren't getting the job done. Their failure to solve the problems of environmental change, racism, inequality, tyranny, terrorism, and crime in real life is bad enough. But when they fail in the movies, the time has come for the kids to take charge.

A major cause of this trend for junior world saviors is the young adult fantasy book industry and its gold mine of franchises pushing that theme. Among the first authors to do so, C. S. Lewis pitted youngsters against superhuman adversaries in his seven-volume *Chronicles of Narnia*, published from 1949 to 1954. Although the series of adaptations started out strong with *The Lion, the Witch, and the Wardrobe* (2005), Lewis's religious themes grew more blatant in subsequent sequels, and the franchise faded with *Prince Caspian* (2008) and *Voyage of the Dawn Treader* (2010). Plans to produce an adaptation of the fourth book in the series have been shelved, so it might be a while before we hear from Narnia's bossy God stand-in, Aslan the Lion.

William Golding's *Lord of the Flies* came out at about the same time as Lewis's series in 1954, and was adapted into a stark, critically well-received film in 1963, directed by Peter Brook. It posited a less magical scenario than Lewis's books, unless you're talking about the kind of primitive magical thinking explored in James Fraser's opus *The Golden Bough*. But both authors—one Christian and the other existential—confront the same failure of adults to deal with disaster, the former drawing on the desolation of World War II, the latter on the angst of the Cold War.

Speaking of the Cold War, no film from that period has scared me as much as William Cameron Menzies's *Invaders from Mars* (1953). Like many sci-fi films of that era, the film begins with an alien spacecraft arriving on Earth. The ET intruder makes itself at home in the backyard of ten-year-old David, burying itself in a sandpit. Who has not felt dread about the sinister sandpit in their backyard? The boy tells his father about the visitor, and when he checks it out, he returns much changed from the affable '50s dad he used to be.

What follows is a kiddie precursor to *Invasion of the Body Snatchers* (1956). Deftly shot from the point of view of the young protagonist, the film evokes the trauma experienced by all kids when they realize that their parents, and perhaps all grown-ups, are zombies whose bodies have been taken over by malevolent entities. With none of the adults to be trusted, it looks like David might have to deal with the problem on his own.

I had flashbacks to this movie when watching Gavin Hood's 2013 adaptation of Orson Scott Card's 1985 (based on a 1977 short story) young adult sci-fi novel *Ender's Game*. The drilled-in-the-base-of-the-skull implant from *Mars* makes a comeback in this film, with a twist (literal and painful, as it turns out). Young Ender, whose uncanny talents qualify him as a prime candidate at age thirteen to lead an armada of starships against an alien menace, has had such a device inserted into his brain. This time it's not a probe designed to control adult humans, but one installed by adults into gifted youngsters like Ender to monitor their every experience. This is a superego with a vengeance.

Although the grown-ups may be omniscient, they are not omnipotent. In fact, they're desperate. The alien hordes have invaded twice before, and each time the planet has come close to annihilation. Earth's leaders, a consortium of tyrants, hope to end the threat once and for all with a devastating preemptive attack on the enemy's home planet.

For some reason, only kids have the conceptual skills or hand-to-eye co-ordination—associated these days with veteran video game aficionados (Card, his opinions about gay rights notwithstanding, was prescient about a lot of things)—to handle such a complex mission in outer space. Mentored by wily Colonel Graff (Harrison Ford), Ender alternates between neediness and resent-ment when it comes to the adults who have commandeered him. He is especially hostile when his training requires him to draw on his lethal skills to dispatch rival child-warriors during his Spartan-like training period. At one point he confronts Graff with the question, Are the aliens the enemy or you?

That same quandary comes up in the four-film adaptation (2012–2015) of Suzanne Collins's best-selling *The Hunger Games* trilogy (2008–2010), especially in the second film, *The Hunger Games: Catching Fire* (2013), directed by Francis Lawrence (who demonstrated his postapocalyptic touch in the 2007 adaptation of Richard Matheson's zombie apocalypse classic *I Am Legend*).

In the futuristic dystopia of Panem, a latter-day Rome called "the Capitol" oppresses and exploits its twelve fief-like districts. An uprising against the ty-rants seventy-five years earlier had failed, and ever since, as punishment, each district must send two young warriors called "tributes" to fight to the death in the annual "Hunger Games"—a case of "circenses," as it were, but not much in the way of panem for the starving masses.

One such tribute, Katniss Eberdeen (Jennifer Lawrence), will prove to be Panem's sole hope of salvation. But before the games begin, her Graff-like mentor, Haymitch Abernathy (Woody Harrelson), warns her, "When you're in the arena don't forget who the enemy is." They're not her fellow tributes, he is implying, but the oppressive system that has set them up as sacrificial pawns—and that system might include the beleaguered districts' leaders as well. As is the case in *Ender's Game*, the enemy remains ambiguous, and, by the end, it is unclear who is manipulating whom, especially with the late Philip Seymour Hoffman as the seductive and reptilian head gamemaker, Plutarch Heavensbee.

Poor Katniss; she doesn't need all this. She just wants to run away with hunky Gale Hawthorne (Liam Hemsworth) to the primal, paradisal outback beyond the electric fences and live off the land, not unlike the two kids in Wes Anderson's day-dreamy *Moonrise Kingdom* (2012). But two obstacles stand in her way. First, there is the diabolical autocrat of the Capitol, President Snow (Donald Sutherland). He wants to manipulate the adulation she earned by winning the previous games with her partner, Peetah Mellark (Josh Hutcherson), into gaudy romantic fantasies. These would provide a "distraction so people forget what their real problems are," as Haymitch puts it. Then there are the people themselves, who see her as a symbol of revolution and hope.

Either way, it doesn't allow Katniss much of a private life. Nor has Jennifer Lawrence had much time to herself offscreen, either. She's become as big a celebrity in the glitzy world of pop culture, as is her character Katniss in the fictitious Panem. It's a postmodern paradox: The film critiques the celebrity culture distracting young people from what is really going on in an imaginary world, but in the real world of showbiz, the films' pop piffle provides the same distraction. Such is the fate of youth sacrificed to save the meta-world—and profit Hollywood studios.

Meanwhile, in comic book fantasyland, the adult superheroes have also come up short in doing their duty. From the DC Extended Universe (the Warner Brothers franchises based on characters in DC comic books, also known as the DCEU) comes *Batman v Superman: Dawn of Justice* (2016), in which the iconic pair of the title have been manipulated into a squabble by evildoers. In the resulting chaos and petulance, the latter ends up dead.

Superman's demise leaves the Earth at risk from pesky alien menaces, so in the sequel, *Justice League* (2017), every remaining costumed character in the DC catalog—Batman, Aquaman, Wonder Woman, the Flash, to name a few—unite to form the eponymous organization. Even with their combined resources and the wobbly assistance of a resurrected but addled Superman, they are barely able to save the day. In the requisite post-credit teaser sequence, it is suggested that their work is far from over, and another sequel is in the works.

In the rival Marvel Cinematic Universe (the interlinked movies produced by Disney featuring Marvel comic book characters, going by the acronym MCU), the situation is also unstable. In *Avengers: Infinity War* (2018), Iron Man, Captain America, Thor, Spider-Man, Black Panther, and others in the title tag team crowd the screen to battle a baddie called Thanos and thwart his scheme to enslave or kill every living being. As can be imagined, with that many super egos in the room, there are a lot of spats and hurt feelings, and things do not go well.

When these childish adults fail to fulfill their responsibilities, can the kids rally to save the day? In two animated films, one from each studio, they endeavor to do so and make fun of the genre's conventions and artifices in the process.

From the DCEU comes *Teen Titans Go! to the Movies* (2018) (based on the Cartoon Network series *Teen Titans Go!*), starring a motley band of adolescent wannabes led by Batman's disaffected ex-sidekick Robin (whose attempt to be superheroic without any superpowers is reminiscent of the kid in 2010's sardonically satiric *Kick-Ass*). No one respects them as superheroes because they are just goofy kids, but they get their chance to prove their worth when the real superheroes (from the DCEU, at any rate) are lured away from their day jobs to make movies.

Back at the MCU, in *Spider-Man: Into the Spider-Verse*, an inner-city a kid from New York City is bitten by a radioactive spider, and as anyone following the Spider-Man saga knows, he soon develops arachnid-like abilities. Not a moment too soon, because the real Spider-Man has been killed battling his nemesis the Kingpin, and the new kid must save the world from the alternative universes spun out by Kingpin's supercollider.

Both *Teen Titans Go!* and *Into the Spider-Verse* are smart, fun, and super self-reflexive, but they, too, take place in an alternative universe, one several removes from the one we inhabit with our real-world problems and where adults have likewise failed to fulfill their responsibilities. One such adult is the dad in Debra Granik's *Leave No Trace* (2018), a PTSD victim from some forgotten conflict who has fled civilization to live with his teenage daughter in the wild. Fortunately, although she has no superpowers, his daughter has common sense and courage, and knows that, except maybe in the movies, the real world is a place you can't escape but must confront and change.

―⁂―

Superpowers Run in the Family in *Incredibles 2* (2018)
Michael Sragow[3]

Levity plus ebullience equals buoyancy. That's what Brad Bird proves in his Incredibles movies as they take off in the opening minutes and keep soaring for two hours. In *Incredibles 2*, he doesn't merely use an introductory set piece to hook an audience, but to establish the bold outlines of his story and a pace and standard of invention for the movie to come. There may be more lyrical directors working in animated features, but no one else has Bird's knack for crafting ingenious narratives that generate trust and affection, and filling them with feats of comedy and courage that test characters and thrill audiences. Achieving edge-of-your-seat hilarity in the sequel to his 2004 smash Bird extends and sustains his vision of infusing an American family with the New-Old-World sophistication of Connery-era James Bond; the try-anything derring-do of *Mission: Impossible* (Bird directed the best one, *Ghost Protocol*, in 2011); and, most important, the energizing team spirit shared by all great heroic squads from the Three Musketeers to the Silver Age's Justice League of America.

In this ongoing extravaganza, set in an alternate reality resembling the precounterculture 1960s, the government continues to prohibit Bob Parr / Mr. Incredible (Craig T. Nelson), his family, his best friend, Lucius Best / Frozone (Samuel L. Jackson), and all other "supers" from exercising their powers. (The reason: costly and time-consuming court suits. For example, a man who attempted suicide sued Mr. Incredible for saving his life because he ruined his death.)

In the first film, Bob rebels against his job at a blandly corrupt insurance company and back-channels a return to superheroism. He ends up on a quest to defeat a superhero-hating techno-wizard named Syndrome (Jason Lee), with the help of his wife, Helen/Elastigirl (Holly Hunter), their junior-high-age kids— super-swift Dash (Spencer Fox, now Huck Milner) and invisible-girl Violet (Sarah Vowell)—and even their infant Jack-Jack (Eli Fucile), whose powers become apparent only at the last minute (and only to Syndrome, not his family). Along with Frozone, they savor the excitement of pooling their gifts to defeat a dangerous enemy, even if it means flouting the law.

Incredibles 2 picks up where the first film leaves off, with the government ban on superheroism still in place. But the Incredibles won't give up their adrenalized family bonding without a fight. So when a monstrous driller explodes from the streets of Municiberg and proclaims, with witty Birdian brio, "Behold the Underminer! I am always beneath you, but nothing is beneath me"—and then starts tunneling into a bank vault—Mr. Incredible, Elastigirl, Dash, and Violet barrel, stretch, sprint, and float into the fray.

Bird crafts set pieces that multitask while pushing jeopardy to the limit, like having an enormous drill bit almost chew its way into Municiberg City Hall. The beginning swiftly reacquaints us with each Incredible (and Frozone, too), but we also learn in a brisk prologue that Violet's junior-high crush and prospective first date, Tony Rydinger (Michael Bird), caught a glimpse of her in costume, sans mask. He ran straight to Rick Dicker (Jonathan Banks) of the NSA (the National Supers Agency), who, as the movie starts, takes Tony's testimony, then wipes his memory clean of all things Violet. When Violet figures out why Tony stood her up on date night, she endures an uproarious bout of superheroine self-hatred. She discovers that a garbage disposal is no match for her indestructible crime-fighting costume. The family comedy humanizes and enlivens the trenchant action farce.

If *The Incredibles* was a pop epic, *Incredibles 2* is a mom-and-pop epic. When telecommunications tycoon Winston Deavor (Bob Odenkirk) makes legalizing superheroes his cause, he and his design-genius sister Evelyn (Catherine Keener) decide that their best propaganda bet is Elastigirl. Cost–benefit analysis proves that she battles evil more efficiently than Mr. Incredible, who tends to wreak huge collateral damage. So while the Deavors put up Bob and the kids in one of Winston's deluxe homes (rock formation in the living room, moveable floors atop indoor pools), they move Elastigirl to New Urbem, a media capital where she'll find juicy criminal targets and plenty of markets for interviews and footage taken with her body cam.

Bird depicts the Deavor's flattery of Helen/Elastigirl with genial social-sexual awareness. Evelyn tries coercing her into saying that she feels relieved to emerge from Mr. Incredible's shadow. But Helen doesn't go there. She knows she has more flexibility and finesse than her husband, but she also recognizes the difference between a feminist plumping for equality and an executive playing the gender card. Bird is no one-size-fits-all entertainer when it comes to ideas or topical notions. He tries them on and resists stretching them out. In *The Incredibles*, the antisuperhero forces stand for the leveling powers of mediocrity. In *Incredibles 2*, Rick Dicker explains the superheroes' predicament this way: Politicians don't understand people who simply do good because it's right.

Given the range Bird has exhibited in such films as *The Iron Giant* (1999) and *Mission: Impossible—Ghost Protocol* (2011), it's completely credible how well he balances Elastigirl's ballooning fame and Bob's skyrocketing responsibilities as a brand-new Mr. Mom. While Elastigirl zeroes in on an arch-villain called Screenslaver, who appears to hypnotize people via video monitors or TV screens, Bob busies himself learning New Math to help Dash with his homework or striving to repair Violet's puppy-love life. He takes her and Dash and Jack-Jack to a family restaurant ("The Happy Platter") owned by Tony's parents. It's a sign of Bird's old-school entertainment chops (and perhaps Vowell's aural expertise) that the biggest laugh in the movie comes from Violet's spectacular nose-spritz the moment she realizes Tony is her waiter.

Elastigirl's exploits are mesmerizing. She can turn her body into a slingshot or a paraglider, or five strands of a spider's web. When her snappy new motorcycle, the Elasticycle, becomes a pair of unicycles, she can stretch enough to ride one on each side of a tunnel. Her part of the story confirms Bird's status as a toy master. That's not merely because of her eye-popping gimmicks, but also because her antagonists let him toy with notions of whether screens are enslaving Americans and superhero fantasies weakening them.

On the other hand, Bob gets belly laughs. Seeing this big fellow try to corral Jack-Jack is as funny as Dustin Hoffman babysitting for Jessica Lange's kid in *Tootsie* (1982). When Jack-Jack explodes with multiple talents (including levitation, telekinesis, laser-blasting, and self-cloning), the kaleidoscopic chaos clarifies the film's most potent message: Moms and dads should treat parenting as an adventure. In a blissful guest-star interlude, that glorious perfectionist Edna Mode (voiced again by Bird himself), couturier to the truly super superstars, develops a maternal streak. She crafts for Jack-Jack his own suit full of sensors that track when he's about to become a devil child or a laser-blaster. "Combustion Imminent," reads the monitor, before Jack-Jack bursts into flames. Whenever that happens, the suit can put out the fire with blackberry lavender retardant.

Bird entwines parody, slapstick, sentiment, and character in the unselfconscious spirit of entertainment that has always characterized our popular art at its best. His movie is a rousing, eclectic grabbag of forms-within-a-form, encompassing everything from mock-newscast to family sitcom. He studs the film with in-jokes. When Jack-Jack flips on the TV we see and hear the intro to *The Outer Limits*: "There is nothing wrong with your television set. Do not attempt to adjust the picture. We are controlling transmission ..."

But it's the way-out jokes that get you. He develops a half-dozen new supporting supers, including Reflux ("Medical condition or superpower? You decide"), who stops bad guys with his molten stomach acid. What's impressive about Bird is that he doesn't sell anyone short or give into stereotypes, even when it comes to a slick wheeler-dealer like Winston Deavor. *Incredibles 2* spins like a pop-art pinwheel because Bird boasts a coherent and scintillating vision. He turns an action comedy about superhumans into a jamboree of human possibilities.

Margaret O'Brien and Judy Garland in *Meet Me in St. Louis*

9

—∞—

HOME MOVIES

For good or ill, families are inescapable, in movies as much as in life. Even their absence is defining. They come in many forms, and not just the nuclear variety. For those lucky (or in tragic cases, unlucky) enough to have them, they are the first social unit they will belong to and a microcosm of all to come. Whether traditional or unconventional, nurturing, neglectful, or abusive, they leave a mark on children that will shape their lives.

Who better to provide insight into the meaning of family than an orphaned bear from Peru? The CGI version of the beloved children's book character and the stuffed animal he inspired comes to the screen in *Paddington* (2014) and *Paddington 2* (2018). Found by the kindly Brown clan in the London train station from which he takes his name, he is adopted and proves his worth as he helps his new family, serves the community, and saves his own skin.

As I write in my essay "The Family Values of *Paddington* (2014) and *Paddington 2* (2017)," the films "preach the requisite virtues of family, individuality, and environmental responsibility" but also cast a "spell of wonder—at the quotidian world, at the magic of the imagination, and at the power of simple decency." And they're funny—what Paddington does with a toothbrush is truly gross and hilarious.

Winnie the Pooh may exceed even Paddington in popularity, but he has his paws full trying to help the grown-up version of his young owner in Marc Forster's *Christopher Robin* (2018), reviewed by Michael Sragow. Married, middle-aged, and with a son of his own, the former innocent of the title has come on hard times. Time for his childhood companion, Pooh, to pay a visit and remind him of what's really important. Like honey, for example. And, as Michael Sragow observes, "instinctive self-knowledge, unselfconscious poise, and authenticity."

When there are no talking bears around to provide guidance, family life can get messy. Based on the fictionalized memoir by Kaylie Jones, daughter of author James Jones, *A Soldier's Daughter Never Cries* (1998) shows a family responding to challenging circumstances with minimal melodramatics. The film's understated style, says David Sterritt, "is a key to its success, and the family's also. *A Soldier's Daughter Never Cries* achieves its greatest drama by *avoiding* drama" and thus "sensitively portray[s] one of contemporary film's most underexplored subjects: a functional family where people really love one another."

A similar family is featured in *Meet Me in St. Louis* (1944), Vincente Minnelli's musical featuring Judy Garland as Esther, the stalwart second eldest of the Smith sisters, famously performing "Have Yourself a Merry Little Christmas." But Little Tootie (Margaret O'Brien), the youngest sibling, doesn't quite harmonize with the rest, especially when the family must move. "Minnelli revisits his own memories with a matchless view of the demons that lurk in the shadows of a sunny childhood," writes Levy. "The dark tone, particularly Tootie's obsession with death, stands out."

Set in Edwardian England at about the same time as *Meet Me in St. Louis*, Lionel Jeffries's adaptation of E. Nesbit's 1906 children's classic *The Railway Children* (1970) also boasts a supportive family, but they face a crisis more harrowing than moving to another city. In the midst of Christmas dinner at their cozy London home, two mysterious men take the father away, leaving his wife and three children to fend for themselves. Luckily, they find a haven in a stone house near a railway station, and new people, rousing adventures, and ingenious plot twists temper their hardship. In "Life without Father in *The Railway Children* (1970)" Sheila Benson writes, "Among the three Railway Children—brave, resourceful, bickering, and marvelously curious—family bonds frequently fray, but they never truly snap."

In Russian director Andrei Zvyagintsev's *Loveless* (2017), family bonds don't snap; they never existed in the first place. A divorced couple in a Moscow apartment argues about the custody of their twelve-year-old son, Alyosha. The twist: Neither wants him, and they don't care if he can hear them saying that. Stricken, he runs away, and no one tries very hard to find him. Peter Rainer sees in this domestic tragedy a microcosm of the entire country. "The sense of apocalyptic doom pervading this movie is felt on both a political and a personal scale," writes Rainer. "Alyosha, with his pugnacious, beseeching face, is not only a lost boy: In the movie's terms, he also represents the loss of something spiritually significant in modern Russia."

If the family in Hirokazu Kore-eda's *Our Little Sister* (2015) is any indication, Japan has the edge over Russia, spirit-wise. Three adult daughters attend their father's funeral and leave with the thirteen-year-old stepsister—the daughter their father had with his mistress—they never knew they had. Despite some residual resentment and domestic adjustment, they welcome her into their home.

As David Sterritt found with *A Soldier's Daughter Never Cries*, this film also succeeds by downplaying the drama and making it real. "While its stakes could not be more emotionally charged," Horton writes,

> its approach . . . is matter-of-fact. It has no evil relatives, no heartless officials. There are quarrels, and a selfish mother and a couple of thoughtless boyfriends, and death, rearing its head at the beginning and the end. But even death is part of the flow, part of the process of getting along and finding a place in the world. In fact, the only villain here is a syrupy musical score.

—⁘—

The Family Values of *Paddington* (2014) and *Paddington 2* (2017)

Peter Keough

Film adaptations of classic children's characters can be judged by the quality and quantity of their fart jokes. Take, for example, *Shrek the Third* (2007), a film that stinks on many levels.

By that measure, *Paddington* (2014), Paul King's live-action plus CGI version of Michael Bond's beloved bear books, scores high. Its one reference to flatulence, although enough to earn a PG rating, is quite demure. True, a lot of marmalade gets spread around, and at times the zaniness gets slap-sticky, but it's all good clean fun.

Paddington falters, however, when it comes to that other pitfall of children's films—the quartet of uplifting, politically correct Hollywood platitudes that includes family bonding, being yourself (which, when you think about it, is a contradiction of the first), protecting the environment, and respecting those different from oneself. The didacticism doesn't bang heads here as much as in other films of this sort, but it detracts a little from *Paddington*'s many charms.

The latter includes Paddington himself, voiced with wistful courtesy and innocence by Ben Whishaw. As generations of readers know, he has stowed away on a cargo ship from his home in Darkest Peru and finds himself alone in the London train station from which he will eventually take his name. The Brown family—father Henry (Hugh Bonneville), wife Mary (Sally Hawkins, as quirky and lovable as a children's book character herself, and one of best things in the movie), and siblings Judy and Jonathan (Madeleine Harris and Samuel Joslin)—are only mildly puzzled when they come across this stranded, talking bear. After some huffing from Henry, they take him home.

In the episodic first book of the series, what follows is a mishmash of misadventures in which Paddington confronts some confounding aspect of the civilized world, makes a mess of it, and inevitably comes out on top. The second film offers lots of that, too, at times improving on the original, as Paddington's wranglings with a bathtub, escalator, or toothbrush (truly gross) expand cleverly into Rube Goldberg devices of disaster reminiscent of the intricately constructed gags of silent comedy.

But unlike books, kids' movies need plots, or at least the adults who make them think they do. *Paddington* starts out with a black-and-white newsreel backstory reminiscent of *Up* (2009) and then borrows liberally from *101 Dalmatians* (1996), with Nicole Kidman in the Cruella DeVil role as Millicent, the dominatrix-like curator of a natural history museum who wants to get Paddington stuffed. This premise serves adequately as a structuring device, despite such smarty-pants sour notes as a riff from the *Mission Impossible* (1996) theme music during one of Millicent's more acrobatic wicked deeds.

What can stop this epitome of the evils of environmental despoliation and intolerance? Nothing less than sticking together as a family and being yourself, of course. Paddington demonstrates the value and appeal of these virtues—but not when it makes speeches about them.

The doughty, beloved bear returns in King's *Paddington 2* (2017), as do all the elements that distinguished the first film, including the gross toothbrush, the marmalade, the platitudes, the delightfully inventive action sequences, and the irresistible, benevolent charm.

It opens with a brief origin recap in which the infant Paddington is rescued from a rushing river by his ursine foster parents, Aunt Lucy (Imelda Staunton) and Uncle Pastuzo (Michael Gambon), who embrace the orphan cub as their own and introduce him to marmalade sandwiches. Paddington shows his appreciation with a burp, the closest the film gets to exploiting a young audience's weakness for dyspeptic humor.

Years later, in London, Paddington has become a favorite of not only the Brown family, but also the entire community, as he selflessly and often inadvertently helps his neighbors to lead better lives. Only mean Mr. Curry (Peter Capaldi), the martinet founder and sole member of his own self-styled community-watch group, and an embodiment of xenophobia, is untouched by the goodness of the innocuous Peruvian bear and denounces him as a foreign "un-desirable." Unlike in real life, however, where such attitudes are valuable political currency, here Mr. Curry is roundly disdained and ignored.

Ever grateful to his now-aged Aunt Lucy (Uncle Pastuzo has sadly passed away) for not only saving his life, but also filling him with homespun wisdom and sending him off to London, Paddington is determined to get her the perfect gift to mark her one-hundredth birthday. He finds it in an antiques shop—an old pop-up book of twelve London landmarks—a city Aunt Lucy has always dreamed of visiting but never did.

The book brings the city to life, and then some. It expands to create scenarios that are wishful fantasies or dazzling flashbacks. It whooshes the characters and the viewer into a wondrous version of an everyday, drab London. It also provides the device that propels the intricate and well-constructed plot. In effect, the film itself is a cinematic pop-up book, brought to life by the film's ingenious set-pieces, spectacular cinematography, sleek editing, and expertise with CGI effects.

Since the book is a rarity and its price is beyond Paddington's means, he sets off on a series of odd jobs, including assisting a barber and working as a window washer, which allows fertile opportunities for some well-choreographed and hilarious slapstick gags reminiscent of great physical comedians like Buster Keaton and Jackie Chan. Unbeknownst to Paddington, however, his money-raising efforts allow Phoenix Buchanan (Hugh Grant, hamming it up and loving it), a narcissistic actor and master of disguise and deception, the opportunity to steal the book for himself. Adding to the injustice, circumstantial evidence and the deceitful testimony of Buchanan and Mr. Curry results in Paddington's conviction and sentence to prison.

Can the gentle Paddington's good nature survive incarceration in a vast Victorian hellhole as dehumanizing as something out of Dickens, filled with hardened criminals, including killers, thieves, and an ex-restaurant critic? Through the miracle of Aunt Lucy's marmalade recipe and by invoking her sagacious sayings ("If you look for the good in people, you'll always find it," etc.), he converts these hard men into an extended family, starting with the meanest and most feared of the lot, "Nuckles" [sic] McGinty (a fierce but endearing Brendan Gleeson).

Meanwhile, his family on the outside is hard at work finding the real perpetrator of the crime. Led by the redoubtable Mrs. Brown, they pursue Buchanan from one London landmark to the next in action sequences that fuse the pages of the stolen book with the actual locations. It's like a combination of Jon Turteltaub's *National Treasure* (2004) and Martin Scorsese's *Hugo* (2011).

Unlike many kids' movies, which try to amuse adults with crass pop references or double entendres, *Paddington 2* instead unobtrusively alludes to such classic films as Alfred Hitchcock's *The 39 Steps* (1935) and Francois Truffaut's *The 400 Blows* (1959). This should engage viewers of all ages, without being condescending to the young or winking and nudging the ribs of grown-ups. Overall it creates a spell of wonder—at the quotidian world, the magic of the imagination, and the power of simple decency—elevating its lessons well above the usual, gaseous Hollywood sentimentality.

—m—

Bearing the Burden of Growing Up in *Christopher Robin* (2018)
Michael Sragow[1]

A Winnie the Pooh movie should be warm and fuzzy. *Christopher Robin*—the story of how the endearingly calm Winnie the Pooh reconnects to the workaholic grown-up (Ewan McGregor) of the title—is just as warm as it needs to be and a bit fuzzier than it ought to be. Although it lacks the sustained, crazy logic of a first-rate flight of imagination, it's still witty and affecting.

Director Marc Forster's fantasia on familiar themes begins where A. A. Milne's two Pooh books end. Pooh the bear (Jim Cummings), Eeyore the donkey (Brad Garrett), Piglet (Nick Mohammed), Rabbit (Peter Capaldi), Owl (Toby Jones), Tigger (Cummings again), Kanga (Sophie Okonedo), and Roo (Sara Sheen)—stuffed animals brought to life in real Sussex woodlands, with computer animation that respects their identities as toys—bid a bittersweet farewell to young Christopher (Orton O'Brien) on the day before he leaves their Hundred Acre Wood for boarding school.

Owl and Rabbit bicker about who's cleverer or wiser; woebegone Eeyore recites his elegiac poem, "POEM" ("Do we care? / We do. / Very much."); Piglet sweetly bequeaths "haycorns" for Christopher to remember him by; and Pooh and the boy wander to what Milne called their "Enchanted Place," where, the author wrote, "They could see the whole world spread out until it reached the sky." There Christopher explains that what he likes doing best is nothing, although he won't be able to do nothing any more. Pooh promises not to forget him, not even when Christopher is one hundred and Pooh therefore is ninety-nine.

After this funny, poignant prologue (drawn from Milne), the movie deftly illustrates, in swift dramatic vignettes and chapter headings of sepia and cream, how Christopher becomes the one who forgets their friendship. The early loss of his father, front-line service in World War II, and the pressures of depressed postwar England squeeze the stuffing out of the boy. We pick up the main story when he's in his thirties and looks fifty. Now chief of the efficiency department at an upscale luggage manufacturing company, he struggles to provide for his wife, Evelyn (Hayley Atwell), and their nine-year-old, Madeline (Bronte Carmichael). Evelyn despairs that she never sees him smile. Madeline asks him to read a bed-time story, hoping for *Treasure Island* (good taste, that girl), but he reaches for a history book instead. The breaking point comes when Christopher sends Evelyn and Madeline on a planned trip to his family's rural cottage and stays behind in London to work. He must cut twenty percent of the company's operating budget by Monday. Can he save his marriage, his family, and the jobs of his coworkers, too? Maybe, just maybe—with the aid of Madeline, the Hundred Acre Wood crowd, and, especially, Winnie the Pooh.

The plot of Christopher Robin follows the Disney *Mary Poppins* (1964) template: To redeem his soul and preserve his home, the man of the house must relearn how revitalizing it can be to fly a kite or, in this case, a balloon. What brings Winnie the Pooh to London is not a blast of the East Wind à la *Poppins* but some accidental magic. Madeline lifts her father's drawing of Pooh out of a box she finds filled with his childhood keepsakes and leaves it for him on the kitchen table. Dashing off to his job, Christopher spills honey all over it. That's when Pooh awakens in his house, far away inside a tree. Out of honey and unable to locate his pals, Pooh seeks his erstwhile human buddy. Pooh goes to the boy's former tree house, daring to use the "door through which Christopher Robin is known to appear"—and finds himself in London. The ensuing adventures re-unite Pooh and Christopher, and send them hurtling back and forth between the bustling metropolis and the Hundred Acre Wood.

I love the way the director, Marc Forster, presents the story's turning point so matter-of-factly and inexplicably. The bear's sleep cap falls over his eyes like a sleep mask, so when he wakes up, he wonders where he is. As soon as he can see, he goes looking for honey. It's both droll and moving that his appetites for food and affection lead him in the same direction.

But what is really happening here? Partly because of that sleep cap, I as-sumed that Christopher's neglect of his old playmates had put Pooh into deep hibernation and the others into limbo. For a while, even the forest looks to be in a grey funk, as if Christopher had personally depressed an entire magic kingdom. Yet the characters carry on as if it's merely an exceptionally foggy Windsday. Too much stuff just happens—Forster doesn't provide an imaginative framework to deepen or enrich the whimsy. Of course, it's a difficult thing to do, given that wool-gathering is part of the characters' charm. But the film's five writers have not mastered the challenge. It's as if they can't see the Hundred Acre Wood for the trees.

Maybe they were all having too much fun varying Milne's slapstick strokes (the adult Christopher gets stuck in a portal the way Pooh usually does) or paying homage to the fifty-year-old Disney cartoon shorts (Tigger gets to deliver his signature ditty: "The wonderful thing about Tiggers / Is Tiggers are wonderful things / Their tops are made out of rubber / Their bottoms are made out of springs"). They do their best work when they're most inventive: Madeline has a delightful moment when Pooh, Eeyore, Piglet, and Tigger pretend to be her stuffed pets in a train car, yet she still orders five cups of tea.

Forster and his team do excel at fleshing or furring out the film's call for go-getters to stop and smell the tea leaves. The script's demand for compulsive adults to cease messing up their family life would be harsh were it not for Pooh's perfection as a foil. Although he famously sighs that he's a "bear of very little brain," he's actually honest and wise, as Benjamin Hoff demonstrates in his classic 1982 best seller *The Tao of Pooh* (a probable influence on this movie). Christopher declares that he enjoys doing nothing, but the bear is the one who sees its existential value: "Doing nothing often leads to the very best kind of something." Except for his relentless pursuit of honey, which inevitably leaves havoc in its wake, Pooh doesn't try to force the outcome of events. "Sometimes if I am going somewhere and I wait, somewhere comes to me," Pooh says. He exemplifies instinctive self-knowledge, unselfconscious poise, and authenticity.

He's also tremendously entertaining, thanks to his sea otter–like capacity for solving problems through play. Christopher realizes that to restrain him from becoming a public spectacle in the city, all he must do is get Pooh to "play naptime." Pooh invents his own game on the train to the country, "Say What You See," and appears to enjoy reciting, "House . . . tree . . . grass." He boasts a full share of malapropisms, like hearing "efficiency" as "a fish in the sea." His literal yet original use of language restores the sting to tired figures of speech. After Christopher says that some employees may be "let go," Pooh asks whether that's what he did to Pooh for a couple of decades—let go of him.

Cummings, Pooh's cartoon voice for thirty years, still finds fresh ways to evoke his human-ursine sensibility. When Christopher asks him to be a less "exuberant" version of himself, Pooh swiftly interjects "ex-Pooh-berant" under his breath. The model-makers and animators match Cummings's variety and delicacy: They achieve maximum feeling via minimalist facial expressions, for example, the slightest upturn of his mouth or tug of his round cheeks. Brad Garrett is equally soulful as Eeyore: No one could be better at bringing doleful overtones to upbeat declarations. Garrett is never more uproarious than when Eeyore proclaims, at the end of his poem, "If anybody wants to clap, now is the time to do it."

McGregor does all he can to enliven Christopher, a human on the verge of a nervous breakdown. His first laugh, when he boldly jumps into a fearsome stream from his youth and learns that the water now comes to his shins, is a wonderful thing. The strong, dramatic Atwell and the blissfully unaffected young Carmichael help him meet the task of embodying a conflicted family in story-book circumstances.

Forster, who first won acclaim for *Monster's Ball* in 2001, has put together a varied resume, including the weighty adaptation of Afghan American novelist Khaled Hosseini's *The Kite Runner* (2007) and the arty Bond film *Quantum of Solace* (2008). The Forster films I like contain fantastic elements. Magical realism redeems *Finding Neverland* (2004), sportive metafiction supports intelligent comedy in *Stranger Than Fiction* (2006), and graphic-novel zombie horror engulfs us in *World War Z* (2013). Forster creates an exact heightened atmosphere for each illusion to thrive, which is what he does in *Christopher Robin*. The film is not as vibrant or virtuosic as those other British talking-bear movies, the superb *Paddington* (2014) and *Paddington 2* (2017), but that may be inevitable, given Pooh's pastoral tradition. *Christopher Robin* is ambitious yet snug, and borderline sentimental: I wish Christopher didn't have to spell out that Pooh is a bear "of a Very Big Heart." But the movie generally honors Milne's idylls.

At times this film resembles 2017's *Goodbye Christopher Robin*, which tells how the real-life boy came to feel exploited by his parents and a new celebrity culture. But that film ended up whiney and reductive about Pooh power. Forster's movie restores Milne's magic and humor. So, I say, "Two cheers for Christopher Robin!" If anybody else wants to clap, now is the time to do it.

A Family Melodrama without the Drama in *A Soldier's Daughter Never Cries* (1998)
David Sterritt

The longtime team of director James Ivory, producer Ismail Merchant, and screenwriter Ruth Prawer Jhabvala earned great acclaim for such literary adaptations as *A Room with a View* (1985) and *Howards End* (1992), and Indian dramas like *Shakespeare-Wallah* (1965) and *Heat and Dust* (1983). But sometimes the group told stories with less exotic pedigrees. *A Soldier's Daughter Never Cries* (1998) is based on a fictionalized memoir by Kaylie Jones, whose father was James Jones, author of such major novels as *From Here to Eternity* (1951) and *The Thin Red Line* (1962).

In her book, the younger Jones recalls her family's life in Paris when she was a child in the 1960s, her struggle with jealousy when her parents adopted a French boy surrendered by his unmarried mother, and the household's move to the United States not long before her father's death. The movie follows the same trajectory and uses the same pseudonyms (Bill, Marcella, and Channe Willis) that Jones gives her family in the book. Rather than transfer the memoir to the screen in a literal-minded way, however, the filmmakers divide the story into three chapters named after their pivotal characters.

The first one, "Billy," introduces Bill (Kris Kristofferson) and Marcella (Barbara Hershey) as loving, somewhat bohemian parents with a taste for drinking and partying. It also shows the complicated feelings that hit Channe (Leelee Sobieski) when six-year-old Benoît (played by Jesse Bradford in later scenes) joins the clan. The second chapter, "Francis," focuses on Channe's adolescent friendship with a classmate (Anthony Roth Costanzo), who seems like a living catalog of gay stereotypes—dressing flamboyantly, doting on his mother (Jane Birkin), eager to succeed in the "opera business" when he grows up—until he abruptly tells Channe he loves her with a passion. The third chapter, "Daddy," finds the Willis clan setting down new roots in New Hampshire, where Bill's heart weakens, Marcella's drinking grows, and Channe slowly adjusts to unfamiliar American ways.

In their most daring and brilliant decision, the filmmakers omit the step-by-step details of what happens between the three chapters, letting each one sketch a portrait of Channe at a particular stage of life. At first it seems strange that Francis vanishes so completely after chapter two that his name is never even mentioned, but then you realize that life works the same way, with an array of friends, colleagues, and acquaintances continually coming and going as we grow, change, and evolve throughout the years. The gaps and uncertainties also remind us that the film is based on a memoir, and some of the things we never learn about the characters—does Marcella appreciate Bill's writing? what holds their marriage together?—are things that Channe herself wouldn't know or understand as a girl. By letting us fill in the blanks on our own, *A Soldier's Daughter Never Cries* remains true to real experience and signals that its deepest concern is with the meanings and mechanisms of memory itself.

The theme of memory resonates most movingly in the final scene. In a prologue before chapter 1, we see Benoît's teenage mother (Virginie Ledoyen) writing her thoughts in a journal that she gives to the Willises, and during the film we see Marcella urging Benoît to overcome his reluctance and read it. In an epilogue at the end, after Bill has died and the others have come to terms with their sad loss, Marcella gives her effort one more try. As she and Channe enjoy a sunny day nearby, Benoît finally picks up the journal and opens it.

It's the perfect setup for a Hollywood-style revelation or catharsis or burst of emotion—but Benoît then closes up the journal, shoves it aside, and walks away to enjoy the sunshine with the others. *A Soldier's Daughter Never Cries* achieves its greatest drama by *avoiding* drama, sensitively portraying one of contemporary film's most underexplored subjects: a functional family where people really love one another and would rather live in a contented present than dredge up the discontented past. Few movies capture the essence of family so warmly, so gracefully, so intelligently.

Not Such a Merry Little Christmas in *Meet Me in St. Louis* (1944)
Emanuel Levy

Meet Me in St. Louis, made in 1944, marked a turning point for director Vincente Minnelli, as well as the Hollywood musical genre. Although coming out of MGM's factory, it was the first time since Rouben Mamoulian's *Love Me Tonight* (1932) that a musical film had been filtered through and was the expression of its director's unified vision.

In his third credited film—and first masterpiece—Minnelli fuses brilliantly the elements of a musical (songs, performances, cinematography, décor, and costumes) in service of his singular sensibility. Stylistically, the film demonstrates Minnelli's fluid camera, relying on swirling movement and smooth dissolves rather than sharp cuts and elaborate montage, attributes of the Busby Berkeley style.

Set in St. Louis at the turn of the twentieth century, *Meet Me in St. Louis* is a nostalgic film in which the memory of a harmonious past and the promise of a glorious future lend the present a warm glow. The film unfolds as a family album in which each scene presents an aspect of daily life in an idealized way. Its formal organization into seasons is in complete harmony with the family's life.

The concluding act, set in the spring, a period of renewal, shows the family at the Louisiana Purchase Exposition, informally known as the St. Louis World's Fair. Looking at the glittering lights with awe, Judy Garland's character, Esther Smith, says, "I didn't dream anything could be so beautiful! It's right in our own back yard! I can't believe it! Right here where we live. Right here in St. Louis!"

Minnelli shot the film in Technicolor, rendering glorious color with extreme intensity and brightness, which contributes to his lush mise-en-scène. Notice the striking red hair of Esther and her sister Rose (Lucille Bremer). He makes sure that in every sequence, Judy Garland stands out in the crowd, wearing a red gown at Christmas, a black one in the Trolley sequence, and so on.

Hugh Martin and Ralph Blane's songs emerge naturally from the characters' feelings or situations, but they never impede the action. The songs illustrate personal romances or social gatherings, which coexist in harmony. Except for one, "You and I," Judy Garland sings all the songs in solo or as part of the group; however, then as now, audiences mostly remember Judy's heartfelt renditions of "The Boy Next Door," "The Trolley Song," and, particularly, "Have Yourself a Merry Little Christmas," songs that later became a staple at her concerts.

The film shows the Smith family at times of unity and celebration: Halloween and Christmas. It ends with family's visit at the St. Louis World's Fair, a confirmation to audiences of 1944 that in staying home, nothing had been sacrificed by the Smiths. Although a secular event, in its function, the World's Fair becomes another religious holiday.

Every act begins with a similar candy-box title card, then moves in toward the house. The story seldom departs from the home, and when it does, it's for communal occasions, for example, the trolley sequence to see the fair's construction or the Christmas dance. Home is a self-sufficient place, making all other institutions peripheral, and even threatening.

The ideology of the film, justified perhaps by the time in which the tale is set and the time in which it was made (during World War II) is admittedly conservative, celebrating a unified three-generational family. Minnelli places at the center the family's women, serving as symbols of social order, stability, and continuity, a reflection that in 1944, most American men were mobilized in the war effort.

The men, on the other hand, present a threat to the family's unity. Initially, the patriarchal Mr. Smith wants to take the family away to New York, and his son Lon wishes to attend college in the East. Moreover, significantly, the grandfather sides with the women and is often seen in the kitchen, which is a typical women's domain.

Taking a mythical approach, *Meet Me in St. Louis* tries to reconcile the dichotomies of art versus reality, stability versus change, small-town America versus the big city, extended versus nuclear family, East and West, past and present. At the end, the World's Fair becomes both a dream image and hometown reality for the Smith family.

That said, the film can't really (or completely) conceal that the family's unity is in danger and that change is just around the corner. The lyrics of Judy Garland's song "Have Yourself a Merry Little Christmas"—"Someday soon we all will be together, if the Fates allow / Until then we'll have to muddle through somehow"—signify that the old way of life will never be the same.

Interestingly, the MGM top moguls at first were reluctant to make the musical, arguing that it was plotless and that there was no real drama or conflict. For her part, Judy didn't want to make the film, claiming that at twenty-one she should not be playing adolescents anymore. A brilliant, if insecure, performer, Judy was also fearful that that the youngest sister, Tootie, was really the starring role. Judy was right. The prized juvenile Margaret O'Brien (MGM's answer to Fox's Shirley Temple) stole every scene. Giving the movie's most extraordinary performance, O'Brien won a special child Oscar that year.

From first frame to last, *Meet Me* is a delectable, beautifully evoked entertainment. For the first time in musical history, nostalgia was used in the service of art. The industry showed its appreciation with four Oscar nominations, one of which was for George Folsey's luminous cinematography.

Minnelli's favorite sequence, and the reason for doing such a nostalgic picture, was the ominous Halloween sequence. Dressed in grotesque costumes, Tootie says she's a "horrible ghost who died of a broken heart." When none of the kids wants to take on the local ogre, Mr. Braukoff, Tootie volunteers for the job. After flinging flour in his glowering face, she shouts, "I hate you," then tells her friends, "I killed him. I'm the most horrible!" In this impeccably directed scene, Minnelli revisits his own memories with a matchless view of the demons that lurk in the shadows of a sunny childhood. The dark tone, particularly Tootie's obsession with death, stands out. In the course of the story, Tootie buries her dolls, which died of mysterious illnesses; she accuses the boy next door of trying to kill her when he pulls her from the path of an oncoming trolley; and she "kills" Mr. Braukoff on Halloween. Tootie is so distraught about her father's imminent job transfer that she literally goes berserk and, in hysterical frenzy, demolishes her family of snowmen (possibly standing in for her own family).

Released in the fall of 1944, to glowing reviews, *Meet Me in St. Louis* became MGM's second-highest-grossing film (after *Gone with the Wind*), even more popular than Judy Garland's 1939 musical *The Wizard of Oz*.

—◊◊◊—

Life without Father in *The Railway Children* (1970)

Sheila Benson

Lionel Jeffries's lively, loving film of E. Nesbit's enduring 1906 novel *The Railway Children* is a tribute to the deepest bonds of family, set in the Yorkshire country-side in 1905, a more innocent time and place. Made in 1970, director-screenwriter Jeffries's adaptation stages the adventures of three uprooted London children with crisp straightforwardness, buoyed by Johnny Douglas's rollicking score, heavy on music hall piano. There is a nice modesty to Jeffries's work, nothing show-offy about it, even when half a hillside is tumbling onto railroad tracks or a train is rushing into a tunnel where we know someone is trapped. He also understands the power of withholding—of making an audience want something, want it even more, then finally giving it to them. The way Jeffries handles the *giving* is what has made the film a classic.

The Railway Children is a case where the writer, largely unknown in the United States, has a hallowed place in British fiction, and it behooves her director/adaptor to tread carefully. E. (for Edith) Nesbit's more than forty books for children—still in print, every one, after more than a hundred years—may turn to magic at times and even to time-travel, but they are anchored in recognizable Edwardian settings, not fantasy worlds. And of them all, *The Railway Children* is the most securely anchored in the recognizable everyday.

It's clear from the rich Christmas opening sequence that Jeffries, a notable character actor himself, respects, even relishes, every detail of Edwardian family life. This is not Uncle Walt, having his way with P. L. Travers.

Jeffries sets things in motion in an upscale parlor crammed with every delight and invention, as the Charles Waterbury family gathers for Christmas night dinner: ebullient, mutton-chopped Father (Iain Cutherbertson); Mother (Dinah Sheridan, exemplary); eldest daughter Bobbie (Jenny Agutter); her younger sister Phil (Sally Thomsett); and their younger brother Peter (Gary Warren), clutching his perfect model train engine.

As befits the best melodramas, everyone's life is changed with a knock at the door. Without explanation, the three children and their mother watch as their "perfect" father (a high-level foreign office diplomat) is taken away in a carriage by two official-looking men.

With their father's disappearance shrouded in mystery, certainly from his children, and in drastically reduced straits, Mother moves the family to a three-chimneyed stone house high in the Yorkshire countryside. From there it's a short run and tumble down to the railway station, where gleaming brass and mahogany steam engines stop daily. For London-bred children—and train lovers— it's heaven. (Middle-class Edwardian "poor," we discover, still require that Cook functions in the kitchen and that there is someone other than Mother to wash and iron the girls' pinafores every day. Mother, modeled on Nesbit herself, sets about writing children's stories, which seem to pay exactly as well then as now. When she sells one, there are buns for tea.)

As the children's remarkable adventures begin, the train station, its tracks, its tunnels, even its passengers become part of the fabric of their daily lives. And there at the station they find Perks, the harried station master (the great Bernard Cribbins), a character as richly dimensional as any in Dickens, and as rewarding to revisit.

The Railway Children is crisscrossed like train tracks by a series of fortuitous meetings. Meeting Perks leads to meeting his struggling wife and their great many children (as well as an agonizing misreading by the *Railway* trio of how Good Works can backfire). Meeting a collapsed foreign gentleman at the station leads to restoring a dissident Russian writer to his wife and children. Meeting the elegant, silk hatted Old Gentleman, who regularly rides the train, leads to, well . . . more-or-less the jackpot of chance encounters. *Family* unifies them all, warming us in its afterglow.

Among the three Railway Children—brave, resourceful, bickering, and marvelously curious—family bonds frequently fray, but they never truly snap. Jenny Agutter's soulful Bobbie is the film's grounding performance. At fifteen, she's the most aware of their mother's struggles and most deeply affected by the loss of her father. Balancing at the edge of maturity, at once compassionate and yearning, Agutter glows.

Garry Warren's Peter manages a nice balance between brashness and brotherly concern. And as slightly dense Phil, "who *means* well," Sally Thomsett is just dim enough. (Agutter and *The Railway Children* have become inseparable. She played Bobbie in TV versions before and after Jeffries's film and moved up to the role of Mother for BBC in 1970.)

You may notice the bones of E. Nesbit's politics poking their way through this turn-of-the-century fabric. Nesbit and her husband were founding members of the socialist Fabian Society, and Bobbie seems to have gone to their meetings, and taken notes.

Forever needing the services of the local village doctor (to treat life-threatening influenza, the perilous health of the escaped Russian writer, the broken leg of a dashing sixteen-year-old athlete) Bobbie proposes that the doctor create a "club" for his patients, just like the one their Cook belongs to: "She only pays two pence a week for her doctoring!" Bobbie says presciently.

In a film with more than its share of harrowing moments, Jeffries saves the fullest rush of emotion for his conclusion, holding back, making the audience peer through smoke and steam, until Bobbie's call of "Daddy, oh my Daddy!" comes through the mist—enough to crack the most hardened heart.

—∽∿∽—

A Child Is Lost in *Loveless* (2017)
Peter Rainer[2]

The single most powerful moment in any movie I saw in 2018 occurs roughly ten minutes into *Loveless* (2017), an Oscar nominee for Best Foreign Film (it lost to *A Fantastic Woman*) from extraordinary Russian director Andrey Zvyagintsev. A divorced couple, Zhenya (Maryana Spivak) and Boris (Aleksey Rozin), are arguing bitterly in the apartment they share with their twelve-year-old son Alyosha (Matvey Novikov). The fight concerns custody but with a catch: Neither parent wants to care for the boy. Zhenya is involved with a wealthy older man and is looking to sell the apartment; Boris has a young and very pregnant girlfriend. The rancorous back-and-forth suddenly cuts to a brief shot of little Alyosha, weeping and fearful. He has been listening to the fight behind a door.

We barely get to know Alyosha before he vanishes from the movie. His unexplained disappearance is first noted by his school authorities, and not by his mother, who spent the previous day with her lover. The crisis brings together Zhenya and Boris, but only in more rancor and recrimination. They are enraged by their own feelings of blame and guilt, and, perhaps, also by the dawning realization that, on a deeper level, the loss of Alyosha absolves them from caring for him.

This is Zvyaginstev's fifth feature. Like his most celebrated previous movies, *The Return* (2003), which was about a father who returns to his wife and two sons after a mysterious twelve-year absence, and *Leviathan* (2014), about a corrupt rural mayor who forces a family from their home, it can be approached as both domestic drama and allegory. Set in 2012, in suburban Moscow, the missing-boy scenario is periodically interrupted by news reports from the television about conflicts in Ukraine. The sense of apocalyptic doom pervading this movie is felt on both a political and personal scale. Alyosha, with his pugnacious, beseeching face, is not only a lost boy: In the movie's terms, he also represents the loss of something spiritually significant in modern Russia, which, as portrayed by Zvyaginstev and his cowriter, Oleg Negin, looks ghastly and grayed out.

The police, believing they are dealing with nothing more alarming than a truant, are of no great help in locating Alyosha. It is left to a well-organized band of volunteers, who tack up posters and fan out across the wooded surrounding terrain, to attempt his recovery. It is dispiriting to note that their mobilization has become second nature: There are so many lost children in the city that one of the first places the volunteers check is an abandoned building where runaways often seek shelter.

Zvyaginstev has always been wildly ambitious, sometimes to a fault, and *Loveless* is perhaps his most encompassing indictment of Russian society. Not all the indicting is equally successful. Those TV bulletins about Ukraine, for example, are too on-the-nose. He is at his most effective when the political and the personal are seamlessly conjoined—when we see, for example, how the graspingness of modern society is perfectly reflected in the formidably selfish Zhenya, a beauty salon owner who seems epoxied to her mobile phone and cares only for material gain. Her connection to her rich lover, who affectionately calls her the "most wonderful monster in the world," is the height of cynicism. And then there is Boris, who works as a middle manager in a tech company. He is terrified that his ultra-religious boss, who requires his employees to be married with kids, will discover his divorce. (Boris seems less concerned about the revelation of Alyosha's disappearance.)

Is the vast comfortlessness of this film's view of Russia justified? The Soviet era, which is what modern Russia, with its capitalist oligarchs, broke away from, was not, after all, the good old days. (This film could not have been made in that era.) The *imposed* bleakness in *Loveless* can seem overly coercive. Nowhere, it seems, is there a safe harbor. Even the volunteers with the search party aren't blameless: They won't explore the nearby lake because they draw the line at dredging bodies.

When Alyosha's parents visit Zhenya's mother (Natalya Potapova) in the hope that the boy fled there, it's almost comically awful to discover that the old lady is even more venomous than Zhenya. (Boris calls her "Stalin in a skirt.") This, at least, helps explain why Zhenya is the way she is—she, too, was an unwanted child.

In the end, Zvyaginstev would have done better, I think, to include more of the beauty that has gone out of this world, if only to heighten its loss.

—◠◡◠—

A Child Is Found in *Our Little Sister* (2015)
Robert Horton[3]

Three adult sisters stand on a small-town road, gazing at the discharge from a nearby chimney. "Smoke from a crematorium is so old-fashioned," one of them remarks—not as a put-down, but more as a dreamy observation. The ashes inside the chimney are what remains of their father, but the sense of detachment is understandable; he abandoned his family fifteen years earlier to be with another woman and have another child. The sisters have come to his town for a dutiful funeral visit. As quickly as possible, they will return to their seaside city of Kamakura, where they share a house.

They will not get away without complications, which is how Hirokazu Koreeda's wonderful new film (based on Akimi Yoshida's award-winning graphic novel *Umimachi Diary*) takes flight. The title *Our Little Sister* refers to the father's other daughter, the now-adolescent Suzu (Suzu Hirose). In a blunt but necessary narrative contrivance, the little girl's mother is also dead, so her only blood relatives are her three half-sisters. Is there room in the Kamakura house for one more? Of course there is. But given the resentment the older sisters still feel toward their father's exit from their lives and given that Suzu is the living embodiment of that abandonment, inviting the girl to join their lives will be a difficult challenge.

Or maybe not that difficult. One of the things I like most about this movie is that while its stakes could not be more emotionally charged, its approach to drama is matter-of-fact. It has no evil relatives, no heartless officials. There are quarrels, and a selfish mother and a couple of thoughtless boyfriends, and death, rearing its head at the beginning and the end. But even death is part of the flow, part of the process of getting along and finding a place in the world. In fact, the only villain here is a syrupy musical score.

The three older sisters have distinct traits, perhaps formed by their abandonment. The responsible oldest, Sachi (Haruka Ayase), is a nurse whose romance with a doctor has distinct complexities. Her sober demeanor contrasts with that of middle sister Yoshino (Masami Nagasawa), who likes sake and hooking up with irresponsible men. Youngest sister Chika (Kaho) barely remembers her father and seems the happiest of the three—content with the steady paycheck from a shoe store and the jovial company of her goofball boyfriend, an ex-mountaineer who lost a few toes to frostbite. Everyone's basically all right—or at least "it isn't anyone's fault," as one character says. That's as close as Kore-eda comes to a statement of meaning.

Kore-eda, whose previous films include the superb *Nobody Knows* (2004) and *Like Father, Like Son* (2013), is a scrapbooker. Toward the end of this film, someone asks what memories the group will recall at the moment of death (a subject that takes up the entirety of Kore-eda's 1998 film *After Life*). *Our Little Sister* is like a collection of those moments: running for a train, walking down a street on a summer day, picking plums for bottling plum wine. Another would have to be the scene where Suzu sits with her new sisters in their favorite seafood place, watching them chatter about this and that in the unforced manner of family; as the scene goes along, you see the realization spread across Suzu's face that she is now a part of this imperfect but vital organism, a role previously unknown to her. If this description has not made it clear, good luck staying dry-eyed during this movie.

Another reason I loved this film is the presence of food. That fish joint unexpectedly becomes a central location, but there's also a lot of cooking and consuming in general. This fits my still-developing thesis about how the greatest directors focus on food prep and dining as central elements in their worldviews. Hitchcock knew all about it; so did Yasujirô Ozu (whose 1953 masterpiece *Tokyo Story* is strongly evoked here). In *Our Little Sister*, plum wine and whitebait toast have very specific, sometimes heartbreaking connections to people and experiences. That's sufficient drama for this gentle beauty of a film.

Elsie Fisher in *Eighth Grade*

10

—⚉—

FROM CRITIC TO CHILD

Even film critics grow up, but they retain that dreamy wonder that colored their first glimpse of the big screen and got them excited about the medium in the first place. The essays in this chapter explore the connection between that sensibility and how it helps in understanding the nature of movies and the way both children and adults respond to them.

In his essay about the great Japanese animator Hayao Miyazaki's inexhaustibly imaginative *Howl's Moving Castle* (2004), Jonathan Rosenbaum finds himself tapping into his earliest memories. "It gave me back a few flashes of myself as a child," he writes, "bringing back images from dreams I'd long forgotten—dreams of distant lands and immense aerial vistas."

One lesson learned from drawing on one's own youthful experience is that a successful children's film neither condescends to the audience nor overindulges in adult sophistication and irony. According to Kenneth Turan in his essay "Hip Heroes," the live-action comedy *Elf* (2003), about a grown-up human raised as a worker in Santa's workshop, and the animated *Shrek* (2001), about the ogre from William Steig's classic children's book, pull off that balancing act. He explains how these two films combine an ironic point of view with an innocence that appeals to both adults and children. The secret? Although savvy and sophisticated, the filmmakers don't pander to either audience, nor do they indulge in sentimentality. The two films, writes Turan, "are examples of the good things that can happen when hipsters do it on the square. Genuinely sweet, as well as wised up, they both bring sophisticated glee and a sense of innocent fun."

Auteur Howard Hawks mastered this knack for tapping into both adult sophistication and youthful simplicity. In *Hatari!* (1962), he tells the story of wranglers played by John Wayne, Red Buttons, and Elsa Martinelli, who capture wild animals on the Serengeti for zoos. Watching the film as a grown-up, Charles

Taylor recalls one of the concerns youngsters might have watching a film of this kind. "No harm comes to any of the wild animals in the film," he reassures the kid in all of us. Instead, he reflects on the positive glow the film puts on what being a grown-up can be. "[F]or adults . . . it can be like seeing the confident, charismatic self you always wanted to be," he writes. "For kids, it makes being an adult look like fun."

The adults in the films I write about in "Borderline Taste" don't act very grown up, but that was why I thought they were fun. I recall how, when I was a teenager, watching such buffoonery in *The Russians Are Coming! The Russians Are Coming!* (1966) with my parents brought us closer together. Years later, as a film critic, an assignment to review *¡Three Amigos!* (1986) jolted me back to the goof-iness I enjoyed back then and helped me bond with my nephews as we competed in imitating the best lines from the movie.

For David Fear, the Pixar animated feature *Inside Out* (2015), in which an eleven-year-old girl's emotions are personified as characters, not only helped him understand the emotions his own daughter was going through at the time but reminded him of his own feelings when he was her age. "Movies helped me process emotions when I was young," he writes. "And then, decades later, with . . . a daughter nearly the age of the kid onscreen, it helped me process them again."

Roger Ebert might have been one of our greatest film critics, but even he had to consult at times with the experts—the kids themselves. He watched *E.T. the Extra-Terrestrial* (1982) with his two grandchildren "to see how a boy on his fourth birthday, and a girl who had just turned seven a week ago, would respond to the movie." When one of the children noted that the audience was seeing things the way E.T. would see them, Ebert recognized that a key to the movie is point of view. "Almost every single important shot is seen either as E.T. would see it or as Elliott would see it," he writes. "And things are understood as they would understand them." In other words, the child empathizes with the other-ness of the alien because both find themselves lost in a threatening, confusing world run by grown-ups.

Two movies helped Mary Pols bond with her son, detailed in her essay "Watching *Boyhood* (2014) with a Boy and *Eighth Grade* (2018) with an Eighth Grader." While she and her ten-year-old son watched the former film about a boy growing up in a twelve-year period, she had an insight into the film's great-ness. "*Boyhood* speaks to a central tenet of childhood, namely that is a place of both helplessness and magic," she writes.

Four years later, she and her now-eighth-grade boy watched *Eighth Grade* (2018). In a scene where the heroine, Kayla, rebuffs a bullying sexual advance, her son reacted with relief. He knew that what the boy was trying to do was wrong and what she does was right. "He got it," Pols writes. "On screen, Kayla got it too. She said no. This most vulnerable-seeming of girls . . . knew her own self-worth and stood up for herself. She transcended the stereotypes I grew up with. She was of my son's generation."

Where the Kids Are: *Howl's Moving Castle* (2004)
Jonathan Rosenbaum[1]

Sometimes movies earmarked for kids are a lot more nuanced, sophisticated, and mature than the ones that are allegedly for grown-ups. As a nonparent, I often avoid PG fare, but *Howl's Moving Castle* (2004) suggests that maybe I shouldn't.

Every character in *Howl's Moving Castle*—derived from an English novel by Diana Wynne Jones—is both lovable and seriously flawed, and although a war does rage around them, the only villains are the faceless forces on both sides that keep it going.

The castle in *Howl's Moving Castle* is a weirdly animated amalgam of thing, creature, and place. So is much of the rest of Hayao Miyazaki's wonderful movie—whether it's a flame named Calcifer (the voice of Billy Crystal), a scarecrow named Turnip Head, the endless stretch of steps leading to the royal palace, or a spectacular paradisiacal meadow. Everything and everyone are undergoing perpetual transformation in this enchanted universe, where magical spells serve either to clarify or conceal certain traits, but people, things, and places persist.

Most radically changed is Sophie, the heroine, who's transformed by the obese Witch of the Waste (Lauren Bacall) from a withdrawn eighteen-year-old hat maker (Emily Mortimer) into Grandma Sophie (Jean Simmons), the castle's take-charge housekeeper. Grandma Sophie's romantic feelings for Howl (Christian Bale), the young wizard and master of the moving castle, periodically make her look eighteen again—to us and to herself, if not to the other characters. The greedy Witch of the Waste, who's made herself young, is returned to senile old age as a punishment, but then she's unexpectedly adopted and even indulged by the household of the moving castle. Howl, a sloppy if handsome cartoon prince, goes from being a brash warrior to an angry pacifist while periodically sprouting wings and undergoing other physical transformations.

Miyazaki, born in 1941, has a refreshing and persuasive way of relating youth to old age and callowness to wisdom. Rather than presenting them succeeding one another and fighting for supremacy, he shows them coexisting peacefully. And he does this with characters so nuanced and real one keeps discovering new things about them at every turn.

A recent daylong reunion of my grammar-school class gave me back a few flashes of myself as a child. *Howl's Moving Castle* did the same thing, bringing back images from dreams I'd long forgotten—dreams of distant lands and immense aerial vistas. I can't swear these were dreams I had as a kid, but it's irrelevant, because in some way we're always children when we dream. And as adults we're always rediscovering and revising our childhood—which is related to why Grandma Sophie keeps recovering her eighteen-year-old self and then teaching that self a thing or two.

According to Richard James Havis in the *Hollywood Reporter*, *Howl's Moving Castle* has made $192 million in Japan. Yet, its success in the United States is uncertain. "Plotting is so multifaceted that it will confuse children," he writes, "and it lacks the clear-cut heroes and villains typical of animation."[2] Does this mean he thinks Japanese children are more sophisticated and less easily confused than American children? Or that the $192 million was paid only by Japanese grown-ups?

I'm less concerned about kids anywhere finding joy in this movie than I am about American adults who worry about the absence of clear-cut heroes and villains. The uncommon respect shown both kids and adults in *Howl's Moving Castle*—and its distaste for violence and war—is an ideal rebuttal.

—⁓—

Hip Heroes: *Elf* (2003) and *Shrek* (2001)
Kenneth Turan

Unlike Frog and Toad, "Elf" and "Shrek" are not friends. They probably don't even know each other. But if introduced, they would likely get along famously. Even though one is human, the other animated, they have a lot in common.

Both *Elf*, the 2003 live action film directed by Jon Favreau, and 2001's *Shrek*, directed by Andrew Adamson and Vicky Jenson for DreamWorks Animation, are examples of the good things that can happen when hipsters do it on the square. Genuinely sweet, as well as wised up, they both bring sophisticated glee and a sense of innocent fun to what could have been traditional family films that were DOA.

The fable of what transpires when a young man raised by elves goes back to investigate his human roots, *Elf* was written by David Berenbaum and was an early success for star Will Ferrell. Ferrell's exactly right as Buddy, who as an infant at an orphanage snuck into Santa's bag and became the first human to penetrate the fastness of Santa's North Pole workshop. Adopted by Papa Elf (an amusingly dry Bob Newhart), Buddy grows up convinced he's an elf himself, even though several factors point strongly in a different direction.

For one thing, Buddy, lacking a true elf's nimble fingers, might just be the worst toymaker in North Pole history, a self-described "cotton-headed ninny muggins." Papa Elf takes pity on him and lets him work on Santa's sleigh, which runs on Christmas spirit measured by the uncannily accurate Clausometer.

Then there's the matter of his size. At six-foot-three, Buddy is bigger than your normal elf, a whole lot bigger, a size difference that director Favreau, determined to keep things old school, shows via the venerable technique of forced perspective rather than the use of modern CGI.

There is one area, however, where Buddy is an elf all the way, and that is in his bottomless good cheer. Despite having to wear the typical elf costume of bright green suit and conical hat over yellow tights and pointy shoes, Buddy radiates cheer like it's never been radiated before. He's always ready with a hug, even for angry raccoons, and when he says, "I just like to smile, smiling's my favorite," you know he's not just blowing smoke up Santa's chimney.

Since *Elf* is something of a one-joke movie, it's essential that Ferrell get this limitless innocence right, and he does. His Buddy, a cheerful combination of Stan Laurel and Tom Hanks in *Big* (1988), is an endearing elf Candide, a true naïf who can't help but make the best of everything.

While this kind of attitude is fine for the North Pole, where Edward Asner's Santa is the only person allowed to get cranky, the challenge for Buddy and this film is to make it creditable in a "magical kingdom called New York City," for— once he finds he's a human and learns that his mother is dead—that's where Buddy heads, determined to find the father who doesn't know he exists. "This is a golden opportunity," Papa Elf tells him like he means it, "to find out who you really are."

Not for nothing, however, does Buddy's father, Walter Hobbs (James Caan), have a prominent place on Santa's naughty list. The Simon Legree of the children's book world, he's too busy repossessing books from kindly nuns and shipping out stories without the final pages to pay much attention to his wife, Emily (Mary Steenburgen), or ten-year-old son, Michael (Daniel Tay). Clearly a big dose of Christmas spirit is in order.

Ditto for comely young Jovie (the always welcome Zooey Deschanel). She's not a real elf, but even though she plays one in Gimbels toy department, she is a tad on the disaffected side and in need of the kind of infusion of good cheer only the genuine article can provide.

Naturally, New York being New York, everyone is not happy with Buddy's attitude, which, *Elf* amusingly illustrates, can be unexpectedly trying. A dwarf children's book writer (Peter Dinklage) gets furious when Buddy insists he's an elf, and a department store Santa goes ballistic when Buddy, alive to the impersonation, hisses at him, "You sit on a throne of lies!"

As for *Shrek*, it's got an attitude all its own. This gleeful piece of wisenheimer computer animation doesn't have much patience for traditional once-upon-a-time fairy tales: The only time one appears, its pages end up in the hero's outhouse.

That would be a fierce ogre with a name that's Yiddish for fear and whose debut in cartoonist William Steig's 1990 children's book about a cheerfully ugly monster who's "tickled to be so repulsive" has become something of a classic. *Shrek* is blessed with Eddie Murphy as a motormouth talking donkey named, well, Donkey. Murphy (working from a script by Ted Elliott, Terry Rossio, Joe Stillman, and Roger S. H. Schulman) is spectacular here, and he's in good company.

Mike Myers, using a Scottish accent that echoes one of his Austin Powers characters, brings not only sharp comic timing, but also a kind of sensitivity to the role of Shrek, an ogre who's more troubled by the world's disdain than he was in the book. And Cameron Diaz is appropriately feisty voicing Fiona, a princess with a secret and a woman who hasn't let being trapped in a tower affect her attitude or her style.

And although Steig's book did without a classic villain, *Shrek* adds a dandy one in Lord Farquaad, a tiny Richard III type (wonderfully voiced by the tall John Lithgow) whose enormous head is packed with evil thoughts, like how best to give the third degree to a gingerbread man who's reluctant to talk.

Farquaad is the ruler of a super-sanitized place called Duloc, which he's determined to turn into the most perfect kingdom on earth. As part of this quest for perfection, Farquuad places a bounty on fairy-tale characters like Pinocchio and the Three Bears, and forcibly exiles them. Donkey is one of them, and when he's saved by Shrek, who he admires as a "mean, green fighting machine," he decides the two of them should be buddies. Freaks, he declares "gotta stick together," adding, with perfect animated logic, "every monster needs a sidekick."

Shrek doesn't quite see it that way. He's a privacy-loving Garbo type who just wants to be left alone, which is why he keeps his property posted with "Beware of the Ogre" signs. So when all those dispossessed fairy-tale types invade his swamp, Shrek stomps off to Farquaad's castle to complain.

That miniature man is having crises of his own. His magic mirror informs him that to have the perfect kingdom, he must marry a princess. In one of *Shrek*'s many pop culture references, the mirror parodies *The Dating Game* by presenting him with a choice of three bachelorette princesses, including one, Snow White, who comes with the advisory "though she lives with seven other men, she's not easy."

Farquaad settles on Fiona, and when Shrek presents his case, he tells the ogre that he can have his swamp back if he rescues the princess from her dragon-guarded castle. So off Shrek sets on what turns out to be a most unconventional quest with the determined Donkey tagging along. "Yes, he talks," Shrek says of his annoying companion. "It's getting him to shut up that's the trick."

Some of *Shrek*'s best moments are when it goes off message and simply fills the screen with sharp riffs on the fairy-tale characters it keeps running across. There's fun to be had with three blind mice, as well as three little breakdancing pigs, and a classic run-in with Robin Hood and his chorus line of merrymen that includes a great visual reference to *Crouching Tiger, Hidden Dragon* (2000).

Smartly constructed to appeal to children and their parents, *Shrek* is a fractured fairy tale that not only knows there's no substitute for clever writing, but also has the confidence to take that information straight to the bank, where it will likely find *Elf* making a deposit at the next window. That's how Hollywood friendships are formed.

Being a Grown-Up Is Fun in *Hatari!* (1962)

Charles Taylor

The first thing you should know about showing Howard Hawks's 1962 *Hatari!* to a kid is that no harm comes to any of the wild animals in the film. Oh, a crocodile is picked off while planning to eat one of the characters. But no one ever got sentimental about a crocodile. And a rogue elephant is shot, but we come upon the scene afterward, and it's the beginning of one of the movie's happiest subplots, as the Italian photographer played by Elsa Martinelli adopts the dead mother's baby, the first of a trio of tiny trumpeters that will earn her the name "Mama Tembo" from the local Warusha tribe.

The animals that the hunters in the movie go after don't wind up stuffed in a den inhabited by bloated old guys who wear safari shorts and harrumph a lot.

They're captured for zoos. (You can complain that zoos aren't the best places for wild animals, just like you could complain about the movie's gags about women being indecisive or emotional. But all that would do is deprive you of a terrific movie for the sake of proving you're superior to the past.) The hunting scenes are breathless, shot (by Russell Harlan) and edited (by Stuart Gilmore) to give us a simultaneous sense of the breadth of the Tanganyikan (now Tanzanian) landscapes (the movie was shot on location) and the chase between beast and machine going on in the foreground. The hunters use jeeps by which they come alongside the animals and lasso them, slowing down to allow the prey to come to a gradual stop. For some captures, John Wayne, as the head of the group, is strapped into a seat right on the left bumper, and Harlan's camera is mounted behind him, making us feel that we're peering over his shoulder and feeling each jolt of the landscape. There's a special thrill in knowing those are really the film's actors so close to rhinos, wildebeests, and giraffes.

As with any Hawks movie, however, the most lasting pleasure comes from the interplay between the actors. This group—including Wayne's Sean Mercer, a German race-car driver (Hardy Krüger), an enigmatic French drifter (Gérard Blain), a former bullfighter (Valentin de Vargas), a veteran hunter (Bruce Cabot), the young woman who runs their business (Michèle Girardon), a Brooklyn cabbie (Red Buttons) who now dodges wildlife behind the wheel instead of other Checkers at rush hour, and the photojournalist (Martinelli) sent to document their work—is one of the ad hoc communities that populate Hawks's films. His characters are wanderers by nature, their truest roots the connections they form with other people.

As in the great Hawks films about these groups—*Only Angels Have Wings* (1939), *To Have and Have Not* (1944), *The Thing from Another World* (1951), *Rio Bravo* (1959), and *El Dorado* (1967)—there is an episodic, rambling structure, all about how these bonds are tested, how each member of the group wins the respect of the others by demonstrating their professionalism, competence, and special talents, and about how human weakness is acknowledged without defining people by their flaws. In the language of Leigh Brackett's screenplay, these people talk bluntly to one another—about their skills, their love lives—but never without compassion. Honesty, delivered with the expectation that people are capable of living up to the best in themselves, is, in Hawks's world, how adults treat one another.

For kids that experience translates to time spent with a group of endearing characters who tell stories; crack wise; show off; play with the compound's pet cheetah, Sonia; herd ostriches back in their pen; and, in the case of Martinelli's Dallas, bathe, feed, and tend to her gaggle of infant pachyderms. The damnedest talent on display is that of Red Buttons's Pockets (the characters have names like Brandy, Pockets, Chips, Dallas, and The Indian), who comes up with a plan to launch a rocket-propelled net over a tree of monkeys bound for captivity. Wayne, who shows the sense of humor that's always so becoming to him, isn't afraid to let Sean become a flustered, easily manipulated lug around Dallas. (The women have the upper hand here. When they have to prove themselves, as Dallas does, it's not because of their sex but because they are untested.)

A friend with whom I tried to share the charms of *Hatari!* said afterward that he felt that he'd seen a Disney movie. I suppose that the animals and some of the silly gags might impart a touch of that, minus the treacle and suffocating sterility (these characters drink and smoke; Martinelli chain-smokes).

But if kids can enjoy *Hatari!* it's also very much an adult movie. It's about the identity to be found in work, about being true to yourself and being accepted for that (even if your integrity sometimes rankles), about the codes we use to describe romantic and sexual attraction, about finding an amity between the modern world and the natural world. (Dallas is inducted into the Warusha tribe at one point, painted to look like one of them and expected to take part in a dance ceremony. But no one makes a brotherhood speech or proclaims, "We are all African.") For all its casualness, all the ease and languor of its presentation, it's a sophisticated picture. For adults, it can be like seeing the confident, charismatic self you always wanted to be. For kids, it makes being an adult look like fun.

—⟶⟨⟨⟨⟵—

Borderline Taste: Crossing Generations with *The Russians Are Coming! The Russians Are Coming!* (1966) and *¡Three Amigos!* (1986)
Peter Keough

Sometimes it takes something dumb to jolt critics into the state of mind that first drew us to movies. A pratfall, a sight gag, or an outbreak of flatulence can do the trick, evoking the childish sensibility that precedes and inspires subsequent analysis, evaluation, and judgment.

Years back as a critic at the *Chicago Reader*, I was losing that faculty. I was reviewing esoteric films, like Peter Greenaway's *A Zed & Two Noughts* (1985), which is about amputation, sex, symmetry, and decomposition; Agnès Varda's *Vagabond* (1985), in which a homeless woman gets drunk and freezes to death in a ditch; and Hou Hsiao-Hsien's *A Time to Live and a Time to Die* (1985), in which a guy peels his long-dead grandmother off of a mat. Not that I was complaining—these are masterpieces—but it had been awhile since I had seen a dumb comedy.

So when I was asked to review John Landis's ¡*Three Amigos!* (1986), I appreciated the break. Not that I would condescend to the material by lowering my critical standards.

Set in 1916, the film follows the adventures of the three performers of the title—Lucky Day (Steve Martin), Dusty Bottoms (Chevy Chase), and Ned Nederlander (Martin Short)—silent-era stars of a once-popular series of two-reelers who have lost their appeal and been dumped by their studio head. But an opportunity arrives from a Mexican village requesting their services, and they travel there thinking that their clients are expecting their trademark live performance—a skit involving acrobatics, singing, dancing, and fake heroics with blank ammunition fired against imaginary bad guys.

After a series of mistaken identity mix-ups and a slow-witted misinterpretation of increasingly alarming events, they eventually recognize that the bad guys are, in fact, real bad guys and that the villagers, thinking the Amigos are actual do-gooders, had hired them to protect them, with what they assumed would be real guns and bullets. A combination, I mused, of *Seven Samurai* (1954) or *The Magnificent Seven* (1960) with *Blazing Saddles* (1974) and *The Inspector General* (1949).

So now I have barely begun watching the movie and already I'm making comparisons to Akira Kurosawa, Nikolai Gogol, and Mel Brooks. And then there was the whole art versus reality business; this film, I told myself, would be a gold mine of erudite analysis. I began taking notes on allusions, irony, metaphor, structural ingenuity, self-referential generic metacommentary, and so on.

In no time I was thinking that the film was, in a sense, a self-reflective deconstruction of its own form. I also considered the genre approach: Like all examples of genres in decline—in this case the western (or maybe Chevy Chase movies)—*Amigos!* draws on and combines various film conventions from other genres to reflect the irresolvable conflicts of society, in particular, cultural inclusion versus xenophobia. In doing so, it lampoons the propensity of Hollywood—and what is Hollywood if not a glittery microcosm of society itself?—to stereotype outsiders, especially those foreigners who seem vaguely threatening to our security and way of life. Hence the fearsome El Guapo (played by Alfonso Arau, who also played one of the Mexican banditos in Sam Peckinpah's 1969 western *The Wild Bunch*) subverts the clichéd image of Mexicans as being swarthy, ferocious, and sneaky when he beams with gratitude because the members of his gang remembered his birthday and have given him a gift ("A sweater!" he exclaims).

But beyond the sociopolitical context, the film does not simply explore cultural xenophobia, the fear of the other that represents the dark sides of our own natures, but rather a fear of existence itself. Existence *as* the "other," the signified that lies beneath the illusory signifier. In other words, the bad guys aren't shooting blanks but genuine lead bullets that can kill them. "This is real!" Lucky Day whispers with incredulity, adding, "I've been shot already!"

I don't know if it was that scene (it was only a flesh wound) or maybe the one with the sweater that did it, or maybe it was when the Amigos enter a saloon full of menacing tough guys who have mistaken them for notorious gunslingers and who are intimidated so much by the innocuous trio that they join in on a chorus of "My Little Buttercup." Probably it was the scene in which Ned Nederlander schmoozes with a group of bewildered Mexican children and brags about his tête-à-tête with Dorothy Gish ("You *know*," he says, "Lillian's sister"). But at some point, I noticed someone laughing too loud, and too often, and in an unnervingly monotone, maniacal manner.

It was me. Other people in the audience were getting nervous. So I tried to suppress the laughter, focusing more and more on the subtext and context, and the neglected auteurist status of John Landis, director of such neglected classics as *Trading Places* (1983) and *The Blues Brothers* (1980). In vain. The eerie laughter continued, intermittently, until the end of the movie.

Later I discussed the film with my teenaged and preteen nephews, who were big fans. Usually I got the feeling that these kids talked about movies with me out of politeness—their taste tended toward *Star Trek IV: The Voyage Home* (1986) and *Police Academy 3: Back in Training* (1986). But now we had *¡Three Amigos!* in common, and before long we were entertaining one another with lines from the movie ("Sew, very old one! Sew like the wind!") and imitating the Amigos' trademark salute of slaps to the chest followed by a hip thrust and a grunt.

This bonding with my nephews reminded me of my fourteenth birthday, when my parents took me to see a movie to celebrate the occasion. I chose the 1966 Norman Jewison comedy *The Russians Are Coming! The Russians Are Coming!* In it, a Soviet submarine runs aground near a fictional New England coastal village. The crew haplessly struggles to extricate their ship. After being detected, the crew members arouse a paranoid and hostile response from the locals. It escalates into a confrontation that might trigger World War III.

I wanted to see it because it promised wacky, off-color humor (fart jokes had not made their breakthrough on the screen yet—if they had this film would probably have had some). This I didn't mention; instead I pointed out that it had serious themes, like not judging people from a different background even when they are armed with submachine guns. In other words, an instructive film despite the crude comedy.

Whatever the reason, we all had a good time, and I was not the only one laughing. Afterward we discussed how wrong it is to be prejudiced against foreigners, even if they are from a country that has pledged to bury you, and about how connecting on a basic human level, as when both the townspeople and the crew of the sub join together to rescue a kid hanging from the roof of a building, can open the door to a reconciliation between two enemy nations.

Very edifying. Mostly, however, I remember that we entertained ourselves by repeating some of the funniest lines, like when the guy with the thick Boston accent says, "Hurry up, Naw-min, they're openin' up the bah!" We even chuckled over borderline-obscene moments, like when Carl Reiner is tied up face-to-face with a matronly switchboard operator. I think that, as when I would later discuss *¡Three Amigos!* with my nephews, my parents found themselves drawn back to what they first loved about movies—that they offered refuge from the world, a place full of thrills, adventure, and, more importantly, silly laughter.

And believe me, at that time we could use a laugh about the big dread in the back of everyone's mind. It was just a few years earlier that we watched President Kennedy give a doom-laden speech on TV during the 1962 Cuban Missile Crisis. The next year he was assassinated. I felt the terror of impending annihilation. They didn't talk about it, but I knew my parents felt the same. It did not go away, that fear that no one was safe from sudden death and that faceless enemies could end the world with a push of a button.

But after seeing this movie, the fear eased a bit. After all, how scary can the commies be when the meanest of the bunch, the captain of the sub (Theodore Bikel) is just a big lovable goof? And that his second in command is a nice guy played by Alan Arkin?

And then there is the love story. It happens after the Russians try to dress like the indigenous population to infiltrate the community and somehow commandeer a boat that they can use to extricate their sub from its predicament. As expected, the plan unravels, and one of the sailors, played by hunky John Philip Law, gets separated from the rest. He meets a local girl, and they fall in love. Now if two young people from countries poised to annihilate one another manage to overcome their differences and become sweethearts, surely there is chance for world peace.

So for a little while in 1966, that dumb comedy brought my parents and me a little closer together. And we found relief from the dread that haunted us all.

It's the magic of movies. As Robin Wood explains in his classic analysis *The American Nightmare: Essays on the Horror Film* (1979), "That which bourgeois ideology cannot recognize or accept, [it] must deal with (as Barthes suggests in *Mythologies*) in one of two ways: Either by rejecting and, if possible, annihilating it, or by rendering it safe and assimilating it, converting it as far as possible into a replica of itself."[3]

Or as Lucky Day in *¡Three Amigos!* puts it, "In a way, all of us have an El Guapo to face. For some, shyness might be their El Guapo. For others, a lack of education might be their El Guapo. For us, El Guapo is a big, dangerous man who wants to kill us."

All of the Feels: *Inside Out* (2015)
David Fear

It starts, as so many things do, with eyes opening. A newborn baby greets her parents and the world in all its gauzy, fuzzy, soft-focus glory—and then there is light. Enter Joy, a sprite in a green dress stepping out of the darkness, the first sensation that this girl, Riley (voiced by Kaitlyn Dias), will ever know. Then Sadness, a scowling blue buzz-killer in a turtleneck, shows up; cue tears. As Riley turns into a toddler, others join the party: Fear, a bug-eyed, anxious wreck in what's admittedly a smart bow tie and sweater vest combo; Disgust, all hair-flips and hand gestures with a too-cool-for-preschool vibe; and Anger, a squat fireplug crossed with an overcaffeinated air-traffic controller who tends to literally blow his top.

We're used to seeing animals and inanimate objects being anthropomorphized in kids' movies: Bring on the dancing teakettles and surfer-dude turtles! But not feelings. The five main players of *Inside Out* are Riley's primary emotions, voiced by Amy Poehler (Joy), Phyllis Smith (Sadness), Bill Hader (Fear), Mindy Kaling (Disgust), and Lewis Black (Anger). They are the ones that will color her memories and drive her interactions in her formative years; help her establish the building blocks of her identity, represented here as islands ("Hockey Island," "Family Island," "Goofball Island"); and keep her safe from broccoli. They will be there when she makes friends, wins at sports, and holds forth in her imagination about lava-flooded living rooms. And they will also be there when, at age eleven, she's forced to move from Minnesota to San Francisco for her dad's job and everything she knows and loves is gone, and everything falls apart.

You can essentially divide the history of animated features into before and after Pixar—the effect of the Bay Area–based production company has been that profound in terms of expanding how smart, savvy, and deep you could go with the form and still sell it to the masses. And while the company has its share of movies that fit a more traditional template (were it not for the animation style itself—*A Bug's Life* (1998) and *Cars* (2006) could pass as straight Disney flicks)—the movies you most associate with the Pixar "brand," for lack of a better word, are ones that tap into magnificent-to-melancholy associations with childhood. This is the company that can make you feel the sorrow of discarded toys. It can make you see that the monsters under your bed might really be cuddly and protective, and serve a function. You do not feel the pathos of *Up* (2009) without that preamble of puppy love, which sets up everything.

More importantly, you do not make the single best movie about the rush of conflicting emotions that characterizes prepubescence without extraordinary curiosity and empathy for what children experience. When asked about *Inside Out*'s ground-zero inspiration moment, filmmaker/Pixar MVP Pete Docter mentioned his own daughter, Elie, who voiced the precocious child version of *Up*'s lady love (named, coincidentally, Ellie). "She was kind of like that character," he notes, until she turned eleven. "Then there were a lot more reclusive, quiet moments. I wondered what was going on inside her head," he said in a 2016 interview with the *Guardian*. If you use the resulting movie as a sort of speculative map, what's possibly going on in the head of most eleven-year-olds is the sense that Sadness had a knack for tainting the happiness of bygone days, that Joy is lost deep in the subconscious where the wild things are, and that, once both of those emotions AWOL, there's nothing to feel but the occasional bursts of Rage, Revulsion, and Apprehension. The foundation for the teen years to come, in other words.

It's at the point that Joy and Sadness find themselves sucked into the memory banks that the movie threatens to become a recognizable version of a typical big-screen 'toon, with the duo having to race back through Riley's brain to the control center before their host does something truly self-destructive. But even then, *Inside Out* keeps throwing curveballs into the cerebral journey. It's tough to think of a better representation of a tween's identity going through seismic upheavals as the sight of those mental islands crumbling into dust and leaving a void. And it's mind-boggling to imagine a more beautifully out-there sequence than Joy, Sadness, and an old imaginary friend named Bing-Bong (bless you, Richard Kind) taking a "shortcut" through Abstract Thought and ending up as Cubist cutouts of conceptual deconstruction. Think of it as a sort of Fisher-Price's My First Nonobjective Fragmentation for kids.

And while other great set pieces and visual jokes abound as they take the Train of Thought back home—notably a dream factory that's set up as, what else, a movie studio—the scenes that are taking place outside Riley's head make the balance between silly and sorrowful work. The scene of this new student telling folks about herself and having sadness cast a shadow over everything, leading to a humiliating outburst in front of her entire class, is so painful it's almost impossible to watch. Ditto the sequence after that, a wordless interlude between kooky brain shenanigans in which the eleven-year-old shuffles along with her lunch tray and sits by herself, marinating in loneliness. It may be possible to stave off tears throughout the film's various emotional low points and nostalgia pangs until Riley, reunited with her parents after almost running away, says, "I know you don't want me to but . . . I miss *home*." The way she draws that last word out into something like a plea, you can feel the dams behind your eyeballs burst.

To watch *Inside Out* as an adult is to feel your heart break when this scene comes up. (Multiply that feeling by a hundred if you're a parent, by 1,000 if you're the parent of a girl, and by infinity and beyond if said daughter is eleven when you first see it.) But one of the great things about this movie is the way it captures an authentic feeling of being that age, experiencing that longing, wanting stability *and* independence, wanting the comfort of your childhood and what comes after, of letting go of childish things yet keeping the fundamentals that turned the girl into the young woman intact. It makes you feel Riley's happiness and sadness and anger and agony—the battle of emotions jockeying for the control board—regardless of how old you are, your gender, your own upbringing, the whole nine.

Yet, it can't help but make you think of your own color-coded core memories, of what it felt like to be that age, of your own doubts and bad decisions and delirious moments that helped you build your own identity islands. For me, so many of those memories are attached to the movies—the gliding marbles of giddiness and intense secondhand grief and other by-proxy feelings, so much of it being transmitted to a young film addict just like the characters in Riley's noggin, in front of a screen. Movies helped me process emotions when I was young. And then, decades later, with my wife and a daughter almost the age of the kid onscreen, as a baby opened its eyes and Joy emerged out of the shadows, it helped me process them again.

—〰—

E.T. the Extra-Terrestrial (1982)
Roger Ebert[4]

Dear Raven and Emil:

Sunday we sat on the big green couch and watched *E.T. the Extra-Terrestrial* (1982) together with your mommy and daddy. It was the first time either of you had seen it, although you knew a little of what to expect because we took the "E.T." ride together at the Universal tour. I had seen the movie lots of times since it came out in 1982, so I kept one eye on the screen and the other on the two of you. I wanted to see how a boy on his fourth birthday, and a girl who had just turned seven a week ago, would respond to the movie.

Well, it "worked" for both of you, as we say in Grandpa Roger's business.

Raven, you never took your eyes off the screen—not even when it looked like E.T. was dying and you had to scoot over next to me because you were afraid.

Emil, you had to go sit on your dad's knee a couple of times, but you never stopped watching, either. No trips to the bathroom or looking for lost toys: You were watching that movie with all of your attention.

The early scenes show a spaceship landing, and they suggest that a little creature has been left behind. The ship escapes quickly after men in pickup trucks come looking for it. Their headlights and flashlights make visible beams through the foggy night, and you remembered the same effect during the ride at Universal. And the keys hanging from their belts jangle on the soundtrack. It's how a lost little extraterrestrial would experience it.

Then there are shots of a suburban house, sort of like the one you live in, with a wide driveway and a big backyard. A little boy named Elliott (Henry Thomas) is in the yard when he thinks he sees or hears something. We already know that it's E.T.

The camera watches Elliott moving around. And Raven, that's when you asked me, "Is this E.T.'s vision?" And I said, yes, we were seeing everything now from E.T.'s point of view. And I thought you'd asked a very good question, because most kids your age wouldn't have noticed that the camera had a point of view—that we were seeing everything from low to the ground, as a short little creature would view it, and experiencing what he (or she) would see after wandering out of the woods on a strange planet.

While we were watching, I realized how right you were to ask that question. The whole movie is based on what moviemakers call "point of view." Almost every single important shot is seen either as E.T. would see it or as Elliott would see it. And things are understood as they would understand them. There aren't any crucial moments where the camera pulls back and seems to be a grownup. We're usually looking at things through a child's eye—or an alien's.

When Elliott and E.T. see each other for the first time, they both jump back in fright and surprise, and let out yelps. We see each of them from the other's point of view. When the camera stands back to show a whole scene, it avoids showing it through adult eyes. There's a moment, for example, when Elliott's mom (Dee Wallace Stone) is moving around doing some housework and never realizes that E.T. is scurrying around the room just out of her line of sight. The camera stays back away from her. We don't see her looking this way and that, because it's not about which way she's looking.

Later, we do get one great shot that shows what she sees: She's looking in Elliott's closet at all of his stuffed toys lined up and doesn't realize one of the "toys" is actually E.T. We all laughed at that shot, but it was an exception; basically we looked out through little eyes, not big ones (for example, in the scene where they take E.T. trick-or-treating with a sheet over his head and we can see out like he can through the holes in the sheet).

Then, in the scenes that really worried you, Raven, the men in the trucks come back. They know E.T. is in Elliott's house, and they're scientists who want to examine the alien creature. But there isn't a single moment when they use grown-up talk and explain what they're doing. We only hear small pieces of their dialogue, as Elliott might overhear it.

By then we know Elliott and E.T. are linked mentally, so Elliott can sense that E.T. is dying. Elliott cries out to the adults to leave E.T. alone, but the adults don't take him seriously. A kid knows what that feels like. And then, when Elliott gets his big brother to drive the getaway car, and the brother says, "I've never driven in forward before!" you could identify with that. Kids are always watching their parents drive and never getting to do it themselves.

We loved the scene where the bicycles fly. We suspected it was coming, because E.T. had taken Elliott on a private bike flight earlier, so we knew he could do it. I was thinking that the chase scene before the bikes fly was a little too long, as if Steven Spielberg (who made the film) was trying to build up too much unnecessary suspense. But when those bikes took off, what a terrific moment! I remember when I saw the movie at Cannes; even the audience there, people who had seen thousands of movies, let out a whoop at that moment.

Finally, in the scene at the end, E.T. has phoned home, and the spaceship has come to get him. He's in the woods with Elliott. The gangplank on the ship comes down, and in the doorway we can see another creature like E.T. standing with the light behind.

Emil, you said, "That's E.T.'s mommy!" And then you paused a second, and said, "Now how did I know that?"

We all laughed, because you made it sound funny, as you often do—you're a natural comedian. But remembering it now, I asked myself—how did Emil know that? It could have been E.T.'s daddy, or sister, or the pilot of the ship. But I agree with you it probably was his mommy, because she sounded just like a mommy as she made the noise of calling E.T.

And then I thought, the fact that you knew that was a sign of how well Steven Spielberg made his movie. At four, you are a little young to understand "point of view," but you are old enough to react to one. For the whole movie, you'd been seeing almost everything through the eyes of E.T. or Elliott. By the last moments, you were identifying with E.T. And who did he miss the most? Who did he want to see standing in the spaceship door for him? His mommy.

Of course, maybe Steven Spielberg didn't see it the same way, and thought E.T. only seemed like a kid and was really 500 years old. That doesn't matter, because Spielberg left it open for all of us. That's the sign of a great filmmaker: He only explains what he has to explain, and with a great movie the longer it runs, the less has to be explained. Some other filmmaker who wasn't so good might have had subtitles saying, "E.T.? Are you out there? It's Mommy!" But that would have been dumb.

And it would have deprived you, Emil, of the joy of knowing it was E.T.'s mommy and the delight of being able to tell the rest of us.

Well, that's it for this letter. We had a great weekend, kids. I was proud of how brave you both were during your first pony rides. And proud of what good movie critics you are, too.

Love,
Grandpa Roger

—ᶆ—

Watching *Boyhood* (2014) with a Boy and *Eighth Grade* (2018) with an Eighth Grader
Mary Pols

In the summer of 2014, I watched writer/director Richard Linklater's *Boyhood* with my then-ten-year-old son. *Boyhood* is rated R for a handful of minor reasons: There are sexual references and teen drug and alcohol use. I'd already seen enough of it on our screening link to know that the R rating was, as so often is the case, ridiculous. I'd also seen enough of it to feel strongly that the movie would be the healthiest and most important viewing experience he'd have that year.

As a longtime movie critic who also happened to be a single mother, I often pushed the limits of appropriateness with him and sometimes for logistical reasons—I'd take him alone on occasions when I had to go to work and didn't have a sitter. I regret *Old Dogs* (2009), which he sensibly hated, but not *Blue Jasmine*

(2013), which he equally sensibly appreciated. Never horror and never anything violent, those are the rules. But when I have shared sophisticated fare with him, it's sometimes been a cultural choice. For starters, I'm trying to grow a good man.

When he was little, and particularly when he was about ten, I wanted him to see the world beyond the classic nuclear family and the kind of "others" sanctified by Disney (the plucky motherless children, whether human or animal). We live in a small New England town. It's not exactly *Peyton Place* (the 1957 movie was shot ninety minutes from where we live), but it's a fairly conventional place filled with mostly traditional, seemingly happy, intact families. We've lived here since 2010, and among his peer group I have yet to encounter another mother in my precise— but according to national statistics—rapidly growing demographic: single mother from the get-go, never married. The few parents who do get divorced get discussed enough to make me think it's likely we've been the subject of discussion ourselves. Or, at least, puzzlement. It took one of my son's soccer coaches the entire season to get his head around my lack of husband. Like how'd you get that kid? Even in the early part of the twenty-first century, we'd been considered a little off.

Because of that, I'd made a low-key habit of seeking out films or television that would specifically highlight that we—my son and I—are not so very "other" as we might seem, living how and where we do. Some of them have been obvious choices—I love how subtle Pixar is about that missing father (yet seemingly well-adjusted kids) in *Toy Story* (1995)—but others, like *About a Boy* (2002), which makes comedy out of the stereotype of the romantically desperate and overwhelmed single mother, are not your average mother–son comfort cinema.

Neither is *Boyhood*, but beyond the simple miracle of its making, it is astonishingly comforting. The loose narrative is built around Mason (Ellar Coltrane), a boy growing up with his struggling single mother (Patricia Arquette) and slightly older sister, Samantha (Lorelei Linklater, the director's child). Occasionally their dad, Mason Sr. (Ethan Hawke), comes by. There's an uptight stepfather who it seems the mother selected mostly for the contrast with Mason's father, who is groovy, aimless, and a big talker. (It initially seems that he may be desirous of time with his children primarily to lecture them on how to be cool, but he turns out to be a decent and not-so-distant father.) No one dies or shoots drugs, and the only violence in the movie is the type children are all too familiar with: domestic. I was mostly concerned that the length of the movie, 165 minutes, would be too much. But from the opening scene, in which the mother chastises Mason for not turning in the homework she knows he did—it's in the bottom of his knapsack—my son was captivated; this film, with its encompassing look at childhood, seemed to be about *him*. Not him projected into an adventure involving flying dragons, but him going to school, forgetting his homework.

You can't talk about *Boyhood* without addressing what most would call its major cinematic innovation and its (rare) detractors a gimmick; the movie was shot in short spurts in the course of twelve years. It's time lapse and long-form, and extraordinary, even as it dwells in the mundane shuffle of an average lower middle-class life.

Coltrane grows up on-screen, from a boy of about six to an awkward 'tween and then to a young man going off to college. Is he a good actor? I only know that I wanted to look at him the way you want to sit on the beach and watch the ocean. Arquette has twelve different hairdos and waist sizes. Hawke changes only in his levels of seediness; he appears to bathe more as the years go on. They shift shapes, but the performances are both flexible and steady. They give everything that Linklater needs.

The children move in and out of phases of beauty and awkwardness, then awkward beauty and back into beauty—not because they look like pretty Hollywood kids, but simply because the passage of their growth is being recorded and thus celebrated. No one has ever done anything quite like it. Michael Apted's documentary series, in which he visits the same group of British boys and girls every seven years beginning with 1964's *Seven Up!* seems a likely inspiration, but those movies are more like sequels. Linklater's *Before* trilogy (*Before Sunrise, Before Sunset, Before Midnight*) spanned an eighteen-year filming period from 1995 to 2013—with much more substantial breaks—using the same characters and actors (Hawke and Julie Delpy).

My son was so used to the lies of cinema that he wavered back and forth between thinking this was documentary or some sleight of hand involving excellent look-a-like casting before finally grasping (I think) that this was fiction vitally focused on what reality looks and feels like.

Outside of something like *My Dinner with Andre* (1981), which has put more viewers to sleep than anyone would ever admit, never has a movie seemed to have such gentle patience with characters. And never has a movie made less of a big deal about the surprise twists that come the way of every human being. Mason Sr. goes from being the kind of bohemian semidad who smokes his way through a meal with his small children, reassuring them he's going to be around more (he's not particularly assuring) to a responsible professional (he's an actuary, one of those legendarily reliable jobs) and settling down with a lovely young woman who comes from a deeply religious family. Big changes like this are simply presented and never really discussed.

The anticipation or dread we are so used to as moviegoers (here comes the joke, the kiss, the confrontation in the dark alley) is so ingrained that it's almost puzzling when the Big Bad refuses to show up. Mason hanging out with older teenaged boys in an abandoned or unfinished house? Surely someone will set fire to it or get arrested for trespassing; that's what the narrative culture of Hollywood movies has taught us. Instead they do what teenagers have been doing for time immemorial. They drink some booze, tell a few off-color jokes, and then go home.

Linklater grew up with a young, single mother who, like Arquette's character, went back to school with her children in tow and was married a few times. The film is autobiographical, but it's also collaborative; as the years went on the writer/director invited input from his growing young stars. He even incorporated Coltrane's budding love of still photography into the narrative. The parlance of divorce and rifts is present but understated. The parents keep track of each other through the children, looking for signs and proofs of change in the person. Early on, there's an element of testing these new waters, as when Mason Sr. tries to flirt with Olivia (he gets nowhere) and you can see him wondering, do we still have it? If I call her Liv, the way no one else does, will she melt? Later, the relationship gets less touchy and more practical. Mason asks his father if he has a job. "Mom wanted to know," he says. Probably she'd like some child support.

Clearly things were very bad between them in the past. Maybe once it got as ugly between them as it got between Ted (Dustin Hoffman) and Joanna (Meryl Streep) in *Kramer vs. Kramer* (1979). But we don't see it. This is one of Linklater's many smart strategies; he doesn't show it because on some level, it doesn't exist for Mason. He's still too young to carry many memories forward from before the split, as evidenced by how vague both kids are about their dad when he first comes to visit. They've adapted to his absence, the way that children do.

In this movie big events often happen offscreen, although Linklater doesn't shy away from the drama of Olivia's breakup with Bill (Marco Perella), the pompous alcoholic she marries. The camera approaches from Mason's viewpoint as he arrives home, presumably from school, and spots her weeping on the garage floor. "Your mother had a little accident and now she's being dramatic," Bill tells the kids, then turns to her and says, "Get off the fucking floor, Olivia." In movies as we know them, this scene would end with a young son challenging the lousy stepfather, puffing out his bantam chest, defending his mother, and getting cuffed for it. But that's not the way it works in real life, most of the time, does it? Most of the time, a kid hangs his head, fumes in silence, and tries to get through the days. There are peaks in all our dramas, but few climax as neatly as they do in the movies.

The heartbreak Linklater focuses on here is not so much what Olivia is going through—although it doesn't look pleasant—but what Mason and Samantha lose in the deal when she takes them away. They like their stepsiblings, Randy and Mindy, who through some unhappy fate seem to live with their creep of a father full-time. (Explanatory dialogue is not *Boyhood*'s style.) "Are we ever going to see them again?" Samantha asks as the car pulls away from the house where they lived with Bill, whereupon Olivia tells them not to look back and delivers the kind of maternal lie that has fueled many a therapy session: "It's going to be okay," she says.

And so it is. But also is not. *Boyhood* speaks to a central tenet of childhood, namely, that it is a place of both helplessness and magic. The freedoms are incredible. (Six years where one's primary responsibility is to learn how to read? Sign me up, again.) But there's always a fence looming up in front of you when you least expect it. You are rudderless, and your primary purpose lies in observation. More often than in any other future time in one's life, this is *shared* observation, a state of living in the utter now with one's peers, lost to us as adults. There is one small scene in *Boyhood* that conjures this so vividly that I started to cry even though there was nothing remotely sad on the screen.

Mason and his middle school tribe, including stepsiblings, are walking down the street when they encounter an older boy who inexplicably unleashes a stream of invectives, "shit," "fuck," what have you, at them. They keep walking, looking back, confused, curious, taking it all in. You almost hear them thinking—*some people are messed up, but we're here together.* The mood of the scene took me back to Linklater's *Dazed and Confused* (1993), the truest movie ever made about high school, where he showed an uncanny ability to look into his characters, to show us exactly how the world appears to them. We see their gaze and go into it at the same time. We feel it.

There are many irritating things parents say to their children over and over again that focus on the idea of the future and the passage of time. "When you're my age, you'll see what I mean," we say to our sons and daughters. "You're getting so big," we say. "Weren't you a baby just yesterday?" To our children this is like every voice in the Charlie Brown cartoons. *Wah wah wah wah.* I don't want to wait thirty years to understand what you're saying, they think. I want to understand right now. And no, I wasn't a baby just yesterday. I was *me.* I am always me. And only me. It's almost impossible for any of us to truly see ourselves shift as we grow and evolve as adults, but we regularly ask our children to grasp this concept.

We can't help ourselves because witnessing the swift passage of time on someone we grew from our seed and egg is so astonishing. Of course we want to remark about it. Richard Linklater and his faithful troupe of actors, who showed up every year for twelve years to spend three days shooting what had to be an amorphous-sounding movie, finally put all that into something we can grasp. And the beauty of it is, our children can, too.

As the last thirty minutes of the film approached, my son refused, despite obvious exhaustion, to tear himself away and go to bed. It was the story of him, and of all of us, and maybe, for the first time, he really saw that connection. During the next year or so, *Boyhood* became comfort food to him. Then it showed up on Netflix, and he'd watch it on a day when he was home sick. I'd come in and sit next to him for a little while and get teary at some point. Those points shift as our lives shift forward, and as our good-bye scene comes closer, I find myself more and more moved by Olivia's quasi-indignant speech about her approaching funeral as Mason packs up for college. It's gone from funny to poignant. My son is fourteen now. He already towers over me. His evolving beauty is a kaleidoscope I can't get enough of yet am only allowed to look into surreptitiously.

We've lived a lot since he was ten. There was, briefly, a stepfather candidate who hurt us both, and after his departure I tried to look to the future for reassurance, imagining us time-lapsed forward, as Olivia and Mason were. I made a conscious decision that there would be no more comings and goings in my romantic life, or rather no more comings so there would be no goings. I learned something from Olivia.

My son and I don't see many movies together anymore. The other day, in one of those in-sync moments (him forced into making chocolate chip cookies but not minding it so much, me cleaning up around him), I asked why he keeps turning me down to go to the movies. He's a freshman in high school. It doesn't take a rocket scientist to answer this question, but I asked it anyway. I gave him options. Was it because a) there really wasn't much he wanted to see or b) he was afraid someone he knew would see him at the movies with his mother? Or maybe c), that he just doesn't like me that much anymore. "Mostly a," he said. "A little bit b. Not c at all."

It was a good moment. He also told me movies just don't seem very "original" anymore. "Interesting," I said, wondering to myself whether a world with Fortnite had rendered movies obsolete to him. He'd got his first PlayStation® six months ago. But it wasn't that, he said. Too many sequels and superheroes, he explained. "And all the horror movies. It just seems like they're all the same." He's not wrong.

I'm missing seeing movies with him. I am still a journalist, but when I was a working movie critic, bringing him to screenings knit us together, creating a steady stream of connections between what was in my mind and his. There are still some leftovers from that era. When we left *Black Panther* (2018) on a snowy February day, both of us elated, I reminded him that he'd met the director five years earlier when Ryan Coogler's first movie, the heartbreaking *Fruitvale Station* (2013), was just coming out. There was no school that day, and I'd had to go to Boston to interview Coogler at the Ritz-Carlton. My son sat reading in a chair outside the room where we did the interview, and as Coogler and I came out, I introduced them. Coogler was memorably kind.

But this year, his *Black Panther* is one of just a few films we've seen together, including *Mary Poppins Returns* (2018) and *Eighth Grade* (2018), the former he grudgingly agreed to see only because his slightly younger cousin wanted to. ("Dude, Lin-Manuel Miranda is in it.") We saw *Eighth Grade* just a few weeks after my son finished eighth grade (the real thing) in a movie theater where we were the only people in the audience.

Even with the hype I'd absorbed in advance, writer/director Bo Burnham's brilliantly humanist movie was a revelation. The last week of eighth grade for Kayla Day (Elsie Fisher, making her debut) unfolds as a series of looming mini-disasters. Kayla makes earnest videos offering advice to her peers, the kind of thing one could imagine being shared on social media as a shaming device. They're not. They made us cringe in the theater—and my son sit up at the realization that the use of "Gucci" as teen slang extends beyond his small town—but in the social media-saturated world Kayla lives in, they're a barely noticed blip (unlike Burnham, still in his twenties, who was discovered, or rather uncovered himself, as a teenaged viral YouTube sensation).

Later Kayla attends a swimming pool birthday party, a horror movie scenario. Most of the girls are sylphs in bikinis. Wearing a one-piece bright green bathing suit that clings to her still-soft adolescent stomach, Kayla is less than perfect and almost naked in front of her crush, Aiden (Luke Prael), whose presence reduces her to embarrassing blather. But he's not mean; you can see, Aiden is just a kid, too. It's clear that Kayla was only invited because the mother of the birthday girl likes her father Mark (Josh Hamilton, giving an adorable and utterly authentic performance, a hard combination to pull off).

Very little happens, but the movie holds you rapt. It's about surviving, both the acute misery of adolescence and the bigger picture stuff, like the absence of a mother, explained, only slightly, late in the movie. (She bailed when Kayla was a baby. Mark dealt.) When a boy jerks off in health class under his sweatshirt, my son dissolved in laughter. I turned to him. "Does this happen at your school?" I asked. "No, but it could," he said. When Kayla is befriended during step-up day by a mentor from the high school she'll be attending, I assumed the girl, Olivia (Emily Robinson), would ditch her afterward, that there would be some social dismissal that would cut deep. Instead the girl is kind and helpful, and seems to genuinely like Kayla.

But that new friendship leads to the most fraught encounter for Kayla's character. After a night out with Olivia and her friends, Kayla gets a ride home from a boy who has been eyeing her all night. She's flattered, as anyone would be, but the kid, Riley (Daniel Zolghadri), slides into the backseat with her and starts asking her about her sexual experience. She exaggerates for him, playing along at first. Then he takes off his shirt. The danger feels real. He's almost a man. She's clearly still a child. I thought about *Fast Times at Ridgemont High* (1982), which I'd introduced my son to at thirteen, having thought of it as one of the funniest movies I'd ever seen back when I was a teenager. Seeing it thirty-five years later, I realized it treats date rape like something normal. I thought afterward, did I just cause this to be incorporated into *his* cultural DNA?

A voice came from next to me in the theater. "Don't do it, Kayla," my son said. "He's bad."

My heart leapt. He got it. On-screen, Kayla got it, too. She said no. This most vulnerable seeming of girls, a little pudgy, pimply, unmothered, knew her own self-worth and stood up for herself. She transcended the stereotypes I grew up with. She was of my son's generation.

Whenever the movie comes up in conversation, my son tells people that it is at least 90 percent accurate to what eighth grade is really like. "Like, the closest thing I've seen to it," he says. What *Eighth Grade* reminded me most of, in its truth-telling, its refusal to make everything black and white, and its desire to explore the minor moments that make up a life, was *Boyhood*. The *Eighth Grade* screener arrived at our house in late fall as awards season was beginning. These are the packages my son rips open, and he crowed about its arrival. A few days later, as I saw him settling in on the couch with a blanket and the remote, I asked, "Are you going to watch *Eighth Grade*?"

"You know, I feel like watching *Boyhood* instead," he said. It made sense. That was his movie. *Eighth Grade* reminded him of it as well, obviously. I sat down next to him and cried fresh tears for all that is behind us. But not for what lies ahead. I don't know what will happen to him, or us, but I think he'll be fine along the way.

APPENDIX

MPAA RATINGS

About a Boy (2002)   PG ("for brief strong language and some thematic elements")

Actress (1991)   not rated

Adolf Hitler: My Part in His Downfall (1973)   not rated

The Adventures of Robinson Crusoe (1954)   not rated

After Life (1998)   not rated

A.I. Artificial Intelligence (2001)   PG-13 ("for some sexual content and violent images")

Airport (1970)   G

Alice in Wonderland (2010)   PG ("for fantasy action/violence involving scary images and situations, and for a smoking caterpillar")

American Graffiti (1973)   PG

American Honey (2016)   R ("for strong sexual content, graphic nudity, language throughout, and drug/alcohol abuse—all involving teens")

American Psycho (2000)   R ("for strong violence, sexuality, drug use, and language")

Apocalypse Now (1979)   R ("for disturbing violent images, sexual content, and some drug use")

The Apple (1998)   not rated

Appropriate Behavior (2014)   not rated

Avengers: Infinity War (2018)   PG-13 ("for intense sequences of sci-fi violence and action, language, and some crude references")

The Aviator (2004)   PG-13 ("for thematic elements, sexual content, nudity, language, and a crash sequence")

Babe (1995)	G
Babe: Pig in the City (1998)	PG
Bambi (1942)	G
Bambi Meets Godzilla (1969)	not rated
Bande de filles (*Girlhood*, 2014)	not rated
Barry Lyndon (1975)	PG
Bashu, the Little Stranger (1989)	not rated
Batman (1989)	PG-13
Batman Begins (2005)	PG-13 ("for intense action violence, disturbing images, and some thematic elements")
Batman v Superman: Dawn of Justice (2016)	PG-13 ("for intense sequences of violence and action throughout, and some sensuality")
The Battle of the Rails (1946)	not rated
The Beast from 20,000 Fathoms (1953)	not rated
Beauty and the Beast (1991)	G
Beauty and the Beast (2017)	PG ("for some action violence, peril, and frightening images")
Bee Movie (2007)	PG ("for mild suggestive humor and a brief depiction of smoking")
Before Midnight (2013)	R ("for sexual content/nudity and language")
Before Sunrise (1995)	R ("for some strong language")
Before Sunset (2004)	R ("for language and sexual references")
La Belle et la Bête (1946)	not rated
The Belles of St. Trinian's (1954)	not rated
Bicycle Thieves (1948)	not rated
Big (1988)	PG
The Big Sky (1952)	not rated
Black Narcissus (1947)	not rated
Black Panther (2018)	PG-13 ("for prolonged sequences of action violence and a brief rude gesture")
Blade Runner (1982)	R
Blazing Saddles (1974)	R
The Blossoming of Maximo Oliveros (2005)	not rated
Blue Jasmine (2013)	PG-13 ("for mature thematic material, language, and sexual content")

The Blue Lagoon (1980)	R
The Blue Planet (2001)	TV-G
The Blues Brothers (1980)	R
Bombshell (1933)	not rated
The Boxtrolls (2014)	PG ("for action, some peril, and mild rude humor")
The Boy in the Striped Pajamas (2008)	PG ("for some mature thematic material involving the Holocaust")
The Boy with Green Hair (1948)	not rated
Boyhood (2014)	R ("for language including sexual references, and for teen drug and alcohol use")
Brokeback Mountain (2005)	R ("for sexuality, nudity, language, and some violence")
A Bug's Life (1998)	G
Cape Fear (1962)	not rated
Captain America: Civil War (2016)	PG-13 ("for extended sequences of violence, action, and mayhem")
Captains Courageous (1937)	not rated
Cars (2006)	G
Cast Away (2000)	PG-13 ("for intense action sequences and some disturbing images")
Cat People (1942)	not rated
Charles Laughton Directs "The Night of the Hunter" (2002)	not rated
Charlie and the Chocolate Factory (2005)	PG ("quirky situations, action, and mild language")
Children of Heaven (1997)	PG
Children of Men (2006)	R ("for strong violence, language, some drug use, and brief nudity")
Chinatown (1974)	R
A Christmas Carol (1951)	not rated
A Christmas Carol (1971)	not rated
Christopher Robin (2018)	PG ("for some action")
Chronicles of Narnia: The Lion, the Witch, and the Wardrobe (2005)	PG ("for battle sequences and frightening moments")
Chronicles of Narnia: Prince Caspian (2008)	PG ("for epic battle action and violence")

Chronicles of Narnia: Voyage of the Dawn Treader (2010)	PG ("for some frightening images and sequences of fantasy action")
Circus Angel (1965)	not rated
Citizen Kane (1941)	PG
The City of Lost Children (1995)	R ("for disturbing and grotesque images of violence and menace")
Clash of the Titans (1981)	PG
A Clockwork Orange (1971)	R
Close Encounters of the Third Kind (1977)	PG
Close-Up (1990)	not rated
Clueless (1995)	PG-13 ("for sex-related dialogue and some teen use of alcohol and drugs")
Coraline (2008)	PG ("for thematic elements, scary images, some language, and suggestive humor")
Le Corbeau (1943)	not rated
Corpse Bride (2005)	PG ("for some scary images and action, and brief mild language")
The Count of Monte Cristo (1954)	not rated
The Countess of Monte Cristo (1948)	not rated
The Court Jester (1955)	not rated
Creed (2015)	PG-13 ("for violence, language, and some sensuality")
Cronos (1993)	R ("for horror violence and language")
Crouching Tiger, Hidden Dragon (2000)	PG-13 ("for martial arts violence and some sexuality")
Cry Freedom (1987)	PG
The Curse of the Cat People (1944)	not rated
Dangerous Moonlight (1941)	not rated
The Day My Aunt Was Ill (1997)	not rated
Dazed and Confused (1993)	R ("for pervasive, continuous teen drug and alcohol use, and very strong language")
The Deep End (2001)	R ("for some violence and language, and for a strong sex scene")
The Departed (2006)	R ("for strong brutal violence, pervasive language, some strong sexual content, and drug material")
Desperate Search (1952)	not rated

The Devil's Backbone (2001)	R ("for violence, language, and some sexuality")
Diary of a Teenage Girl (2015)	R ("for strong sexual content including dialogue, graphic nudity, drug use, language, and drinking—all involving teens")
Do the Right Thing (1989)	R
Doctor Zhivago (1965)	PG-13 ("for mature themes")
Dr. Strangelove or: How I Learned to Stop Worrying and Love the Bomb (1964)	PG ("for thematic elements, some violent content, sexual humor, and mild language")
Dreamchild (1985)	PG
Dumbo (1941)	G
Edward Scissorhands (1990)	PG-13
Eighth Grade (2018)	R ("for language and some sexual material")
El Topo (1970)	not rated
Elephant Boy (1937)	not rated
Elf (2003)	PG ("for some mild rude humor and language")
Enders Game (2013)	PG-13 ("for some violence, sci-fi action, and thematic material")
Enemy (2013)	R ("for some strong sexual content, graphic nudity, and language")
Ernest & Celestine (2012)	PG ("for some scary moments")
E.T. the Extra-Terrestrial (1982)	PG ("for language and mild thematic elements")
The 400 Blows (1959)	not rated
A Face in the Crowd (1957)	not rated
Fantasia (1940)	G
Fantastic Mr. Fox (2009)	PG ("for action, smoking, and slang humor")
Fast Times at Ridgemont High (1982)	R
Fight Club (1999)	R ("for disturbing and graphic depiction of violent antisocial behavior, sexuality, and language")
Finding Nemo (2003)	G
Finding Neverland (2004)	PG ("for mild thematic elements and brief language")
Fires Were Started (1943)	not rated

The Fits (2015)   not rated

For Your Eyes Only (1981)   PG

Forbidden Games (1952)   not rated

Forbidden Planet (1956)   G

The French Connection (1975)   R

From Here to Eternity (1953)   not rated

Fruitvale Station (2013)   R ("for some violence, language throughout, and some drug use")

Gangs of New York (2002)   R ("for intense strong violence, sexuality/nudity, and language")

Gentlemen Prefer Blondes (1953)   not rated

Germany Year Zero (1948)   not rated

Get Out (2017)   R ("for violence, bloody images, and language including sexual references")

Gladiator (2000)   R ("for intense graphic combat")

The Golden Voyage of Sinbad (1973)   G

Gone with the Wind (1939)   not rated

The Good, the Bad, and the Ugly (1966)   R

The Good Earth (1937)   not rated

Goodbye Christopher Robin (2017)   PG-13 ("for thematic elements, some bullying, and brief language")

Grand Hotel (1932)   not rated

Gravity (2013)   PG-13 ("for intense perilous sequences, some disturbing images, and brief strong language")

Great Expectations (1946)   not rated

Great Expectations (1998)   R ("for language and some sexuality")

The Greatest Show on Earth (1952)   not rated

The Greatest Story Ever Told (1965)   G

Green for Danger (1946)   not rated

Grumpy Old Men (1993)   PG-13 ("for some sexual references")

A Guy Named Joe (1943)   not rated

Hard Times (1975)   PG

Harry Potter and the Prisoner of Azkaban (2004)	PG ("for frightening moments, creature violence, and mild language")
Heat and Dust (1983)	R
Hell or High Water (2016)	R ("for some strong violence, language throughout, and brief sexuality")
Hellboy (2004)	PG-13 ("for sci-fi action violence and frightening images")
High Noon (1952)	PG ("for some Western violence and smoking")
The Hobbit: An Unexpected Journey (2012)	PG-13 ("for extended sequences of intense fantasy action violence and frightening images")
Hope and Glory (1987)	PG-13
Howards End (1992)	PG ("for mild language, violence, and sensuality")
Howl's Moving Castle (2004)	PG ("for frightening images and brief mild language")
Hugo (2011)	PG ("for mild thematic material, some action/peril, and smoking")
The Hunger Games: Catching Fire (2013)	PG-13 ("for intense sequences of violence and action, some frightening images, thematic elements, a suggestive situation, and language")
I Am Legend (2007)	PG-13 ("for intense sequences of sci-fi action and violence")
I Love Melvin (1953)	not rated
In Old Chicago (1938)	not rated
The Incredibles (2004)	PG ("for action violence")
Incredibles 2 (2018)	PG ("for action sequences and some brief mild language")
Inside Out (2015)	PG ("for mild thematic elements and some action")
The Inspector General (1949)	not rated
Intolerance (1916)	not rated
Invaders from Mars (1953)	not rated
Invasion of the Body Snatchers (1956)	not rated

The Iron Giant (1999)	PG ("for fantasy action violence, language, some thematic material, and smoking")
The Italian Job (1969)	G
It's a Wonderful Life (1946)	PG ("for thematic elements, smoking, and some violence")
Ivanhoe (1952)	not rated
Jack and the Beanstalk (1952)	not rated
Jesse James (1939)	not rated
Johnny Guitar (1954)	not rated
Jour de fête (1949)	not rated
The Jungle Book (1942)	not rated
The Jungle Book (1967)	G
The Jungle Book (2016)	PG ("for some sequences of scary action and peril")
Justice League (2017)	PG-13 ("for sequences of sci-fi violence and action")
The Karate Kid (1984)	PG
Kick-Ass (2010)	R ("for strong brutal violence throughout, pervasive language, sexual content, nudity, and some drug use—some involving children")
The Kid (1921)	not rated
King Kong (1933)	not rated
King Kong (2005)	PG-13 ("for frightening adventure violence and some disturbing images")
The Kite Runner (2007)	PG-13 ("for strong thematic material including the rape of a child, violence, and brief strong language")
Kramer vs. Kramer (1979)	PG
Lady Bird (2017)	R ("for language, sexual content, brief graphic nudity, and teen partying")
The Ladykillers (1955)	not rated
Land of the Pharaohs (1955)	not rated
Lassie Come Home (1943)	not rated
Last Year at Marienbad (1961)	not rated
Lawrence of Arabia (1962)	PG

Leave No Trace (2018)	PG ("for thematic material throughout")
The Lego Movie (2014)	PG ("for mild action and rude humor")
Leviathan (2014)	R ("for language and some sexuality/graphic nudity")
The Life of Birds (1998)	TV-PG
The Life of Mammals (2002–2003)	not rated
Like Father, Like Son (2013)	not rated
Lilya 4-Ever (2002)	R ("for strong sexual content, a rape scene, drug use, and language")
The Lion King (1994)	G
Listen Up Philip (2014)	not rated
Little Dorrit (1987)	G
The Little Kidnappers (1953)	not rated
A Little Princess (1995)	G
The Little Princess (1917)	not rated
The Little Princess (1939)	not rated
Little Women (1933)	not rated
Little Women (1949)	not rated
Little Women (1994)	PG ("for two uses of mild language")
Lonely Are the Brave (1962)	not rated
Lord of the Flies (1963)	not rated
Love Me Tonight (1932)	not rated
Loveless (2017)	R ("for strong sexuality, graphic nudity, language, and a brief disturbing image")
The Lovers' Wind (1978)	not rated
Ma Vie en Rose (1997)	R ("for brief strong language")
Mad Max (1979)	R
Mad Max: Fury Road (2015)	R ("for intense sequences of violence throughout and for disturbing images")
The Magnificent Seven (1960)	not rated
Make Way for Tomorrow (1937)	not rated
A Man Escaped (1956)	not rated
Man of the West (1958)	not rated
Martha Marcy May Marlene (2011)	R ("for disturbing violent and sexual content, nudity, and language")

Mary Poppins (1964)	G
Mary Poppins Returns (2018)	PG ("for some mild thematic elements and brief action")
The Matrix (1999)	R ("for sci-fi violence and brief language")
Meet Me in St. Louis (1944)	not rated
Memento (2000)	R ("for violence, language, and some drug content")
Metropolis (1927)	not rated
Mimic (1997)	R ("for terror/violence and language")
The Mirror (1997)	not rated
The Miseducation of Cameron Post (2018)	not rated
Les Misérables (1935)	not rated
Miss Potter (2006)	PG ("for brief mild language")
Mission Impossible (1996)	PG-13 ("for some intense action violence")
Mission: Impossible—Ghost Protocol (2011)	PG-13 ("for sequences of intense action and violence")
Monsieur Hulot's Holiday (1953)	not rated
Monster's Ball (2001)	R ("for strong sexual content, language, and violence")
Monsters, Inc. (2001)	G
Moonrise Kingdom (2012)	PG-13 ("for sexual content and smoking")
The Most Dangerous Game (1932)	not rated
Mowgli: Legend of the Jungle (2018)	PG-13 ("for intense sequences of action violence including bloody images and some thematic elements")
Mr. & Mrs. Smith (1941)	not rated
My Dinner with Andre (1981)	PG
The Naked and the Dead (1958)	not rated
The Naked Kiss (1964)	not rated
The Naked Spur (1953)	not rated
National Treasure (2004)	PG ("for action violence and some scary images")

The Newton Boys (1998)	PG-13 ("for violence including bloody aftermath of a shooting and language")
The Night of the Hunter (1955)	not rated
No Country for Old Men (2007)	R ("for strong graphic violence and some language")
Nobody Knows (2004)	PG-13 ("for mature thematic elements and some sexual references")
North by Northwest (1959)	not rated
Not as a Stranger (1955)	not rated
Old Dogs (2009)	PG ("for some mild rude humor")
Old Yeller (1957)	not rated
Oliver Twist (1948)	not rated
101 Dalmations (1996)	G
Our Little Sister (2015)	PG ("for thematic elements and brief language")
Paddington (2014)	PG ("for mild action and rude humor")
Paddington 2 (2017)	PG ("for some action and mild rude humor")
Paisan (1946)	not rated
Pan's Labyrinth (2006)	R ("for graphic violence and some language")
ParaNorman (2012)	PG ("for scary action and images, thematic elements, some rude humor, and language")
Performance (1970)	R ("for sexual content, nudity, drug material, and some violence")
Peyton Place (1957)	not rated
The Pickwick Papers (1952)	not rated
Pinocchio (1940)	G
Plane Crazy (1928)	not rated
The Planet Earth (2006)	TV-G
The Planet Earth II (2016)	TV-G
The Playboy of the Western World (1962)	not rated
Pocahontas (1995)	G
The Polar Express (2004)	G
Police Academy 3: Back in Training (1986)	PG
Poltergeist (1982)	PG

Ponette (1996)	not rated
Providence (1977)	R
Psycho (1960)	R
Quantum of Solace (2008)	PG-13 ("for intense sequences of violence and action, and some sexual content")
Querelle enfantine (*Childish Quarrel*; 1896)	not rated
The Railway Children (1970)	G
Rango (2011)	PG ("for rude humor, language, action, and smoking")
Rebel without a Cause (1955)	PG-13
The Red Balloon (1956)	not rated
Red Dust (1932)	not rated
The Red Pony (1949)	not rated
Red River (1948)	not rated
The Red Shoes (1948)	not rated
The Red Turtle (2016)	PG ("for some thematic elements and peril")
Repas de bébé (*Baby's Dinner*) (1895)	not rated
The Return (2003)	not rated
The Return of Frank James (1940)	not rated
The Revenant (2015)	R ("for strong frontier combat and violence including gory images, a sexual assault, language, and brief nudity")
The Rider (2018)	R ("for language and drug use")
Rise of the Planet of the Apes (2011)	PG-13 ("for intense and frightening sequences of action and violence")
River of No Return (1954)	not rated
RoboCop (1987)	R
Rocky (1976)	PG
Roma (2018)	R ("for graphic nudity, some disturbing images, and language")
Rome, Open City (1945)	not rated
A Room with a View (1985)	not rated
Rosetta (1999)	R ("for language")
The Ruling Class (1972)	PG

The Runner (1985)	not rated
The Russians Are Coming! The Russians Are Coming! (1966)	not rated
Saving Mr. Banks (2013)	PG-13 ("for thematic elements including some unsettling images")
Schizo (2004)	not rated
The Search (1948)	not rated
The Searchers (1956)	not rated
The Secret of Kells (2009)	not rated
A Separation (2011)	PG-13 ("for mature thematic material")
Seven Samurai (1954)	not rated
Seven Up! (1964)	not rated
The Seventh Seal (1957)	not rated
Shadowlands (1993)	PG ("for thematic elements")
Shakespeare-Wallah (1965)	not rated
Shane (1953)	not rated
Shock Corridor (1962)	not rated
Shrek (2001)	PG ("for mild language and some crude humor")
Shrek the Third (2007)	PG ("for some crude humor, suggestive content, and swashbuckling action")
Shutter Island (2010)	R ("for disturbing violent content, language, and some nudity")
Sicario (2015)	R ("for strong violence, grisly images, and language")
Sinbad and the Eye of the Tiger (1977)	G
Small Change (1976)	PG
Snow White and the Seven Dwarfs (1937)	G
Solaris (1971)	PG
A Soldier's Daughter Never Cries (1998)	R ("for language")
Song of the Prairie (1949)	not rated
Song of the Sea (2014)	PG ("for some mild peril, language, and pipe smoking images")
Spider-Man: Into the Spider-Verse (2018)	PG ("for frenetic sequences of animated action, violence, thematic elements, and mild language")
The Spirit of the Beehive (1973)	not rated

Spirited Away (2001)	PG ("for some scary moments")
Spotlight (2015)	R ("for some language including sexual references")
Stagecoach (1939)	not rated
Stalker (1979)	not rated
A Star Is Born (1954)	not rated
Star Trek IV: The Voyage Home (1986)	PG
Star Wars: Episode IV—A New Hope (1977)	PG ("for sci-fi violence and brief mild language")
Starship Troopers (1997)	R ("for graphic sci-fi violence and gore, and for some language, and nudity")
The Station Agent (2003)	R ("for language and some drug content")
Steamboat Willie (1928)	not rated
Stowaway in the Sky (1960)	not rated
La Strada (1954)	not rated
Stranger Than Fiction (2006)	PG-13 ("for some disturbing images, sexuality, brief language, and nudity")
Stuart Little (1999)	PG ("for brief language")
Suture (1993)	not rated
Sweeney Todd: The Demon Barber of Fleet Street (2007)	R ("for graphic bloody violence")
Tales of Beatrix Potter (1971)	G
Teen Titans Go! to the Movies (2018)	PG ("for action and rude humor")
The Terminator (1984)	R
Test Pilot (1938)	not rated
The Texas Chain Saw Massacre (1974)	R
The Thief of Bagdad (1924)	not rated
The Thief of Bagdad (1940)	not rated
Things to Come (1936)	not rated
The 39 Steps (1935)	not rated
¡Three Amigos! (1986)	PG
A Time to Live and a Time to Die (1985)	not rated
To Kill a Mockingbird (1962)	not rated
Together (2000)	R ("for nudity/sexuality and language")
Tokyo Story (1953)	not rated

Tootsie (1982)	PG
Toy Story (1995)	G
Toy Story 2 (1999)	G
Toy Story 3 (2010)	G
Trading Places (1983)	R
The Traveler (1974)	not rated
Treasure Island (1934)	not rated
A Trip to the Moon (1902)	TV-G
The Triplets of Belleville (2003)	PG-13 ("for images involving sensuality, violence, and crude humor")
True Grit (2010)	R ("for some intense sequences of western violence including disturbing images")
21 Jump Street (2012)	R ("for crude and sexual content, pervasive language, drug material, teen drinking, and some violence")
22 Jump Street (2014)	R ("for language throughout, sexual content, drug material, brief nudity, and some violence")
The Twilight Saga: Breaking Dawn—Part 1 (2011)	PG-13 ("for disturbing images, violence, sexuality/partial nudity, and some thematic elements")
The Twilight Saga: Breaking Dawn—Part 2 (2012)	PG-13 ("for sequences of violence including disturbing images, some sensuality, and partial nudity")
2001: A Space Odyssey (1968)	G
Umberto D. (1952)	not rated
Under the Skin (2013)	R ("for graphic nudity, sexual content, some violence, and language")
Up (2009)	PG ("for some peril and action")
Vagabond (1985)	not rated
The Valley of Gwangi (1969)	G
A Very Long Engagement (2004)	R ("for violence and sexuality")
The Virginian (1929)	not rated
WALL·E (2008)	G
Waxworks (1924)	not rated
We Are the Best! (2013)	not rated
What Maisie Knew (2013)	R ("for some language")

Where Is the Friend's House? (1987)	not rated
The White Balloon (1995)	not rated
White Mane (1953)	not rated
The Wild Bunch (1969)	R
The Wild Child (1970)	G
The Wind Rises (2013)	PG-13 ("for some disturbing images and smoking")
Winter's Bone (2010)	R ("for some drug material, language, and violent content")
The Wizard of Oz (1939)	PG ("for some scary moments")
Wonder (2017)	PG ("for thematic elements including bullying and some mild language")
Wonder Woman (2017)	PG-13 ("for sequences of violence and action, and some suggestive content")
A World Apart (1988)	PG
World War Z (2013)	PG-13 ("for intense frightening zombie sequences, violence, and disturbing images")
The Wrath of God (1972)	PG
Y Tu Mamá También (2001)	R ("for strong sexual content involving teens, drug use, and language")
The Yearling (1946)	not rated
Yellow Submarine (1968)	G
A Zed & Two Noughts (1985)	not rated

PERMISSIONS

Chapter 1: From Child to Critic

1. "Light in Auggie," published in the *Chicago Reader*, November 16, 2017. Reprinted by permission of the *Chicago Reader*.
2. A version of "The Many Kinds of Movie Wonder" originally appeared in *1000 Films to Change Your Life* (London: Time Out Guides, 2005).

Chapter 2: Adventures in Animation

1. "The Ageless Wonder of *Bambi* (1942)" by Michael Wilmington first appeared on March 14, 2011, on moviecitynews.com. Reprinted with permission of moviecitynews.com.
2. A version of "Raising the Art of Animation to a Higher Level in *Up* (2009)" by Peter Keough appeared in the *Boston Phoenix* on June 9, 2009.
3. "Of Eternity and Beyond: *Toy Story 3* (2010)" by John Anderson first appeared in *America*, July 19, 2010. Reprinted with permission of America Media.
4. *Song of the Prairie* is available on DVD, along with such other Jirí Trnka works as *The Hand*, *Story of the Bass Cello*, and *The Emperor's Nightingale* on Image's *The Puppet Films of Jiri Trnka*.
5. WBUR Boston Online, January 2004. Reprinted by permission of WBUR.
6. "Bear Meets Mouse in *Ernest & Celestine* (2012)" by Michael Sragow originally appeared in the *Orange County Register*, March 5, 2014, and is reprinted with permission of the Southern California News Group.
7. "Ideals Crash to Earth in *The Wind Rises* (2013)" by Michael Sragow first appeared in the *Orange County Register* on February 27, 2014, and is reprinted with permission of the Southern California News Group.
8. Peter Rainer/copyright © 2017, *Christian Science Monitor*.

Chapter 3: Beast Fables

1. A version of "Into the Wild: Four Variations on *The Jungle Book*" by Michael Sragow originally appeared in the Criterion Collection's the *Current* on January 2, 2017.
2. A version of "An Ape Shall Show the Way: *Dawn of the Planet of the Apes* (2014)" by Michael Sragow originally appeared in the *Orange County Register* and is reprinted with permission of the Southern California News Group.

3. "In *Babe* (1995), a Pig Shows the Way" by Carrie Rickey was published in the *Philadelphia Inquirer* on August 4, 1995. Reprinted courtesy of the *Philadelphia Inquirer.*
4. "Accidental Tourist: *Babe: Pig in the City* (1998)" by Stephanie Zacharek originally appeared in a different version on Salon.com on November 25, 1998.

Chapter 4: Dreams, Fantasies, and Nightmares

1. "There's No Film Like *Oz*: The *Wizard of Oz* (1939)" by Michael Wilmington was published on Moviecitynews.com on September 29, 2009. Reprinted with permission of Moviecitynews.com.
2. "A Diabolical Preacher Runs Amok," review of *The Night of the Hunter*. *Life*, August 1, 1955, p. 49.
3. Michael Powell, *A Life in Movies: An Autobiography* (London: Heinemann, 1986), 653.
4. Vincent Canby, "*Poltergeist* from Spielberg," *New York Times*, June 4, 1982, p. C16.
5. David Sterritt, "Two More Films from Spielberg, a One-Man Fantasy Factory," *Christian Science Monitor*, June 3, 1982, p. 19.
6. A version of this review first appeared in the *Boston Phoenix* on February 20, 2007.

Chapter 5: Well Adapted (or Maladjusted)

1. "A Consummate *Christmas Carol* (1951)" by Michael Wilmington was originally posted on Moviecitynews.com on December 24, 2014. Republished with permission of Moviecitynews.com.
2. *Tales of Beatrix Potter* was digitally restored and released as a Blu-ray DVD in 2011, to celebrate the film's 40th anniversary.
3. "Smart Times at Beverly Hills High in *Clueless* (1995)" by Kenneth Turan was originally published in the *Los Angeles Times* on July 19, 1995. Republished with permission of the *Los Angeles Times*.
4. "Henry James's Dark Screwball Comedy: *What Maisie Knew* (2012)" by Gerald Peary was originally posted on the Arts Fuse (Artsfuse.org) website on May 27, 2013. Republished with permission of the Arts Fuse.
5. A version of "From *Neverland* to *Shadowlands*: Hollywood's Romance with Children's Book Authors" by Peter Keough appeared in the *Boston Globe* on December 7, 2013.

Chapter 6: Matters of Life and Death

1. A version of "Holiday Films; Made in Iran: Films about (but Not for) Children" by Godfrey Cheshire originally appeared in the *New York Times* on November 15, 1998, and is copyrighted by the *New York Times* and used here by permission.

Chapter 7: Ordinary Heroes

1. Stuart Klawans, "Shined Shoes," in Luc Sante and Melissa Holbrook Pierson (eds.), *O.K. You Mugs: Writers on Movie Actors* (New York: Pantheon, 1999), 123.
2. Parts of "Growing Up Female in *Lady Bird* (2017), *The Fits* (2015), and *Leave No Trace* (2018)" by Robert Horton appeared in another form in *Seattle Weekly* and the *Daily Herald*.
3. "Perverse Conversion in *The Miseducation of Cameron Post* (2018)" by Robert Horton appeared in the *Seattle Post* and the *Daily Herald* on August 8, 2018. Republished with permission of *Seattle Weekly* and the *Daily Herald*.
4. Transgender politics has shown us how the everyday language we use is structured by a male/female binary inhospitable to those whose identity falls somewhere in between—or altogether elsewhere—and that to affirm the equality of transgendered people requires our willingness to let language take on new shapes and forms. Hence, I take seriously the question of what gender pronouns to assign Ludovic in this essay. In "her" own mind, the character is decidedly not a "boy." Yet, neither does "he" understand "himself" as a fully achieved "girl." *Ma Vie en Rose* strongly suggests that Ludo is working toward a female identity, but to assign him a set of masculine pronouns would participate in the same kinds of repression the movie works to undo, and, on the other hand, to use feminine pronouns would be to make assumptions that Ludo has not yet arrived at. Thus, I have allowed my language to be guided by the way Ludo describes him/herself with the term *garçon-fille* (boy-girl) and use such hybrid pronouns as "s/he."
5. "Flower Power: *The Blossoming of Maximo Oliveros* (2005)" by Godfrey Cheshire originally appeared in *Indy Week* on January 24, 2007. Republished by permission of the author.
6. "Uneasy *Rider*" by Peter Keough was first published in the *Boston Globe* on April 27, 2018.

Chapter 8: Extraordinary Heroes

1. A version of "*Black Panther* (2018) Makes Superhero History" by Peter Travers appeared in *Rolling Stone* on February 6, 2018.
2. "*Wonder Woman* (2017) Enters the Pantheon" by Michael Sragow was first published in *Film Comment* on June 1, 2017. Reprinted with permission from the Film Society of Lincoln Center and *Film Comment* magazine. © Film Comment.
3. "Superpowers Run in the Family in *Incredibles 2* (2018)" by Michael Sragow first appeared in *Film Comment* on June 15, 2018. Reprinted with permission from the Film Society of Lincoln Center and *Film Comment* magazine. © *Film Comment*.

Chapter 9: Home Movies

1. "Bearing the Burden of Growing up in *Christopher Robin* (2018)" by Michael Sragow first appeared in *Film Comment* on August 3, 2018. Reprinted with permission from the Film Society of Lincoln Center and *Film Comment* magazine. © *Film Comment*.

2. "A Child Is Lost in *Loveless* (2017)" by Peter Rainer first appeared in the *Christian Science Monitor* on February 16, 2018. Peter Rainer/copyright © 2018 *Christian Science Monitor*.
3. "A Child Is Found in *Our Little Sister* (2015)" by Robert Horton first appeared in *Seattle Weekly* on August 10, 2016. Reprinted by permission of the *Daily Herald*, which holds those rights.

Chapter 10: From Critic to Child

1. "Where the Kids Are: *Howl's Moving Castle* (2004)" by Jonathan Rosenbaum was first published in the *Chicago Reader* on June 9, 2005. Permission to reprint granted by the *Chicago Reader*.
2. Richard James Havis, "Film Review: 'Howl's Moving Castle,'" *Hollywood Reporter*, February 18, 2005.
3. Robin Wood, "An Introduction to the American Horror Film," in Bill Nichols (ed.), *Movies and Methods*, Vol. II (Berkeley: University of California Press, 1985), 199.
4. "*E.T. the Extra-Terrestrial* (1982)" by Roger Ebert was first published on September 14, 1997, on www.rogerebert.com. Reprinted with permission of the Ebert Company, Ltd.

INDEX

ABOUT THE EDITOR AND CONTRIBUTORS

Peter Keough was film editor of the *Boston Phoenix* from 1989 until its demise in 2013. Other publications he has written for include the *Chicago Reader*, the *Chicago Sun-Times*, the *Chicago Tribune*, and *Sight & Sound*. He was editor of *Flesh and Blood: The National Society of Film Critics on Sex, Violence, and Censorship* (1995) and *Kathryn Bigelow: Interviews* (2013). He currently writes about film and other topics for the *Boston Globe*.

—⟋⟍—

John Anderson is a TV critic for the *Wall Street Journal*, film critic for *America* magazine, and a contributor to the *Los Angeles Times* and *New York Times*. He has authored books on Taiwanese director Edward Yang and Finnish director Pirjo Honkasalo, and his work has appeared in *Variety*, *Newsday*, *DGA Quarterly*, the *Nation*, *Film Comment*, and the *Village Voice*. He is a past member of the selection committee of the New York Film Festival and a three-time chairman of the New York Film Critics Circle.

Sheila Benson, who lives in Seattle, Washington, writes for *Critic Quality Feed* and thanks her lucky stars every day that she's no longer film critic for the *Los Angeles Times*.

Jay Carr, longtime *Boston Globe* film critic, reviewed films for Turner Classic Movies. He was a recipient of the George Jean Nathan Award for Dramatic Criticism and was named Chevalier, Ordre des Arts et Lettres (France) for writings on French film. He served on the Library of Congress's National Film Presentation Board. Carr edited and wrote six essays for the National Society of Film Critics anthology *The A List* (2002). He died on May 15, 2014, at seventy-seven.

Justin Chang is a film critic for the *Los Angeles Times* and NPR's *Fresh Air* radio program. Before joining the *Times*, he was chief film critic at *Variety*. Chang is author of the book *FilmCraft: Editing* and serves as chair of the National Society of Film Critics and secretary of the Los Angeles Film Critics Association.

Godfrey Cheshire is a film critic and filmmaker based in New York City. His writings on film have appeared in the *New York Times*, *Variety*, *Film Comment*, *Cineaste*, *Sight & Sound*, and other publications. He is writer-director of the documentaries *Moving Midway* (2007) and the forthcoming *The Experiment: Black and White at V.E.S.* He is a former chairman of the New York Film Critics Circle and cofounder of the Iranian Film Festival New York.

Morris Dickstein is Distinguished Professor Emeritus of English and Theatre and senior fellow at the Graduate Center of the Center for the Humanities at the City University of New York. He has contributed to numerous publications, including the *New York Times Book Review*, the *Times Literary Supplement*, the *Nation*, *American Film*, and *Partisan Review*, and twice was a finalist for the National Book Critics Circle Award in criticism. His books include *Dancing in the Dark: A Cultural History of the Great Depression* (2009), which received the Ambassador Book Award in American Studies from the English-Speaking Union, and *Why Not Say What Happened: A Sentimental Education* (2015).

Roger Ebert, the first film critic to win a Pulitzer Prize, which he won in 1975, wrote for the *Chicago Sun-Times* for thirty-six years. His national TV programs, *Siskel & Ebert* and *Ebert & Roeper*, played weekly for more than thirty years. Later, with his wife Chaz, he produced the public television program *Ebert Presents at the Movies*. He was the first film critic honored with a star on the Hollywood Hall of Fame and was voted an honorary member of both the Director's Guild of America and the American Society of Cinematographers. Ebert passed away in Chicago on April 4, 2013, at seventy.

David Fear is a critic and film/TV editor for *Rolling Stone* and was a critic/editor at *Time Out New York* from 2004 to 2013. His work has been published in the *New York Times Magazine*, *Esquire*, the *Village Voice*, *Film Comment*, *Spin*, the *New York Daily News*, *Blender*, *Moviemaker*, *Nashville Scene*, and the *San Francisco Bay Guardian*, among others. Fear is a member of the New York Film Critics Circle and lives in Brooklyn.

Robert Horton is the longtime film critic for *Seattle Weekly* and the *Daily Herald* (Everett, WA), and a regular contributor to *Film Comment*. He is author of *Frankenstein* (2014) and *Billy Wilder: Interviews* (2001), and his career appreciation of Frank Sinatra was collected in *Best American Movie Writing 1999* (1999). Horton has been a Fulbright Specialist (Romania, 2016), an adjunct professor at

Seattle University, the curator of the Magic Lantern film program at the Frye Art Museum in Seattle, and a speaker with Smithsonian Journeys. His work is linked on the *Crop Duster* website, https://roberthorton.wordpress.com/.

J. R. Jones has spent more than twenty years contributing reviews to the *Chicago Reader*, where he served as film editor and principal film critic from 2008 to 2018. His book *The Lives of Robert Ryan*, a biography of the actor, was published in 2015.

Andy Klein, a regular critic for KPCC's Film Week, was film editor/critic for the *Los Angeles Reader* until its closure in 1996, and at *Los Angeles CityBeat* until its closure in 2009. He has contributed to the *Los Angeles Herald Examiner*, *Los Angeles* magazine, *American Film*, the *Hollywood Reporter*, *Variety*, *Salon*, *Film Comment*, the *Los Angeles Times*, and the *Christian Science Monitor*, among others. Klein is a member of the Los Angeles Film Critics Association and the National Society of Film Critics.

Nathan Lee is a PhD candidate in the Department of Modern Culture and Media at Brown University and teaches at the Rhode Island School of Design. He is a former film critic for the *New York Times*, the *Village Voice*, *NPR*, and *Film Comment*.

Emanuel Levy (PhD Columbia University) marked his 40th anniversary as film professor, scholar, and critic in 2019. A two-time president of the Los Angeles Film Critics Association, he has served as senior critic for *Variety* and chief critic for *Screen International*, and is currently a contributor to *Financial Times*. In 2003, Levy established the Emanuel Levy: Cinema 24/7 website, at EmanuelLevy .com, which contains more than 25,000 reviews. He is author of nine books, the most recent being *Gay Directors/Gay Films: Almodóvar, Davies, Haynes, Van Sant, John Waters* (2015). Levy is a voting member of the Golden Globes and the National Society of Film Critics, and has appeared on CNN, CBS, PBS, and other networks.

Gerald Peary lives in Cambridge, Massachusetts, and reviews films for the *Arts Fuse*. He was a longtime film critic for the late *Boston Phoenix* and is author of eight books on cinema. Peary is programmer of the Boston University Cinematheque and filmmaker of three feature documentaries, notably *For the Love of Movies: The Story of American Film Criticism* (2009). He is a featured actor in the Andrew Bujalski film *Computer Chess* (2013).

Mary Pols has been a film critic for *Time*, the *Oakland Tribune*, and *Contra Costa Times*. She continues to review books, and her criticism appears regularly in *People* and the *New York Times Book Review*. She is also author of a memoir, *Accidentally on Purpose* (2009). A former Knight Fellow at Stanford, she now lives in her native Maine, where she is editor of *Maine Women Magazine*.

Peter Rainer is the film critic for the *Christian Science Monitor* and a regular contributor to NPR's *FilmWeek*. He was a finalist in 1998 for the Pulitzer Prize in Criticism and previously served as film critic for *New York* magazine, the *Los Angeles Times*, *New Times*, and the *Los Angeles Herald Examiner*. He is author of *Rainer on Film: Thirty Years of Film Writing in a Turbulent and Transformative Era* (2013) and editor of the National Society of Film Critics anthology *Love and Hisses* (1992). Rainer also wrote and coproduced documentaries for A&E on Sidney Poitier and the Hustons, and has appeared as a film commentator on *Nightline* and CNN.

Carrie Rickey is the film critic emerita of the *Philadelphia Inquirer*. She reviews movies for Truthdig.com, where a series she wrote on the history of female filmmakers earned the 2018 LA Press Club award for Best Commentary. Rickey also writes for other publications, including the *New York Times*, *Sight & Sound*, and the *Forward*. *Before Hollywood*, a documentary she produced on the development of cinema in the nineteenth century, won a regional Emmy in 2018.

Jonathan Rosenbaum was film critic for the *Chicago Reader* from 1987 to 2007, and is author, coauthor, or editor of several books, including *Moving Places* (1980), *Midnight Movies* (with J. Hoberman, 1983), *This Is Orson Welles* (editor, 1992), *Placing Movies* (1995), *Goodbye Cinema, Hello Cinephilia* (2010), and *Abbas Kiarostami* (with Mehrnaz Saeed-Vafa, expanded 2nd edition, 2018). He maintains a website archiving most of his work at www.jonathanrosenbaum.net.

Michael Sragow is a contributing editor to *Film Comment* and writes the "Deep Focus" column for the magazine's website. He edited the Library of America's two volumes of James Agee's writings (2005), as well as *Produced and Abandoned: The National Society of Film Critics Write on the Best Films You've Never Seen* (1990). Sragow is author of *Victor Fleming: American Movie Master* (2008).

David Sterritt was film critic for the *Christian Science Monitor* for almost forty years and chair of the National Society of Film Critics for ten years. He is editor in chief of *Quarterly Review of Film and Video*, contributing writer at *Cineaste*, and film professor at the Maryland Institute College of Art. Sterritt served two terms as chair of the New York Film Critics Circle, and his writing has appeared in the *New York Times*, *PopMatters*, *Indiewire*, and many other publications. He has also written or edited more than fifteen books.

Charles Taylor is author of *Opening Wednesday at a Theater or Drive-In Near You: The Shadow Cinema of the American '70s* (2017). His writing on movies, books, popular culture, and politics has appeared in the *New York Times*, *Dissent*, the *Yale Review*, the *Nation*, and many other publications. Taylor lives in New York.

Peter Travers is the longtime movie critic for *Rolling Stone* and the host of ABC's *Popcorn with Peter Travers*, for which he interviews talent from film, TV, theater, and what's streaming on the web. A former chair of the New York Film Critics Circle, Travers appears frequently in print and online to pinpoint what's shaking things up in pop culture.

Kenneth Turan is film critic for the *Los Angeles Times* and NPR's *Morning Edition*. He has been the *Times* book-review editor, director of the *Times* book prizes, and a staff writer for the *Washington Post*. Turan's latest books are *Not to Be Missed: 54 Favorites from a Lifetime of Film* (2014) and *Free for All: Joe Papp, the Public, and the Greatest Theater Story Ever Told* (2010). He teaches at USC and is on the board of directors of the National Yiddish Book Center.

James Verniere is the film critic for the *Boston Herald*. Born in Newark, New Jersey, he has a master's degree from Rutgers University. His work has previously appeared in the Film Registry of the Library of Congress and the National Society of Film Critics books *The A List* (2002) and *The X List* (2005). Verniere has also written for the *Chicago Sun-Times*, the *Los Angeles Times*, *Sight & Sound*, *Film Comment*, and *Heavy Metal* magazine.

Michael Wilmington has been the film critic for the *Los Angeles Weekly*, the *Los Angeles Times*, and the *Chicago Tribune*, where he won or shared two Peter

Lisagor Awards for arts criticism. In 2008, Wilmington became the movie and DVD critic for *Movie City News*.

Stephanie Zacharek is the film critic for *Time* magazine. She was previously chief film critic for the *Village Voice* and Salon.com, and her writing on books and pop culture has also appeared in the *New York Times*, *New York Magazine*, the *Los Angeles Times*, *Rolling Stone*, and *Sight & Sound*. She was a finalist for the 2015 Pulitzer Prize in Criticism.

31901065409825